Presented to

_____

By

_____

On the Occasion of

_____

Date

_____

DEVOTIONS
FROM THE PSALMS

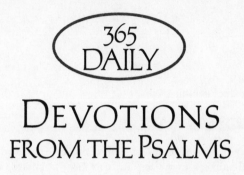

365 DAILY

DEVOTIONS
FROM THE PSALMS

INSPIRATION FROM THE BOOK OF PSALMS

DAN R. DICK

BARBOUR
PUBLISHING

ISBN 978-1-59789-693-1

Cover image © Corbis

Published by Barbour Publishing, Inc., P.O. Box 719, Uhrichsville, Ohio 44683
www.barbourbooks.com

Our mission is to publish and distribute inspirational products offering exceptional value and biblical encouragement to the masses.

Member of the
Evangelical Christian
Publishers Association

Printed in the United States of America.
5 4 3 2 1

Blessed is the man that walketh not in the counsel of the ungodly, nor standeth in the way of sinners, nor sittith in the seat of the scornful.
PSALM 1:1

A time for starting over. A new beginning. A wonderful time to take stock of life and look for ways to improve and grow. Too often, careless resolutions are made that are never kept, and so one year blends into the next with little change. The fact is, all of us have areas in our lives that could stand some improvement. As this new year begins, let us look at our lives with honesty and candor. Let us approach change with a positive spirit, and work toward finding ways to become the people God wants us to be. Most importantly, ask the Lord to guide and strengthen you, for it is through His power that we are able to conquer our failings and turn them into strengths. God is able to see us both as we are and as we can be, and we need that vision in order to truly change. He will steer us away from the ungodly. He will liberate us from the way of sin. He will lead us from scorn to joy. The Lord will do all this and more because of His great and abiding love for His children. Rejoice in the love of God. He has given us a new year, and He also desires to give us a new life.

PRAYER: O Lord, cleanse my soul of all wrong. Help me to grow in the light of Your love. Lift me above what I have been, and set me onto a new path of righteousness and grace.

Amen.

*For the LORD knoweth the way of
the righteous: but the way
of the ungodly shall perish.*
PSALM 1:6

Jeff got so discouraged sometimes. He worked so hard while his roommates messed around, but they always seemed to do every bit as well as he did. Whenever he let up even for a little bit, his grades fell. It just didn't seem fair.

It's hard to look around and see so many undeserving people receive such wonderful rewards. We like to feel that justice is going to be done, but we hardly ever see it. Thankfully, our trust is in the Lord and His promises. Those who receive all their blessings now have nothing more to come, while those who patiently wait upon God and His justice will find themselves face-to-face with an eternity of joy and peace. Nothing escapes the watchful eye of God. He sees the way of the righteous, and He will surely reward them.

PRAYER:
Lord, help me to wait patiently for Your will to be done, and do not let me envy the blessings of others. Keep my eyes fixed upon Your great love. Amen.

The kings of the earth set themselves,
and the rulers take counsel together,
against the LORD, and against his anointed.
PSALM 2:2

Just reading a newspaper or watching a newscast can be a terrifying experience these days. The horrors of our modern world are mind-boggling. We search for some shred of sanity, and we find almost none. World leaders appear to be bent on destruction, and our voices simply aren't heard. In the time of King David, in the time of our Lord Jesus Christ, and in many times since, the rulers of the world have given little heed to the teachings of God or the concerns of His people. For this reason, we, as children of God, need to hold fast to our faith and spread God's Word wherever and whenever we can. The only true stabilizing force we have in this life is the Word of God. God's Word will be our shield and our strength in the most troubled of times. Turn to it daily, and you will be renewed. ✓

PRAYER:
Heavenly Father,
calm my soul,
place Your peace
within my heart, and be a
source of sanity in my life. When
things look most dismal, shine Your light
upon me. Amen.

Be wise now therefore, O ye kings:
be instructed, ye judges of the earth.

PSALM 2:10

Where is the voice of God in our world today? In times past, God's people were listened to, and the influence of the faithful was amazing. Why isn't that so true today?

Not too long ago I heard a man say, "We're too bright for that religious stuff now. We've grown up and are learning to deal with problems sensibly." What could be further from the truth? Without the counsel of the Lord, everything is ignorance. In trying to deal with our problems apart from God, we are creating more problems than we can handle. The answer is not in running from the Lord, but in running to Him.

In our own lives, we need to learn to let the Lord rule. Giving God control of our lives is not a sign of weakness; it is the greatest show of strength we will ever make. Under the guidance of God, we become conquerors in a world that tries hard to break us down.

PRAYER:
O Lord, be close to me, building me up and keeping me ever in Your loving care. Do not let me be swayed from the path You have set me on. Others may fail me, but You never will. Hallelujah! Amen.

Serve the LORD with fear,
and rejoice with trembling.
PSALM 2:11

The fire licked up the outside walls and up into the night. All around the building, firefighters scampered, trundling huge hoses into position to battle the blaze. Jerry stood with sweat pouring down his face and the spray from the hose soaking his body. He loved his work and felt he really served well. He knew the dangers that were involved, but he fought fires anyway. His job was one of the greatest joys of his life.

Not all things that inspire fear should be avoided. A wise person knows his limits and knows what situations he can handle and what ones he cannot. A little fear is healthy. It gives us respect and appreciation. It causes us to not get careless. Fear of the Lord should not drive us from Him; it should help us to understand Him and deal with Him reverently and respectfully. When we encounter our Lord with both joy and trembling, we know Him in a special and meaningful way.

PRAYER:

Lord, help me to never forget Your awesome power, as well as Your awesome love. Allow me to feel a healthy fear, but never let that fear separate me from You. Amen.

Kiss the Son, lest he be angry, and ye perish from the way, when his wrath is kindled but a little. Blessed are all they that put their trust in him.

PSALM 2:12

What a beautiful image is presented when we think of being able to kiss the Son of God. As family members embrace and kiss when they meet, so we are able to look forward to a day when we will be welcomed as family of Jesus Christ. He awaits us in love and care, and we have no need to fear anything, for we will one day be united. In fact, we are already united through the Holy Spirit of God. The Holy Spirit is God's kiss, blown to us on earth, and we can receive it with joy. We will never know greater love than the love God has for us. He sent His only Son to be our Savior and Lord. He gave us all that He had to give, out of His divine love for us. Rejoice in the love of God and let it carry you throughout each day of the year.

PRAYER:

Welcome, dear Lord, into the depths of my heart. Dwell there in love, and never leave me. I am whole only when You are with me. Thank You for loving me so very much. Amen.

But thou, O LORD, art a shield for me;
my glory, and the lifter up of mine head.
PSALM 3:3

I was walking along one day, deeply troubled and feeling quite alone. Pressures and problems seemed too much to bear, and I found nothing to make me feel hopeful. My deep thought was broken by a flutter of wings and a flash of color. A butterfly flitted in front of my face, then alighted on my shoulder. The grace and beauty of the small creature broke through my depression and caused me to smile. The great weight I was feeling in my heart lifted, and I began chastising myself for having been so foolish. In a world where such glory exists, why do we continually allow worldly concerns to occupy so much of our attention? Let God be our glory, and indeed, when we find ourselves most down, He will lift our heads up and show us all the wonders of His magnificent creation.

PRAYER: Lord, protect me from those things that turn my attention from You. Clear the eyes of my heart so they can focus on the splendor of Your creation. Thank You for the blessings of this day. Amen.

H. bday Dad

8

*I will not be afraid of ten thousands
of people, that have set themselves
against me round about.*

PSALM 3:6

All of the customers had been so hateful and bellig-
erent. Nancy thought that if one more unpleasant
person assaulted her, she would scream. To make
matters worse, the store owners were being unreasonable
and hard to get along with. She didn't know how much
more she could take. She rested her chin on her chest and
heaved a heavy sigh. Then, the cross she wore around her
neck caught her eye, and she felt strangely calm. The frustrations of the day melted away as the peace of Christ
settled upon her heart.

In the daily battles we find ourselves engaged
in, it is vital that we remember we have
an ally who is greater than anyone who
might oppose us or wish to make us
unhappy. Jesus Christ became victor
over everything this world could
throw at Him—even death itself.
If we will give Him control
of our hearts, He will be
true to us and grant us
victory in the struggles
we face.

PRAYER:
Father,
You have
made me
a conqueror
through Your Son,
Jesus Christ. Help me to
live as a victor and not as
one defeated. Lift me up to be
a sign to the world that in
Christ we need never be
afraid. Amen.

Happy 1st David

*Hear me when I call, O God of my
righteousness: thou hast enlarged me when
I was in distress; have mercy upon me, and hear my prayer.*
PSALM 4:1

Jeffrey was a quiet man—so quiet, in fact, that many people forgot that he was around. He rode the train into New York every morning with the same crowd of people, never speaking to anyone, sitting alone at the back of the car. One morning a man a few rows up began to choke on a roll he was eating. In a flash, Jeffrey jumped to the man's aid, grabbing him and dislodging the piece of roll. All of the riders were amazed that the quiet man from the back of the train had been able to come forward in a time of emergency.

We are all capable of great things in time of distress. The Lord gives to His children the ability to serve one another, even so much as to save another life. It is important that we continually pray for God to guide our actions and show us ways to serve. When we open ourselves to the will of God, we will be surprised at the wonderful things we can do.

PRAYER: Have mercy upon me, O Lord, and guide all the steps I take. Use me to spread Your glory each day. Strengthen me with supernatural power to serve You always. Amen.

*Stand in awe, and sin not: commune
with your own heart upon your bed,
and be still.*

PSALM 4:4

Jennifer lay in her bed, listening to the approaching thunder. Storms scared her, yet something deep inside thrilled at their coming. She closed her eyes and imagined the thunder as the voice of God spreading across the face of the earth. There was a strange comfort in the thought that God would thunder forth in such a way. Jennifer began to pray to God, confident that He would hear her and be with her. In the wee small hours of the night, Jennifer drifted off, asleep in the loving arms of God until morning.

In the face of the storms of life, we need the confidence that our Lord will be with us and that He will grant us peace. The peace of the Lord is the strongest force on earth, and those who find their peace in the Lord need never fear. Look deep inside and dwell with the Spirit of God in your heart. There you will find the calm that no storm can disturb. ✓

*PRAYER:
O Lord,
grant me
Thy perfect
peace, and lift
me above the storms
of my life. I trust in Your
great love. Be with me, I pray.
Amen.*

My voice shalt thou hear in the morning,
O LORD; in the morning will I direct
my prayer unto thee, and will look up.
PSALM 5:3

The sun had just begun to climb into the sky, and the dew shone brightly on the field below. Though not ordinarily a morning person, Ann always loved those special times when she rose in time to see the sunrise. On mornings like this, who could doubt that there is a God? Ann's heart filled with joy beyond words, and nothing could remove that joy during the day. Taking a Bible, she went to a clearing to sit and to read and to pray.

God gives us special times in order that we might find joy and that we might find Him. He has created a glorious world, and He has freely given it to us. The early quiet of the day is a beautiful time to encounter the Lord. Give Him your early hours, and He will give you all the blessings you can hold.

PRAYER:
I raise my voice
to You in the
morning, Lord. Help
me to appreciate Your new
day, and use it to the fullest. Open
my eyes to the splendor of all Your
creation. Amen.

*Lead me, O LORD, in thy righteousness
because of mine enemies; make thy way
straight before my face.*

PSALM 5:8

Barry hated to be left out of the good times his friends had, but he hated it even worse when they went out drinking and cruising. He didn't like to drink, and his friends always mocked him because of it. Thank goodness for Jean. She had come along and given him an excuse not to go out. She really disapproved of drinking and driving, so Barry could do for Jean what he had never been able to do for himself: say no!

God gives us the reason to say no. In those areas of our life where we are too weak to say no to our friends, we can learn to say no because we know that God wants us to. So many people would lead us from the path of God, many of them unintentionally. Ask the Lord for guidance. In the face of our strongest temptations, God will give us the strength and the reason to resist.

PRAYER:
O God, I find myself in some terrible situations that I don't want to be in. Help me to free myself from those things I know displease You. Guide me, strengthen me, liberate me, I pray. Amen.

O LORD, rebuke me not in thine anger,
neither chasten me in thy hot displeasure.
PSALM 6:1

Child experts have discovered that one of the most traumatic experiences children face is to have their parents scold or punish them in front of their friends. The humiliation that accompanies the punishment can leave deep emotional scars. The actual punishment pales in comparison with the embarrassment the child suffers. Most children would rather face any penalty other than public chastisement.

Just as loving parents guard and protect their children's dignity, so our Lord protects the dignity of His children. To believe that God would punish us in such a way as to rob us of our self-esteem is ridiculous. God would never do such a thing. God does not deal with us in hot anger, for He loves us too much. He watches us closely, guiding us gently and regarding us as valuable creations. We need never believe that God has punished us in order to humiliate us. His own Son was humbled by men and women, but the Lord of all life lifted Him up, and He will lift us up, also.

PRAYER:
Though I face trials and problems, I know that You are not to blame, Lord. You give so much, and You help me in times when I most need You. Have patience with me, God, and help me to grow. Amen.

Have mercy upon me, O LORD; for I am weak: O LORD, heal me; for my bones are vexed.

PSALM 6:2

The closer we get to God, the more glaring are our faults. The brighter the light of perfection that we subject ourselves to, the more flaws are revealed. The better we understand the awesome magnificence of God, the more we expose our own imperfections. As the great men and women of the Bible came to realize, the stronger we become in the faith, the more wretched we sometimes feel.

This, however, is no cause for despair. Our Lord wants nothing more than for us to come to depend on Him. We can only truly become dependent as we acknowledge our inadequacies. As the apostle Paul found out, true strength comes from admitting our weakness, and total healing comes by realizing that without God we are sickly and terminally diseased by sin. Cry out for the mercy of God, and He will strengthen you; ask for His healing and you will be made whole.

PRAYER:
Dear Lord, I try to be perfect and find that I am hopelessly deficient. Nothing I can do will bring me the perfection You intend for me. Fill me with Your Spirit, and do for me all that I cannot do for myself. Amen.

O LORD my God, in thee do I put my trust: save me from all them that persecute me, and deliver me.
PSALM 7:1

G reg couldn't believe his ears. His teacher had just asked the class if anyone belonged to a church youth group. Greg attended one faithfully, but he was too embarrassed to let any of his school friends know about it. Most of the kids in the youth group were considered to be freaks by the "in crowd" at the high school. Only a couple of the other kids were raising their hands. For a moment Greg hesitated; then he slowly raised his hand. To his surprise, no one laughed, and a couple of his school friends even showed interest in his church involvement. Greg began to wonder what he had really been afraid of.

There are so many people in this world who will not understand our faith in the Lord Jesus Christ. They will ridicule us, persecute us, and turn us aside. That does not justify us hiding our faith. We are to shine as a light in this world. If we are proud of our faith, we will find that God will give us special strength to stand up in the face of ridicule. As Scripture says, if we will be proud of the Father, He will be proud of us. If we are ashamed of Him, however, then Christ will also be ashamed of us.

PRAYER:

Lord, You are the brightest light shining in my life. Help me to reflect Your light in all that I do and say. Save me from persecutors, and enable me to be everything You would have me to be. Amen.

The LORD shall judge the people: judge me, O LORD, according to my righteousness, and according to mine integrity that is in me.

PSALM 7:8

If we are honest with ourselves, we have to admit that it's a very scary thought that God might actually judge us according to our measure of righteousness and integrity. Under the careful scrutiny of the Lord, all our blemishes surface, and we are exposed for what we really are: sinners in need of a good cleaning! Praise God that the cleaning is available to us through the blood of the Lamb, Jesus Christ. By the forgiveness of sin offered through the cross and resurrection of Christ, we are made clean and pure and able to pass the scrutinous eye of God. Christ's righteousness becomes the righteousness of all who believe in Him and turn their hearts over to Him. Jesus paid the penalty that would have come to us. We now have no fear of condemnation from the Lord. All we have is the promise of love and forgiveness to those who repent of their sins and follow in the ways of the Lord.

PRAYER: Make me like You, O Lord. In the ways I am lacking, remake me in the image of Christ. Create in me a new and clean heart, and bless the paths I am to walk. Amen.

*When I consider thy heavens, the work
of thy fingers, the moon and the stars,
which thou hast ordained; what is man,
that thou art mindful of him? and the son of
man, that thou visitest him?*
PSALM 8:3–4

A devout man refused to enter a church because he said that he was not worthy to tread on holy ground. Whenever he saw a cross, he burst into tears and turned his eyes away. He humbled himself whenever he could, and he lamented that he would never be good enough to hope for salvation.

One day, a traveling minister entered the hometown of the man. He saw the devout man sitting on the stones outside the church building, and so he stopped to talk. When he found out the man's thoughts, he told him, "God is not looking for worthy men, but willing children. He doesn't want to be surrounded by people trying to impress Him with how much they can love Him. He merely wants people who will receive the great love He has to give. You are wise in saying you will never be worthy, but do not be foolish in not realizing that you are loved. Come, and receive the gift of the Lord. He set the earth and skies in motion, the birds in the air, the fish in the sea, the creatures on the earth; and He did it all for you, my friend."

*PRAYER:
Though I do not
deserve Your great
love, Father God, I
thank You that You give it
so freely. Embrace me as a child,
cradle me in Your strong and tender
arms, and help me remember that I
am Yours. Amen.*

*Thou hast made him a little lower
than the angels, and hast crowned him
with glory and honour.*

PSALM 8:5

There are not many days that go by where I feel very holy. As much as I might like to be a reflection of Jesus Christ, I am afraid that my image is a very dim one at best. For each success I have at walking in the footsteps of Christ, I have a dozen failures where I have strayed from the path. And through it all, God still loves me totally. In my imperfection, God still reveres me and thinks I am good. It boggles the mind to realize that human beings are God's pride and joy. Despite the grief and frustration we must be, God believes in us and helps us to be the best people that we can be. He loves His children and rejoices in their victories. Our Lord created us just lower than the angels, the most perfect of His creations.

Despair not. No matter how inadequate we might feel, we are considered beautiful by our Creator, and in the end it is His opinion, not ours, that makes all the difference in the world.

PRAYER: Grant me spiritual wings that I might soar as an angel on this earth, O Lord. Help me to live up to the intention You had at my creation. Let me wear my crown wisely and proudly, to Your glory. Amen.

I will praise thee, O Lord, with my whole heart; I will shew forth all thy marvellous works.
PSALM 9:1

Audrey loved the little children and they dearly loved her. She would walk with them through the gardens and fields, showing them all the wonders of nature. She would sit with them for hours and tell them stories. She would read to them from her Bible, then explain what she had read. She would remind the children of all the good things God could do. For the main part of her life, Audrey taught little children the reality of God.

To be truly in love with God is a consuming passion. We can't wait to tell the world of the wonderful truth we know. The Spirit of God enters in to our hearts, and our lives are never the same again. Praise the Lord with your whole heart, and show forth all His wonderful works.

PRAYER: Each new day brings new wonders to my attention. Thank You, O Lord, for creating such a beautiful world with so many miracles to behold. Amen.

Lighthouse

> *The LORD also will be a refuge for the oppressed, a refuge in times of trouble.*
>
> PSALM 9:9

Ellen lived in a tiny shack on the edge of a small backwater town. She had no modern conveniences, no car, no electricity, no fancy clothing. She just lived a simple life, giving of herself to others, sharing what little she did have with anyone who needed it. Often people tried to help Ellen, but she just smiled and said she didn't want for anything. When asked why she lived as she did, Ellen said, "God has made sure that I've had enough to get by on. I don't need any more than that. He and I have a nice deal. When He needs me, He lets me know and shows me what I can do; and when I need Him, all I have to do is call. I've faced hard times, but the Lord has always given me strength and given me a place to run to."

The Lord is our refuge and our strength. It takes a great deal of wisdom to realize that. Our lives are much more than possessions and positions. Our lives are gifts from God, given to us and to others for His glory. We need not ask what more God can do for us, but what we might do for God. He will surely let us know.

PRAYER: Father, I sometimes need to escape: from the world, from myself, from the things that tie me down. Be my liberation and my sanctuary. Strengthen me for Your service. Amen.

*And they that know thy name will put
their trust in thee: for thou, LORD, hast
not forsaken them that seek thee.*
PSALM 9:10

The crowd in the office seemed to have no morals whatsoever. Beth could hardly believe some of the things she heard the other employees talking about. They used foul language, spent weekends in drunken fogs, and had no compunction about their loose sexual behavior. Sometimes Beth felt so alone. It was hard to spend so much time out of the day with people she disagreed with so strongly. Her thoughts always turned to her close friends, and she was glad to have others who felt as she did to turn to. Her friends were all Christians, and it really did make a difference. She didn't feel like an outsider when she was with Christian friends. Having such good friends made it easier to deal with the people at work. She wondered what she would do if she didn't have friends who felt as she did.

So many people have no idea what it means to have the Spirit of Christ in their hearts. They believe that their lives are fine just as they are. How sad that they do not know enough to put their trust in God. It is our job, as the voice and hands of God, to let people know of the truth of Christ, so they, too, might come to put their trust in Him.

shine His love light

PRAYER: Make
me an agent of
Your will and
Word. Help me
to teach others by the
example of my life what it means
to be Christian. I will put my trust in
You. Help me to share that trust with
others. Amen.

Arise, O LORD; let not man prevail: let the heathen be judged in thy sight. Put them in fear, O LORD: that the nations may know themselves to be but men.

PSALM 9:19–20

I t is frightening to listen to the decrees made by some of our world leaders. They hold the lives of so many people in their hands, and all too often they seem bent on destruction—not only of themselves, but of as many people as they can take with them. If it were true that they really had the ultimate power, there would be no reason for hope.

We know better, however. The only true power in this world is the power of God, and our fate will not be decided by men and women, but by God. We are created for eternity, and so we do not need to fear the decisions made by corrupt human beings in this age. Our trust is in the Lord of all creation, and in Him there is never reason to fear or doubt.

PRAYER: Father God, sustainer of life and giver of sanity in an insane world, hear the prayers of Your people, and give us peace and confidence of a bright new age to come. Amen.

*The wicked, through the pride of his
countenance, will not seek after God:
God is not in all his thoughts.*
PSALM 10:4

A successful corporate leader once said, "It's not
that I don't believe in God, it's just that I don't
have time for Him. If I did all the things that God
wanted me to do, I'd never have time left for business."
What a telling statement! Being a Christian means so
much more than just believing in the existence of Christ.
Many people believe in Christ, but they consciously remove Him from their hearts and minds. They don't have
time for Him. What a tragedy! Too many people see life
in Christ as slavery rather than freedom. They feel oppressed by the only true liberator that exists.

To understand Christ, we must spend time with Him.
If we reject Him without even getting to know Him, we
rob ourselves of any chance at redemption and salvation.
As Christian people, we need to keep God close by us.
We need to read His Word, dwell upon Him in
our hearts, and speak of Him
wherever and whenever possible.
Keep the Lord close by you, and
you will never feel alone.

PRAYER:

*Be with me, O
my Lord. Plant
Yourself firmly in my
thoughts, and never let me
turn from You. Amen.*

> LORD, *thou hast heard the desire of the humble: thou wilt prepare their heart, thou wilt cause thine ear to hear.*
>
> PSALM 10:17

The jury had argued the merits of the case for hours. Nelson had remained silent through the entire debate, but now he leaned forward and began to speak. Immediately, everyone silenced themselves and turned to listen to what Nelson had to say. Because he had said little previously, his words had a strange impact, and his argument persuaded the jury members.

When someone talks all the time, the tendency is to tune that person out. No one wants to be around someone who chatters incessantly. What a joy it is to find someone who employs an economy of words. The person who speaks infrequently tends to be heard the most.

When we learn to speak to God of the more important desires of our hearts, we can be assured that He is hearing us and will answer our prayers. When we merely chatter on to God about every little annoyance or inconvenience, we may find that He is slower to answer, in hopes that we will learn to take care of problems that are within our own power to solve. Use wisdom in your dealings with God, and you will find your relationship enriched.

PRAYER: Teach me humility and wisdom, O Lord, that I might speak wisely of the things that are most important. Help me to know what I am able to deal with and what I am not. Guide me as I grow. Amen.

*In the Lord put I my trust: how say ye
to my soul, Flee as a bird to your mountain?*
Psalm 11:1

Yani meant well, but sometimes Gail got so mad at her. Gail was a strong Christian, but Yani felt that Christianity was false, and so she kept trying to persuade Gail to try an Eastern faith. Gail had no trouble with Yani believing as she did, but she wanted them to be able to simply share the truth of their separate beliefs in order to grow and learn more. Yani wanted nothing to do with Christian teaching, and she vehemently fought to convince Gail of her erroneous faith. Gail saw no reason to flee from Christianity when in her heart she knew it was right.

We are overexposed to choices. Every day someone will try to tell us that we need one more thing in order to make our lives complete. Ads tell us that we should be dissatisfied with what we have, that we need something different. The truth is, when we find what works, or what is right, or what we like, no one should be able to tell us that we're wrong. Jesus Christ is the Way, the Truth, and the Life, and no one and nothing else can ever take His place. We are already kingdom people. There's no reason to try anything else.

PRAYER:
When I feel surrounded by doubts and I question my faith, Father, reach out to me, that I might know I have nothing to fear. Teach me Your truth each day.

Amen.

The LORD is in his holy temple, the LORD's throne is in heaven: his eyes behold, his eyelids try, the children of men.

PSALM 11:4

Whenever they went to the ocean, Dave remembered Tim and how he had drowned by swimming out too far. Not only did he go out too far, but he swam in an area without a lifeguard. Since that time, Dave always looked for the lifeguard, and he refused to swim if the lifeguard wasn't present. Once, Dave had thought that lifeguards were on the beach to keep people from having too much fun. Now he thought differently.

What comfort there is to know that we are being watched over. This life provides some pretty treacherous waters, and we need to know that there is a divine lifeguard, ready to pull us up at a moment's notice. The Lord watches over us, not to stifle or oppress us, but to ensure us a full, happy, and healthy life. We can tread life's waters knowing that there is nothing to fear, for the Lord is watching.

PRAYER:

When I get in over my head, Lord, be there to lift me up. I need You to watch over me and care for me. I put all my faith in You. Amen.

Help, LORD; for the godly man ceaseth;
for the faithful fail from among the
children of men.

PSALM 12:1

S arah thought that going to a Christian college would be an answer to her prayers. She really looked forward to a community of believers where she could feel at home. She especially wanted to find out what it would be like to date Christian guys who wouldn't try to take advantage of her. Boy, had she been wrong. The guys she went out with at the college were no different from the boys in high school. And a lot of the girls partied all the time. Sarah wondered if there was something wrong with her. Maybe being a Christian wasn't what she thought at all.

Many people face a dilemma like Sarah's. Too many people think that being a Christian means believing but not doing. They act as if being a Christian makes their old behaviors somehow right. Nothing is further from the truth! Being a Christian means living a godly life and rejecting many things that the world says are okay. How sad that the people who do live good lives are the ones who feel like freaks. As the days go on, fewer godly people exist. Thankfully, God is with those who choose the path of righteousness, and He will be with us always.

PRAYER:
I live with a foot
in two worlds,
Lord. Reach out and
pull me into the kingdom,
that I might step from this world into
Yours. Amen.

*The LORD shall cut off all flattering lips,
and the tongue that speaketh proud things.*
PSALM 12:3

A friend of mine tells of a man he worked with who believed that he knew everything there was to know about God. If people expressed their beliefs, the man would criticize and analyze them, telling them what he felt was wrong with their way of thinking. He bragged of all the things he had read, of the people he had met, and the numbers he had led to Christ. His religion was worn as a badge to impress others. However, when things got hard for the man, he found that he was ill-equipped to deal with the pressures.

Our faith in Christ is not to be a source of bragging and pride, but a source of comfort and service. Being Christians doesn't make us better than other people, just better off. We are blessed by the gift of God's love, and we should receive it with humility and grace.

PRAYER:
Creator
God,
You have
made me in
Your image, and
I sometimes forget
how thankful I should be.
All that I am, and all that I
can be, is a gift from You, and
nothing that I have done
on my own. Forgive my
foolish pride. Amen.

For the oppression of the poor, for the sighing of the needy, now will I arise, saith the LORD.

PSALM 12:5

Something is terribly wrong in our world. Some of God's children are ill-fed, homeless, diseased, and abused. Many people do not know the comforts of a home, nor the security of a free state. Who will care for these lowly children of God?

The Bible says that the Lord will rise up in behalf of these people, but it also says that He will do so through His servants and followers. That means that God will provide for His poorer children through the grace of His richer ones. We are called to give from our blessed abundance, that others less fortunate might live. This is not an option for Christians, but a basic mandate upon which our faith is built. We are the hands, the feet, the eyes, and the voice of the Lord. Let us serve Him well.

PRAYER:
Use me as You will, O Lord. Make me an instrument of Thy glory and will. Send the power of Your Spirit into the world through me. Amen.

How long wilt thou forget me, O Lord?
for ever? how long wilt thou hide
thy face from me?
PSALM 13:1

There is no worse feeling than feeling a distance from God. When we cry out in prayer, we need to feel His presence with us. When that feeling is absent, hopelessness and despair set in. We need to know, however, that the Lord has not really gone far from us, but we have pushed Him from ourselves. The Lord is always as close as a prayer, and we need but open our hearts to Him, and His presence will be felt once again. The Lord never hides His face from us, though often He will wait; stepping back like the loving Father that He is, to see whether or not we can struggle through a problem on our own. God wants to see us grow, and He often has to let us struggle a bit in order to allow that growth to occur. Even in those times of trial, however, the Lord is never far away, and He will not allow us to be tried beyond our endurance.

PRAYER: Help me to know that You are with me in every situation at every moment of the day. I need Your comforting presence in my life, O Lord. Without it, I cannot go on. Amen.

Consider and hear me, O LORD my God:
lighten mine eyes, lest I sleep the sleep of death.
PSALM 13:3

Bill was beginning to doubt his faith. He had been confirmed into a church almost twenty years ago, he had once read the Bible regularly, and he still prayed occasionally, always at meals. Still, he felt like he was just stumbling through life like a sleepwalker. Nothing seemed to matter, and Bill felt that his life lacked purpose. There had to be something more, but Bill was wondering what it was.

If the Lord is not a real and vital part of our lives, then we are only half living. God renews us and puts purpose into our being. We are spiritual batteries that constantly need to be recharged. We cannot be recharged apart from the power source: Jesus Christ. The Bible, the church, fellowship with other believers, prayer; these and many other activities draw us close to God and therefore energize our spiritual lives. Draw close to God and feel the power. It's waiting right now, and it is given freely.

PRAYER:
Energize my life
with the power
of Your Holy Spirit,
Lord. Grant that I might live
life fully, not halfway. Open my eyes
to the glorious life I have been given.
Amen.

The fool hath said in his heart, There is no God. They are corrupt, they have done abominable works, there is none that doeth good.

PSALM 14:1

The Reverend Dave Scott stood trembling at the doorway to the sanctuary. During the night, vandals had broken into the church. They hadn't taken anything, but they had destroyed just about everything. Windows were shattered, pews splintered, Bibles ripped apart. Reverend Scott felt a terrible sickness in the pit of his stomach. Who could do such things? Was nothing sacred anymore?

We need to ask ourselves these questions, because we face such situations all the time. Terrible things are done all around us, and often they happen without regard or respect for things we hold sacred. Foolish people hold our God in contempt, and we can only find consolation in the fact that the Lord sees all, and His justice will one day be done. For us, we must hold on to His goodness and His strength so we can endure such inconceivable crimes. Our Lord is greater than the "things" foolish people destroy. His will be done!

PRAYER: O Lord, while the evil days keep coming, grant me strength enough to endure until the end. Remind me that I worship You, and nothing any man or woman can do will ever destroy that. Amen.

The LORD looked down from heaven upon
the children of men, to see if there were
any that did understand, and seek God.
PSALM 14:2

I t won't do you any good. All that talk about God is
just a crutch. Do your best, live for the day; then lie
down and die."

Tim listened to his friend rave on and on, but he never
challenged him. In some ways, he agreed with his friend.
Sometimes Jesus was a crutch, but after all, lame people
need a crutch. Tim felt like he'd been limping through his
entire life before he found Christ. He also believed that
God wanted him to do his best and live for each day, but
he knew there was more to it than that. Even if all his
friends told him that God was a lie, he wouldn't believe it.
God was real, and no one could convince him otherwise.

Arguments against the existence of God can sound
good, but they amount to nothing more than opinion
in the face of fact. We walk by faith, not by sight. God
is looking for faith-walkers. If we will
follow what we know to be true
with our hearts, instead of what
we can be convinced of in our
minds, then God will lead
us and sustain us in
all that we do.

PRAYER:

Be with me, Lord.
All around me are
people who attack
my faith. Dwell in my heart,
and let me feel the reality of Your
presence within. Amen.

3

*Have all the workers of iniquity
no knowledge? who eat up my people as
they eat bread, and call not upon the LORD.*

PSALM 14:4

Cory rode along the street on his bicycle, lighting huge firecrackers and tossing them onto the doorsteps of houses along the way. He would listen for the mighty explosions and then laugh as frightened homeowners came to the door to see what had happened. His terrorizing spree came to an end as one firecracker was too short and a fuse blew up in Cory's hand, severely injuring him.

Do the people who abuse and oppress others really think there is no penalty to pay for what they do? It seems that way. Workers of iniquity who pride themselves on their brilliance and accomplishment are, in fact, some of the most ignorant people alive. Those who do not know the Lord do not know much of anything. True knowledge and wisdom come through love of and respect for the One who died to make our salvation possible: Jesus Christ.

PRAYER: O Lord, steer me away from those who, through ignorance of You, cause pain and destruction. Help me, instead, to build up and defend all that is right and good. Amen.

He that backbiteth not with his tongue,
nor doeth evil to his neighbour, nor taketh
up a reproach against his neighbour.
PSALM 15:3

Ruth attended every church function held, and she never refused to pitch in when there was work to do. She gave liberally of her money, time, and talent. There was nothing she would not do for her church. Even so, she found that others did not welcome her or invite her to join in their special functions. One day she complained to the people she was with, "Too many people think too highly of themselves, and they're jealous of me because I do so much." She began to list by name those whom she meant. Finally, one of her associates stopped her and said, "The reason you're not more welcome is because you always talk about others. You spend a lot of time doing good; then you undo it by gossiping. We get tired of hearing you criticize everyone who doesn't do things like you want them to."

We are called to be Christians in our thoughts, deeds, and words. If the love of God truly dwells in our hearts, then we should show it by the way we treat and talk about others. What we say matters a great deal, and God will judge us based on our words and thoughts, as well as on our actions.

PRAYER:

Lord, help me to love with Your divine love. Keep me from judging others, but never let me forget that to grow, I must continually examine myself.

Amen.

Wow!

*He that putteth not out his money to usury,
nor taketh reward against the innocent. He
that doeth these things shall never be moved.*

PSALM 15:5

The young man was quite proud of himself. He ran a lawn-care service specifically targeted to older people who could not do the work for themselves. But, because he had them in a tough position, he charged them more than he ordinarily could have. Since they couldn't do the work themselves, and they often didn't know anyone else to contact, they had to pay his price. Publicly, he gained the reputation of being a champion of the elderly. Privately, he gloated over his shrewd maneuvering.

The Bible tells us that when we receive our rewards on earth, we have nothing to look forward to from God in the future. Our duty is to love and defend others, not take advantage of them. When we put other people's interests ahead of our own, then we can count on God's favor in the days to come.

PRAYER: You have created everyone equally, Lord, and no one is more precious in Your sight than anyone else. Help me to see the value in all people and do everything in my power to serve them and love them. Amen.

*Their sorrows shall be multiplied that
hasten after another god: their drink offerings
of blood will I not offer, nor take up their names into my lips.*
PSALM 16:4

Ralph had grown up desiring to be wealthy one day. He had worked hard, devoting himself to the pursuit of his precious money. Now he could honestly call himself rich, but he wasn't sure it was all he dreamed it would be. He spent so much of his time protecting what he had accumulated. He lay awake at night worrying about investments, deals, taxes—anything and everything that might ruin his status. His every waking moment was tied up in the acquisition of more and more wealth. On rare occasions, Ralph found himself wishing for just a little peace of mind and a chance to forget about money for a while.

The pursuit of God is one of the few life choices we can make that has no strings attached. We give very little and receive so much. Money, fame, power, and prestige all sound nice, but they require more effort than they are worth. Worse, they pay temporary benefits that fade away, leaving us feeling empty, lost, and alone. Give your life to God, and walk in the ways that He chooses, and you will find that He will bless you continually.

*PRAYER:
Turn me from the
things that cannot
offer me lasting
satisfaction. Turn me instead,
Lord, to the things that are eternal
and holy. Amen.*

I have set the LORD always before me:
because he is at my right hand, I
shall not be moved.

PSALM 16:8

The little boy rode his bicycle like a demon. He would pedal as fast as he could and fly down the street. He still had training wheels on his bicycle, though he did little to balance it. He had long since gained his balance, but he refused to let his parents remove them. Some of his friends made fun of him, but he felt safe and secure, as long as the training wheels were firmly in place.

All of us have times in our lives when we need something or someone to help us. Sometimes these things become crutches to us, but other times they give us the confidence and support we desperately need. God is the only support we truly need, and we can rest assured that He will always be close by. With God before us, we can stand up against anything. He is not a crutch. He's the source of all strength and power.

PRAYER:
Lord, be
my strength.
When I
need help to
get through the day,
be with me and help me
to know that You are there.
Amen.

Thou hast proved mine heart; thou hast visited me in the night; thou hast tried me, and shalt find nothing; I am purposed that my mouth shall not transgress.

PSALM 17:3

Being a teacher for thirty years teaches you an awful lot. Ann had seen just about every trick in the book. The minute her back was turned, children would try all kinds of things. Often she would leave the room for a few minutes, just to see who her problem children were going to be. She would return suddenly and catch them in all stages of misbehavior. There were the exceptions, of course. Some children sat quietly whether she was in the room or not. Those children were rare treasures, but they often helped her keep her sanity.

All of us behave differently when we think we're being watched. Usually, we are on our best behavior when we know that someone else is around. The funny thing is, Somebody is always with us: God. Is God pleased when He sees the way we act when we're alone? It is a wise person who tries to live righteously all the time, both when others are with him and when he is alone. God will help us be the people we are meet to be if we will only ask. No one is more deserving of our best behavior than God.

PRAYER:

Lord, help me to give You my best, not my worst. Keep me very mindful of Your presence, and help me make You proud of who I am becoming. Amen.

Hold up my goings in thy paths,
that my footsteps slip not.
PSALM 17:5

Burt had worked in high-rise construction all his life. Every day he would walk the girders high above the ground with apparent ease. In his lifetime he had seen a number of men plunge from the girders due to a mere moment of carelessness. As for himself, he knew he had been protected. Each morning he began work only after saying a short prayer, asking the Lord to watch his movements through the day, keeping him safe from any mishap.

Though most of us never do anything as dangerous or risky as high-rise construction, we do stand in danger of falling to temptation. A fall like that is as devastating to the soul as a plunge from a high girder would be to our physical being. No matter how careful we try to be, we need someone to catch us when we stumble. God is that Someone. He waits with open arms to catch His children when they fall. Rest easy in the knowledge that God guides your steps. He will protect those who put their trust in Him.

PRAYER: I need Your guiding love, Almighty God. Without it, I am sure to fall. Thank You for being with me, picking me up when I fall. Amen.

The LORD is my rock, and my fortress, and my deliverer; my God, my strength, in whom I will trust; my buckler, and the horn of my salvation, and my high tower.

PSALM 18:2

J ennifer could hardly wait for her shift to be over. The nurses' station was a mad rush, and there was simply no time to even catch her breath. Some nights she wondered why she had ever gone into nursing. The pace was so crazy, and the work was exhausting, both mentally and physically. For a moment, Jennifer closed her eyes and said a quick prayer to the Lord, thanking Him for His great mercy and asking for just enough strength to make it through.

The Lord listens for our prayers, and He responds by giving us the strength we need to meet every situation. He truly is our strength and our fortress. Trust in the Lord, and He will grant you His peace.

PRAYER:

Dear Lord, there are times when I just don't think I can make it. Please grant me Your power to endure and succeed. Help me to remember that real strength comes from You. Amen.

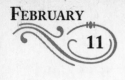
*I will call upon the LORD, who is worthy to
be praised: so shall I be saved
from mine enemies.*

PSALM 18:3

When Charlie was a boy, he used to dream of being like his favorite comic book hero. With super powers, Charlie knew he'd be unstoppable. No one could pick on him, no one could tell him what to do, and everybody would love him. As he grew older, Charlie was sad to realize that no superhero life lay in his future. Superheroes were just myths.

Then, one day, Charlie found a new kind of hero. A friend of his gave him a New Testament and asked him to read it. Charlie was swept into a world where sin and evil came to an end, where good really did win, and where love was the strongest power of all. And the best thing was, everyone who believed could be a hero, too.

We need to choose our heroes carefully. Only one hero is worthy of our praise and allegiance, and that is Jesus Christ. Jesus will save us from our enemies, and He will set all things right. Follow Him, and He will grant you a power beyond belief.

PRAYER:
Dear God,
I follow so
many false
heroes, thinking
they might have
something I need. Help
me to remember that all I
could ever need or want, You
have already given me through
the life of Your blessed Son.
Amen.

He delivered me from my strong enemy,
and from them which hated me: for they
were too strong for me.
PSALM 18:17

Young David was foolish to think he could succeed where the army of Israel had failed. The Philistines were mighty, they were mean, and they were excellent fighters. They had been unstoppable as they marched throughout the lands of the Middle East. What chance did one small boy have against the leader of the mightiest fighting machine in history?

Alone, David would not have stood a chance, but David was not alone. As young as David was, he still had the wisdom to call upon God for help in his time of greatest need. Faith is the most powerful force in the universe, and it knows no age. The faith of a child is every bit as mighty as the faith of an older man or woman.

As we face problems that seem much too great for us to handle alone, we need to understand that the same problem is as nothing to God. God is on our side, and He will surely help us whenever we call upon Him. David would not have faced his Goliath without God on his side. Should we ever face our own Goliaths without Him?

PRAYER:
Lord, send Your might to see me through the storms of life. When trials seem too gigantic to handle, be the source of my strength. Deliver me and comfort me, O Lord. Amen.

The LORD rewarded me according to my righteousness; according to the cleanness of my hands hath he recompensed me.

PSALM 18:20

The children knew what to expect from their teacher. She rewarded those who gave their best effort. It didn't matter so much that they were right all the time. What was important was that they tried to do the best they could. The dullest student was rewarded as often as the brightest, as long as he put forth effort. Year after year, the teacher turned out good students.

Putting forth a great deal of effort is much easier when we can feel we've accomplished something. There is a basic instinct within each of us that likes praise and reward. We need to feel that we are noticed when we do what is good and right. The Lord sees all that we do, and His pleasure is ever with us. His abundant blessings come to all who truly love Him and pursue Him with all their hearts, minds, and souls.

PRAYER:
I will try to do my very best, God. I want to be the person You intend for me to be. Assist me as I struggle to find Your image within myself and shine forth that image for the whole world to see. Amen.

*For thou wilt light my candle: the L*ORD
my God will enlighten my darkness.
PSALM 18:28

Jeffey dutifully tended the lamp that hung by the altar. The flame had not failed in over thirty years. Throughout that time, Jeffey had daily filled the lamp with oil. People throughout the church marveled at his dedication and persistence.

One day Jeffey became sick and had to go to the hospital. Friends stopped in to see Jeffey, and as each one left, he lifted his head and said, "Don't forget the light, okay?"

One woman, puzzled by the urgency of Jeffey's reminder, asked why the little lamp meant so much to him. His eyes grew misty, and he said, "That light means the world to me. When I was young, two lights came into my life: my wife and Jesus. My wife died, but then so did Jesus. The lamp reminds me that so long as it shines, both of them are still alive. I guess it wouldn't matter if the lamp went out, but it's important to me."

God sends light into our lives in many ways. The greatest light of all is love, and we know love through His greatest gift, Jesus Christ.

PRAYER:
Shine forth through the dark reaches of my life, Light of the World. Fill me with Your blessed warmth and glow. Shine through me for others to see. Let me be Your love in this world.
Amen.

He maketh my feet like hinds' feet, and setteth me upon my high places.
PSALM 18:33

Her grace and beauty were breathtaking. The doe paused for a moment; then she sprang forth in a poetic dance of joy. Effortlessly, she scaled the rocky incline, never missing her footing, until she stood out against the autumn sky. Her gentle eyes scanned the horizon, she sniffed delicately, shook her head once, and then was off.

God has equipped His creation with many wonderful and amazing qualities. The doe that can climb steep mountains with nary a misstep, the jaguar that can outrun any prey and turn sharply at its fastest pace, the eagle that can span vast distances in a matter of hours—all these creatures are strong because they use their God-given talents as they were intended to.

There is a lesson to learn from such creatures. We, too, have been given many wonderful gifts and talents. When we affirm the talents we have been given, then God will surely bless us, and we will be a sign to others of His goodness. God has given us hands, feet, wings to fly, power, grace, and a multitude of other gifts. Embrace them, and know that the Lord is good.

PRAYER:

Teach me to use the gifts I have been given. Aid me as I test my wings and struggle to get my footing. Be patient with me, Lord, and touch me with Your touch of peace and grace. Amen.

He teacheth my hands to war, so that a
bow of steel is broken by mine arms.
PSALM 18:34

Angela was the youngest of six children. Her memories of childhood conjured images of constant fighting and competition. She had learned very early how to fight. Her young years had been a painful lesson in the survival of the fittest.

It was only after she left home that she found out that living didn't mean fighting. She met and married a strong Christian man whose strength came not from any physical source, but from a deep and abiding faith in the Lord. He taught her patience and compassion and peace. Her world was turned upside down as she realized that true strength came not from fighting, but from refusing to fight. God granted her a power greater than any she'd known. By her peace of mind and spirit, Angela broke free from the bondage of her past and faced the future with the assurance that nothing could ever defeat her again.

PRAYER:

Lord, remove from me my spirit of competition in trying to be better than other people. Whenever my will says to fight back in anger, let Your spirit prevail with a desire to forgive. Make me strong in Your love.

Amen.

*Thou hast enlarged my steps under
me, that my feet did not slip.*

PSALM 18:36

Brent thought he was going to freeze to death. He had set out to Jill's house during the early throes of the blizzard. It was four miles to her house, but the drifting snow was making progress almost impossible. He was halfway there, so it didn't matter whether he went forward or back; the trip was going to be rough. He could have kicked himself for not being prepared before leaving the house. Now he was paying for it.

As he passed the Johnson house, Ed Johnson leaned out and called to him. As Brent looked up, Ed held out a pair of snowshoes, waving them with a big grin on his face. Brent broke into a smile and struggled over to the Johnsons'. When he was young, Brent thought people in Minnesota were eccentric for keeping snowshoes around. Suddenly, it didn't seem so funny anymore.

There are some situations that arise in our lives that are as difficult to get through as a deep snowdrift or sifting sand. We struggle, and the more we do, the worse off we become. God reaches out to us in those times, gladly lending a hand. He will enlarge our steps, so that we might get over the toughest problems. Believe it.

PRAYER:

Dear Lord, equip me with the means to meet life's problems. Often I flounder around, sinking deeper and deeper into tough situations. Liberate me, and set me back on my feet, I pray. Amen.

The heavens declare the glory of God;
and the firmament sheweth his handywork.
PSALM 19:1

Steve slammed on the brakes and pulled to the side of the road in anger and frustration. Grabbing the map and a flashlight from the glove compartment, he burst out of the car. He knew he was lost, but he didn't have the slightest idea how to get himself found again. He leaned on the roof of the car, tracing out his location on the map. After a few moments, he snapped off the light, closed his eyes, and laid his head against the metal of the car. When he opened his eyes, he was startled by the number and beauty of the stars in the Arizona sky. Like a child, he gazed at the heavens with his mouth hanging open. Never before could he remember such a beautiful sight. A peace came over him that totally removed the rage of a few minutes before. Forgetting the time or the situation, Steve climbed up on the hood of his car, leaning back to soak in the splendor of God's creation.

This day, we need to stop for a moment to open new eyes to the wonder of God's world. If we will only try to see it through His eyes rather than our own, we will find new beauty that we never noticed before. His is a world of wonder and miracles. See it.

PRAYER:

Lord, open my eyes that I might see all that this world is meant to be. Do not let the pressures of the day create a cloud that prevents me from seeing Your beauty. Amen.

*The law of the Lord is perfect, converting
the soul: the testimony of the Lord is sure,
making wise the simple.*

PSALM 19:7

The church conference was going along fairly well. Plans were being made, new officers were elected, and proposals were abounding. Business was getting done. Elaine sat back and watched the proceedings with a sense of awe and disappointment. She knew she was new to church policy and planning, but she still felt that God should have a place in it all. No one seemed to be talking much about Him. What good was a church without God? Finally, when she could stand it no longer, she stood up to address the planning board. She expressed her concern, and a hush fell over the group. It seemed that the absence of God from the conference hadn't dawned on anyone else. From this moment on, the conference took on a different feel, and all agreed it was one of the best ever.

We may not always have the most information or the best background, but we know that nothing of real value can occur apart from the Lord. When God is present, souls are converted, the simple are made wise, and miracles begin to happen. Remember the Lord in all that you do.

PRAYER: As I plan my days and my weeks, Lord, be a central part of all I do. Be with me to decide what is best. Guide me by Your will and Your Spirit. Amen.

*The fear of the LORD is clean, enduring
for ever: the judgments of the LORD are
true and righteous altogether.*
PSALM 19:9

Patty always laughed whenever anyone tried to tell her that what she did was sinful. She would mock her friends, telling them they sounded like old ladies. Gwen couldn't understand how Patty could do the things she did and still call herself a Christian. Gwen was surprised to see Patty standing at her door in tears.

Patty had begun to wake up to the fact that she really was living a wrong lifestyle. The more she thought about it, the worse she felt. She hoped that Gwen could help her. Gwen told her that she was already on the right track to finding help. Realizing that what you do is wrong is the first step. Fearing what might happen because of what you do is the next step. Fear can be a healthy thing for us when it forces us to clean up our lives and walk the straight path. Once on the right path, we can leave fear behind, for nothing can harm us once we are in the Lord's camp. God's judgments are righteous and true, and He will always help us make the changes that allow us to clean up our lives, if we will only ask Him to.

PRAYER:
I need to respect You more, Lord. I need to be reminded that Your way is the only way, so that I won't be tempted to stray. Be with me to guide me. Amen.

Let the words of my mouth, and the meditation of my heart, be acceptable in thy sight, O LORD, my strength, and my redeemer.

PSALM 19:14

Paula put up a good front. Though she couldn't stand Beth, she never said anything bad to her. She kept quiet until she was alone with her other friends. At odd times she would think of Beth, and resentment and contempt would rise up within her heart. Still, Paula was quite pleased with herself that she never let Beth know how she truly felt.

It is not enough that we try to put on a good front when we are around people we don't like. We need to search our hearts for reconciliation and forgiveness. We need to tap into the saving love of Christ, which heals all hurts and is the source of all patience and tolerance. God is interested in both the words of our mouths and the deepest ponderings of our hearts. To appear Christlike on the surface is never enough. To be Christlike at the core of our being, that is the key.

PRAYER: Creator, God, I want to be a Christian to the very depths of my being. Search my heart, and transform it. Let love reign. Amen.

Some trust in chariots, and some in horses:
but we will remember the name of the
LORD our God.
PSALM 20:7

Grayson was as old as the hills. He had farmed the same stretch of land for more than sixty years. Every year, the farms around old Grayson's invested in fancy new equipment and machinery. Grayson farmed with the same equipment year after year—once new, now antique. His neighbors tried to encourage him to upgrade his tools, but Grayson just shook his head. His justification for his stubbornness was simple: If the Lord wanted him to have a bountiful harvest, he would. It wasn't the machinery that made the farm. It wasn't the latest technology. It was the will of the Lord.

His neighbors secretly laughed at the simplistic reasoning of the old man, but time and again they ended up amazed at what he was able to do with his simple means. When harvesttime came round, Grayson held his own with the best of them.

The simple faith of a single man or woman is a mighty thing. Trust in the Lord, and you will marvel at all that can be done.

PRAYER:
Make me faithful,
Lord. I doubt so
often, and I put my
faith in other things. Those
things will pass away, but I know
that You will endure forever. Thank You
for Your love and grace. Amen.

Thine hand shall find out all thine enemies: thy right hand shall find out those that hate thee.

PSALM 21:8

Hiding was useless. Tim knew that he would be found out soon enough. He had pushed his luck just a little too far. At first, stealing had been for fun, just to see if he could get away with it. Then it turned into a kind of sport, until finally he could hardly help himself. Now he'd been seen, and it was just a matter of time till someone caught up with him. What had seemed so cool before seemed pretty stupid now. There was no way out. He was in big trouble.

It seems to be part of human nature to ignore consequences until it is too late. God gives us an awful lot of opportunities to make up our minds whether or not we will follow Him, but we cannot expect Him to wait forever. God knows our hearts this very minute. There is no hiding from Him. If we are not for Him, we are against Him. The choice is ours. Each day gives us a new opportunity to reconfirm our faith in God. Let us take each and every opportunity.

PRAYER: I get tired of hiding, Lord. Seek me out and inspire me to be a better person today than I was yesterday. I want to follow You and walk in the ways of Your Son. Amen.

Be thou exalted, LORD, in thine own strength: so will we sing and praise thy power.

PSALM 21:13

Reverend Davis looked down at his hands and shook his head. He was so tired, and he just didn't feel he had anything left in him that people ought to hear. He couldn't understand it. He'd always tried to do the Lord's work and lead people to Jesus. He had preached the gospel every chance he got. He had even achieved a certain level of fame. No one could deny what a powerful soldier for Christ he had been. Reverend Davis just couldn't make sense out of the fact that God wasn't helping him now, when he needed it most. At least God owed him that.

Too often we fall into the trap of believing that we do God's work for Him. That's not true. The most we can do is open ourselves to let the Lord do His own work through us. When we try to do it for Him, we can only expect to grow weary. However, when God works through us, we will find a new energy and vitality that we have never experienced before. The Lord is exalted through His own strength, not ours. Open yourself to Him now, and let the true power begin to flow.

PRAYER:

Make me an instrument of Your peace, love, and hope, O Lord. Allow me to serve You, not by my own rules, but Yours. Amen.

My God, my God, why hast thou forsaken me? why art thou so far from helping me, and from the words of my roaring?

PSALM 22:1

I lay awake, crying in the night. I thought of all the things happening in my life, and I was frightened by the feeling of aloneness I was experiencing. Never had my life looked so bleak. Suicide wasn't an answer, because I was too afraid to die. I thought God was with me, but my prayers simply faded into the darkness, with no one to hear them. God had abandoned me, and I didn't know what I'd done to deserve it. I rolled over in my bed and noticed a shaft of moonlight shining through the window, coming to rest on a picture of my grandfather. Grandpa would have known what to do. He would have told me to quit feeling sorry for myself and take control of my own circumstances. He never let anything rule over him...except God. Suddenly the light of the Lord broke through my depression. In an instant I realized that God had been with me all along; I had just chosen to look the other way. His divine love broke through on the wings of a moonbeam, and His answer moved through my heart with the memory of my grandpa. Never does the Lord forsake His own. The only distance that is ever between us is the distance that we put there.

PRAYER:
Gift of my life, continue to shower me with Your love. Let me feel Your gentle weight upon my heart, and keep me ever mindful of Your presence in my life. Amen.

O my God, I cry in the day time, but thou
hearest not; and in the night season,
and am not silent.

PSALM 22:2

Prayer is a tricky thing. It was never meant as a "gimme" list by which we can get things from God. It is not a gripe time to vent frustrations and woes. It is not a time to show off our piety. Rather, it is a time to draw close to God in order to be open to His will and guidance. So often we feel that God is not listening because we don't get what we ask for. We want results immediately, and we decide beforehand what we will accept as an answer and what we will not. Who says that we get to make the rules?

The Lord hears us, and He is true to answer us, but He always measures His responses according to His divine wisdom. He knows what is best for us, even when it doesn't agree with what we want. It is natural and human to doubt the Lord sometimes. He understands that. Just don't give up. The Lord breaks through our desert spots to comfort us when we cry.

PRAYER:

Lift me, Lord, into
Your loving arms.
Grace me with the
sweet memory of Your care,
that I might never doubt You in times
of trial. Amen.

Be not far from me; for trouble is near;
for there is none to help.

PSALM 22:11

S am stuck close to his older brother Ed. Some bullies had been bothering him and so he felt wisdom was the better part of valor; he dogged Ed's every step. Ed didn't mind. He kind of liked it. He liked knowing that his little brother trusted him and looked up to him. If it was protection Sam wanted, then protection he would have.

The Lord is never far from us. Once we put our trust in Him, He is true to protect and defend us. He loves us to put our faith and respect in Him. Though life may get stormy and rough, the Lord is there to calm the waters and get us through safely.

PRAYER:

Dear Lord,
be with me
as I face the
challenges of each
new day. Protect me
from those things that can
harm me. Stay close to me, for
I know of no greater strength
than Yours. Amen.

*I am poured out like water, and all my
bones are out of joint: my heart is like
wax; it is melted in the midst of my bowels.*
PSALM 22:14

I had a friend who thought some boys were trying to mug him. In his efforts to run away, he fell down a flight of stairs and landed in a pile of garbage. He suffered many broken bones and scrapes, and required a large number of stitches. As he lay in pain and refuse, he heard the boys draw close. He prayed to God for help. He heard the boys getting steadily closer, and as his prayers increased, the boys moved out of the alley and across to the top of the steps. In the light that shined there, the man saw that the boys were scouts. In a wave of relief and embarrassment, my friend sank back into the garbage and passed out.

It is good to know that even in our own foolishness we can turn to the Lord for help. Often we are our own worst enemies, but that doesn't matter to the Lord. In our brokenness, God reaches out to us and loves us.

*PRAYER:
Lord, I am often
guilty of doing
foolish things.
I hurt myself in so
many needless ways.
Protect me from myself, and in
my times of greatest suffering and
pain, be the source of my comfort. Amen.*

Deliver my soul from the sword;
my darling from the power of the dog.
PSALM 22:20

Perhaps the most pleasing prayer that we offer to God is the prayer that we pray for someone else. A prayer for another person is an unselfish and caring act. It takes the trust we have in God and extends it outward on behalf of other people. It is an example of how we can walk in the footsteps of Jesus. Certainly, God wants us to pray for our personal needs, but we enter into His ministry and love when we send forth our prayers in the names of others.

PRAYER: Hear the concerns of my heart, Almighty God. I care for so many people, and I want to lift them up to Your care. Be with them and give them the blessings that You continue to give to me. Make Yourself real in their lives, Lord. Amen.

Save me from the lion's mouth: for thou
hast heard me from the horns of the unicorns.
PSALM 22:21

Josh huddled close to the tree trunk. It had been hours since he had gotten separated from the rest of his troop. Darkness had come, and then the wind kicked up and a storm approached. In the distance Josh could hear animals fighting. He prayed that they wouldn't pick up his scent and come looking for him. As he hugged his pack closer to his chest, he felt a familiar friend, the Bible his father had given to him. He carried it with him wherever he went. Right now it didn't matter that it was too dark to read it. Josh knew it was there, and that made him feel a bit more secure.

The Word of God can be a powerful source of comfort for us. In times of danger and dread, the Lord will come close to us, to comfort and protect us. Rest in the Lord, and He will save you.

PRAYER:
Lord, be with me
this day. Help me
to see Your presence
everywhere I go. I need to
feel You are near me. Amen.

The meek shall eat and be satisfied: they shall praise the LORD that seek him: your heart shall live for ever.
PSALM 22:26

Stella never asked for very much. She was a quiet woman, and everyone who knew her adored her. She came to all the church functions and sat down by herself, never wanting to impose on anyone. In no time at all, her table was filled with people who wanted to be with her. Her kindness and gentleness attracted people to her. Stella never wanted for company and attention, because her meek spirit shone forth like a beautiful light.

PRAYER: O Lord, please break my spirit of pride and aggressiveness. Let me reflect the peace and tranquility of heart that Your love inspires. In a world of torrent and turmoil, let me stay calm. Fill me with gentleness and meekness. Amen.

The LORD is my shepherd; I shall not want.
PSALM 23:1

On their own, sheep will starve. They do not have enough sense to move on to greener pastures when their own is stripped of foliage. They will wander off into traps, standing helplessly while predators stalk them. Of all God's creatures, few are more helpless than sheep.

It is interesting that God calls us His sheep. We so often think that we have complete control over our lives, and yet we really are helpless. We need to admit our weaknesses. When we admit weakness, that is our strength, because then we understand our need for God. God will protect us, provide for us, guide us from place to place, and never leave us alone. He truly is the Good Shepherd, the best shepherd we could ever hope to find. We need a shepherd. Thank goodness we have the finest.

PRAYER:
Lord, I have difficulty admitting that I cannot do everything on my own. Help me to see that leaning on Your strength is not weakness at all, but power beyond measure. By Your wisdom I am saved.
Amen.

Yea, though I walk through the valley of the shadow of death, I will fear no evil: for thou art with me; thy rod and thy staff they comfort me.

PSALM 23:4

To look at Bess and to listen to her talk, you would never have thought she was dying of cancer. She always had the same smile on her face and a kind word for everyone who came to see her. The other patients spent a lot of time with her, because her spirit seemed to be contagious. She ministered to her roommates by remaining cheerful and positive. Even the thought of death couldn't take Bess's dynamic humor from her.

The love of God can help us to endure many things. Circumstances that ordinarily knock us flat are as nothing when face-to-face with the power of God. Cry out to God in times of affliction, and He will comfort you and lift you above the fear of evil things. Truly, our help is in the Lord.

PRAYER: There is nothing in this life, Lord, that I cannot face as long as You are with me. Amen.

Thou preparest a table before me in the presence of mine enemies: thou anointest my head with oil; my cup runneth over.
PSALM 23:5

Some people never find satisfaction in the things they do have, but spend their entire lives wishing for things they don't have. They are never happy with where their lives are going; they feel empty in their relationships, and therefore they find it impossible to give thanks for the many blessings they have been given.

As Christians, we are people of praise. Every prayer we offer unto God should acknowledge the many wonderful things that He has done for us. Only a blind person can deny the beauty and splendor of this world. God gives good things to His children, and we should be thankful for all that we have.

PRAYER:
Lord, I cannot believe how much I have been given. Help open my eyes to the many blessings that have been bestowed upon me. Make me thankful, Lord. Amen.

*The earth is the LORD's and the fulness
thereof; the world, and they that dwell therein.*

PSALM 24:1

Two families disputed for years about who held claim upon a stretch of fertile land. Harsh words and insults were exchanged regularly, and on occasion, tempers flared to the point of physical violence. Neither family would budge in their conviction that they were the rightful owners. No compromise could be reached, and so the seeds of bitterness took root and flourished between the two clans.

Long after the two families are but faint memories, the land will still be there. How foolish it is to devote so much of our lives to the acquisition of things, when all things truly belong to the Lord. We are but caretakers of what the Lord has made, and it has been given to us for everyone's pleasure. Wise use of our resources and preservation of all creation is the responsibility of all humankind. We have been given many precious gifts, but they are ours for only a while. In time, all things return to the Lord.

PRAYER:

Lord, make me a wise steward of Your creation. Let my actions hurt not one living thing. Help me to build up, rather than destroy. Inspire me to share, to give, and to love. Amen.

babies &
shared Hope

*O my God, I trust in thee: let me not be
ashamed, let not mine enemies triumph over me.*
PSALM 25:2

Gail called herself a good Christian. She read her
Bible, prayed daily, attended church every Sunday, and pitched in whenever her church needed her. God seemed to be a very real part of Gail's life,
and yet, whenever her faith was put to the test, she seemed
to give up. Her answer for everything was, "Well, God
couldn't be bothered with me, I suppose." The truth was,
Gail was afraid to put her full faith in God, for fear He
might let her down. Her feelings of unworthiness blocked
her from putting her trust totally in God.

Trust takes time. We need to practice putting our trust
in the Lord, but when we do, we find a new confidence
that He will be faithful to us. The more we trust, the more
we are convinced that our trust is
well placed. The key to trust is
to try. Try putting your faith in
the Lord, and watch wonderful
things happen.

PRAYER:

*Assist me as I
try to let go of
my doubt and fear
and put my trust in You. I
sometimes become my own worst
enemy, Father. Save me from myself.*

Amen. yep!

Remember not the sins of my youth, nor my transgressions: according to thy mercy remember thou me for thy goodness' sake, O LORD.

PSALM 25:7

Perry had paid the penalty a thousand times. The guilt that he carried with him gnawed at him constantly. When he was a teenager, he had foolishly tossed a firecracker at a friend of his, to scare him. The explosive had gone off in his friend's face, blinding him. Perry played the scene over and over in his mind, even though many years had passed. His friend had forgiven him, and he had even asked forgiveness from God. His pastor told him that the sin was forgiven, but Perry just couldn't forgive himself. *Hardest on ourselves.*

Who are we to hold on to past sins when our Lord has forgiven and forgotten them? As long as we're human, we will have pasts filled with sins abundant. To dwell on them is to make ourselves less than God wants us to be. Ask forgiveness from the Lord, receive it, and move forward in the glory of God's grace. Your sins are forgiven, indeed!

PRAYER: Teach me to let go of the things I have done wrong in the past, Lord. Cleanse me and prepare me for the wonderful life that is to come. May I learn from my mistakes and grow from them without allowing them to control my life, O Lord. Amen.

Learn & grow as we go.

Mine eyes are ever toward the LORD;
for he shall pluck my feet out of the net.
PSALM 25:15

Critical
Fast 40 days

J erry was terrified of heights. He had been all his life. Unfortunately, his new job required that he climb ladders and travel across catwalks high above the ground. With great courage and resolve, Jerry worked on overcoming his fear. Whenever he had to climb or walk the catwalk, he would focus his attention on the end of the line and pretend that Jesus was waiting there with outstretched arms. His fear left him completely, and he was able to scale great heights without concern.

If we will set our sights on the Lord, He will make our steps sure. No snare, trap, or pitfall can stop us when our eyes are on the Lord. He will guard us each step of the way.

PRAYER:

I am uncertain,
Lord, and often
I am afraid. Dispel
my fears, and instill Your
holy confidence in me. I place
my trust in You, that I might walk a
good walk of faith and never stumble.
Amen.

Return from Saluda, S.C.
Billie (Sis) James, Marie
Luke — say "Hi" to ...

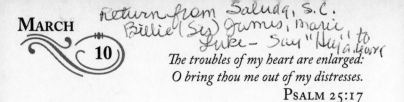

The troubles of my heart are enlarged:
O bring thou me out of my distresses.

PSALM 25:17

Maggie was beside herself with anxiety. The last thing her boss had said to her was that she had to be in the office early the next morning. Her boss and the owner of the company wanted to "have a talk with her about her performance." What did that mean? Was it good or bad? Surely they would have told her if it was good. Maggie just knew she was going to be fired.

Isn't it amazing what we can let our minds do to us? We blow things out of proportion, and it causes such great suffering and distress. When we thrust ourselves into panic and fear, it is good to know that we can turn to the Lord, and He will be faithful to comfort us. Open yourself to His peace, and you will find new serenity.

PRAYER:

I let my mind get carried away sometimes, Lord. Please don't let me get too carried away. I need Your wisdom as an anchor when I set myself adrift in worry and fear. Be my salvation, Father. Amen.

Let me only 'hear' & say Positive. Critical away.

*I have hated the congregation of evil doers;
and will not sit with the wicked.*
PSALM 26:5

Jeremy knew he wasn't cool. Everyone at school told
him so. He wanted to be cool, but he wasn't willing to
do the things people told him he had to do in order to
be cool. He didn't want to smoke, or do drugs, or drink, or
hurt other people. If that was cool, forget it. It just wasn't
worth it inside. If people didn't want to accept him as he
was, then maybe they weren't worth his time, anyway.

Sometimes it's very difficult to say no to evildoers. It
can be very lonely, because so many people love to do what
they know is wrong. It is a very rare individual who will
say no even when it means being rejected. Still, God calls
us to live right and good lives. In
order to do that, we need to steer
clear of evildoers. Call upon the
Lord to give you strength and
conviction. He will answer
your call.

PRAYER:

*All around me I
see people doing
things that are not
pleasing to You. I want
to live a good life, Father, one
that is pleasing to You. Rescue me
from those who would drag me down,
and fill me with Your Spirit. Amen.*

The LORD is my light and my salvation;
whom shall I fear? the LORD is the strength
of my life, of whom shall I be afraid?

PSALM 27:1

The group of demonstrators refused to move along, as the police instructed them. They were committed to their cause, and no amount of threat or coercion was going to sway them. They were standing up for what they believed in. Though many went off to prison, none complained, for they knew they had done what was pleasing to God. By His grace, they had no cause to fear.

God doesn't want worthy people nearly as much as He wants committed people. Those individuals who stand up and say, "Here am I, Lord! Take me," are the ones who please Him most. To those who give their all to the Lord, He will give comfort and peace. They will have no cause to fear anything.

PRAYER:
Make me
a reflection
of Your divine
light, O God. By
Your light all fear is
erased and all darkness
dispelled. Amen.

Though an host should encamp against me,
my heart shall not fear: though war should
rise against me, in this will I be confident.
PSALM 27:3

Each new day brings with it the threat of war somewhere in the world. Many countries have seldom
known peace. Even in America, there are people
who live in fear for the future as we escalate the creation
of new nuclear instruments of destruction. If this world is
our only source of faith, then we are in serious trouble.

Thankfully, our destiny is not tied to this world, but
to the eternal domain of our God. We need fear nothing,
since we have the assurance of an eternal home of peace
and sanity. There is great comfort in knowing that the Lord
is still in control. This world may come to an untimely
end, but the heavens shall endure
forever. Praise God!

PRAYER:
Maker of all good
things, be the
source of sanity in a
world gone mad. In the
face of nuclear terror, be our
support and strength. Keep us safely
in Your care, both this day and evermore.
Amen.

When my father and my mother forsake me,
then the Lord will take me up.

PSALM 27:10

Zachary sat on the front steps, his chin propped up on his hands. His dad was busy with work around the house, and his mom was doing work she had brought home from the office. Neither one of them had any time for him anymore. There was always something else that was more important. Zachary found himself spending a lot of time on his front steps.

Our world can be a lonely place when everyone's too busy to give time to one another. People get lost in the shuffle. Sometimes it happens to us. We need the Lord in our lives so we never have to worry about being alone. The Spirit of God dwells within each one of us, and for that reason, God is never far from us. When the pace of life threatens to bury you, remember the Lord and reach out to Him. He will not leave you lonely.

PRAYER:

Lord, I am reaching out to You. When I feel most alone, be close to me. Help me to always be aware of Your presence. Amen.

Wait on the LORD: be of good courage, and he shall strengthen thine heart: wait, I say, on the LORD.

PSALM 27:14

When I was a few years younger, I began to believe that I would never find another person to share my life with. I had lived as a single more years than I cared to, and I used to pray daily for God to send the right person to me. I said that same prayer for almost seven years. Just at the point where I began to think maybe God wasn't listening, the most wonderful woman I've ever met showed up out of the blue. The Lord worked through the perfect relationship for me, in His own time. Though I battled a continual lack of patience, the will of the Lord prevailed, and I couldn't be happier.

As difficult as it is, waiting on the Lord always pays off in the long run. God knows the perfect solution to all life's situations. All we need do is ask for His divine guidance and help, and He will make all things good. Wait on the Lord!

PRAYER:
Hear my prayers,
O Lord, and fill
me with a patience
that will see me through
even the longest dry spells. I know
that You will do what is best for me.
Amen.

Draw me not away with the wicked, and with the workers of iniquity, which speak peace to their neighbours, but mischief is in their hearts.

PSALM 28:3

A small village depended on its large neighbor to protect and defend it. The small village had no means to defend itself on its own. For years the large village defended the smaller one; but one day, when the small village needed support, the larger village refused, saying they no longer cared what happened. Actually, the larger village wanted to acquire the land of the smaller one, so they had hired a band of soldiers to attack the little village.

This parable is not a piece of simple fiction, but a startling and sad reality in our world today. Deceit is the order of the day. What will ever bring all the sadness and oppression to an end? The Lord God, that's who. The Lord despises evil, and one day all evil will be erased. As kingdom people, we can rejoice in the promise of peace and harmony that God is sure to supply.

PRAYER:
Lord,
search out
the depths
of my heart,
and remove any
deceit that You might
find within me. Purge
my heart of all wickedness.
Count me among the number
of the faithful, not the
mischievous. Amen.

Fasting 1 week

The LORD is my strength and my shield;
my heart trusted in him, and I am helped:
therefore my heart greatly rejoiceth; and
with my song will I praise him.
PSALM 28:7

Karen wanted so badly for the semester to end. She was tired and mentally exhausted. Nothing had seemed to go right. She supposed her grades would be fine, but grades meant very little when you felt so bad about all your classes. Better to be done with it and put it all behind. When the end did finally roll around, Karen felt as if the weight of the world had been lifted from her shoulders. Maybe things weren't so bad, after all.

If we put our faith in God, He will see us through the tough times, and we will emerge from our experiences renewed and wiser. He truly is our shield and strength. Rejoice in His great love for us, and lift your voice in praise.

PRAYER:
Lord, I can get
through anything
if I know that You are
with me. Be close by my side,
teaching me the way I should walk.
Amen.

Give unto the LORD, O ye mighty, give unto the LORD glory and strength.

PSALM 29:1

Scott never forgot where his strength and courage came from. He had battled fires for most of his adult life, and he knew how lucky he had been to never be seriously hurt. He had been in plenty of tough situations, but everything had always worked out. Many of his friends had not been as lucky as he was. He had watched a lot of men he worked with get injured, even die. There were no two ways about it: He had a lot to be thankful for, and he took every opportunity to say a prayer of thanksgiving.

God gives each of us strengths and talents. There is no reason for us to boast or brag. All that we are and all that we can do is a gift from God. Give Him thanks and praise for all you have. The Lord is good to His children.

PRAYER:
I can only marvel at the loving-kindness You have shown to me, O Lord. I thank You for blessing me day by day. Accept my offering of praise and glory. Amen.

*The voice of the LORD is powerful, the voice
of the LORD is full of majesty.*
PSALM 29:4

Stacy loved going to the beach. At night she would lie
awake, listening to the surf pounding on the rocks.
Closing her eyes, she would pretend the sound was
God's own voice thundering through the night. Such
thoughts helped her feel His presence, close and comforting. A voice with such power and might allowed no room
for fear. The owner of a voice like that could do anything.
Indeed, Stacy knew that nothing could
defeat her God—the God who
thundered and roared with the
greatest of power and majesty!

PRAYER:

*Lord, You are
greater than
anything else in
creation. In nature
You display Your power and
might. I stand in awe of all that
You are, even though I understand very
little. Thank You for Your love and
protection. Amen.*

For his anger endureth but a moment; in
his favour is life: weeping may endure for
a night, but joy cometh in the morning.

PSALM 30:5

A dam wailed throughout the entire ride. From the moment the roller coaster started out, he began to whimper. As it approached its first hill, the whimper had become a roar. The ride was torture for him, but as soon as it ended, he was back to normal.

Most things in life are similar to Adam's roller coaster ride. No matter how bad they are, they come to an end, and things get back to normal. God never tests us beyond our level of endurance. He is faithful to see us through each hardship and to bless us richly when our trial is through. The nighttimes of our life may seem dismal and black, but there is always a glorious morning on the rise.

PRAYER:
When
times seem
exceptionally
difficult, Lord,
help me to remember
that they will pass away. No
trial lasts forever, Lord, and
the promise of good things to
come is mine. Amen.

*What profit is there in my blood, when I
go down to the pit? Shall the dust praise thee?
shall it declare thy truth?*
PSALM 30:9

Most people want to be well remembered when
they die. We want to leave a legacy of some kind.
What will our legacy be? Will it be money, or a
building, or a statue? Will it be something that will last a
short while, then be gone? Why can't we leave something
truly important?

The greatest legacy we can leave is a life well lived. As
Christians, we need to be an example of how wonderful
Christ can be. We can honestly usher in the kingdom
of God on earth if we will devote ourselves to leading
kingdom lives. There is profit in the blood of a Christian.
Christ's own blood was shed that we might all inherit
eternal life. If God was willing to shed His own blood for
us, should we be willing to do any
less? God's legacy to us is life
eternal. What will our legacy to
others be?

*PRAYER:
May each day I
live be considered
a gift, Father. Guide
me so that I can live each
gift to the fullest. Let others see You
through me, I pray. Amen.*

For thou art my rock and my fortress;
therefore for thy name's sake lead me,
and guide me.

PSALM 31:3

The rabbit tensed every muscle. The fox had caught its scent and was stealthily moving in for the kill. Timing was everything. The brambles were just yards away, but the fox was fast. As the fox pounced, the rabbit broke into a hopping sprint and wriggled into the brambles. Fox teeth closed on air, mere inches behind.

The rabbit knows where it should go in times of trouble. It is well aware of where its fortress is. Are we as wise as the rabbit? Our fortress is the Lord. In times of desperate need, we should immediately turn to Him. There is no better place to rest and be safe.

PRAYER: Never let me stray too far from Your loving protection, Almighty God. I need You more than I even realize. Open Your arms to me, Lord. Amen.

I have hated them that regard lying vanities: but I trust in the LORD.
PSALM 31:6

E lijah looked at the worshipers of Baal with despair. How could they follow such a loathsome god? Where was their integrity? He could not understand how anyone could turn from the love of the one true God to worship something so evil. The priests of Baal paraded around in fancy robes, and they thrilled their followers with petty magicians' tricks. They had lost sight of religion through pageantry and vanity. Elijah would show them the error of their ways, or at least God would. When God and Elijah were finished, no one could doubt who the real God was.

Elijah's story from 1 Kings 18 is the perfect example of what happens to people who lose sight of God and turn instead to worldly things. Vanity kills faith and undermines humility. Look to the Lord in all things, and you will never have to worry.

PRAYER:

Lord, I am sometimes tempted by the flashy things I see. I forget truth, and I chase after fantasy. Break through my blindness with Your divine light, Almighty God. Amen.

Have mercy upon me, O LORD, for I am in trouble: mine eye is consumed with grief, yea, my soul and my belly.

PSALM 31:9

Beverly felt guilty that she had not been to church for so long. Somehow things had gotten so hectic, and church had just kind of slipped away. Her husband worked six days a week, and she worked Saturday nights, so Sunday became the only day they really had together. The more she thought about missing church, the more guilt she felt; and the more guilt she felt, the harder it was to go back. She was thrilled and surprised when the pastor came by and told her how much they had been missed. When she tried to offer an excuse, he told her that he wasn't there to scold, just to show concern.

We too often let guilt determine what our actions will be, rather than living as forgiven people. The Lord is more than willing to shower His children with mercy and grace. All we need to do is ask with a penitent heart. The Lord will forgive us all that we ask.

PRAYER: Thank You for Your gracious, forgiving love, Lord. I am nothing without Your loving-kindness. Hear me when I call out to You, Father, and be with me. Amen.

*Let the lying lips be put to silence; which
speak grievous things proudly and
contemptuously against the righteous.*
PSALM 31:18

Lisa couldn't quite believe everything the preacher was saying. He went on and on about how members of other Christian denominations were misguided and on the road to destruction. That didn't make sense. How could the pastor know that he was right and everyone else was wrong? He said that God had told him, but surely God talked to others, too. It was terribly confusing.

One day, everyone who speaks in order to hurt others will have to pay for what they say. So many things are said and done in the name of Christianity that are in no way Christlike. Our law is the law of love and forgiveness, not judgment and narrow-mindedness. Ask the Lord to open your heart to those you disagree with, and wonderful things will begin to happen.

*PRAYER:
I know so little,
and I say so
much, Father. Help
me to reach out to people
whom I don't understand or agree
with. Make me an instrument of unity
and fellowship. Amen.*

When I kept silence, my bones waxed old
through my roaring all the day long.
PSALM 32:3

Agnes drank way too much. If anyone ever mentioned it, she got very defensive and came up with all kinds of arguments to prove that she didn't. She had argued so many times, so many ways, that even she began to believe her own tales. The trouble was, the mirror didn't lie. Every time she took a look in the mirror, an older, ill-looking woman stared back. Perhaps the woman in the mirror did have a problem, but not Agnes.

We can only deny our sins for so long before they catch up with us. The Lord wants us to confess our sins, to repent of them, and to fill our lives with other things that will not do us harm. He created life to be lived to its fullest, not to be destroyed. God gives life, not us. We have no right to devalue God's great beauty. Confess sin, and God will renew your life.

PRAYER:

Why do I do such stupid things, Lord? I have so much, and I guess I take it for granted. Let me be honest with myself and with You. Grant me Your forgiveness, and make me clean. Amen.

Be ye not as the horse, or as the mule, which have no understanding: whose mouth must be held in with bit and bridle, lest they come near unto thee.
PSALM 32:9

Miriam did exactly as she pleased, whether it was wise or not. Her stubborn streak was a mile wide, and no one could dissuade her once her mind was made up. On many occasions she had been hurt, simply because she refused to use good sense. Each lesson she encountered she chose to ignore, so very little growing ever took place. In time Miriam grew bitter and angry because her unhappiness grew.

Let's face it. We need guidance. Our willfulness gets us into trouble when we refuse to unite it with common sense. Our Lord is the author of good sense and levelheadedness. It only makes sense that we should turn our lives over to Him. He is faithful to guide and direct us. He teaches and nurtures us, enabling us to be the best that we can be.

PRAYER: Break my willful pride, O Lord, and let me recognize my limitations. Needing guidance is not weakness. Help me to see the strength that can only come from depending on You. Amen.

*Sing unto him a new song; play
skilfully with a loud noise.*

PSALM 33:3

I looked at my watch through bleary eyes, to see that it was just after five in the morning. Downstairs a horrendous noise shook the whole house. I stumbled along to find out what was happening. In the family room, the two small children of friends of mine stood, one with a drum, one with a harmonica, a hymnal spread out in front of them. They were, to their way of thinking, playing a selection of inspirational greats. I couldn't help but smile. At first, the children thought I might be mad at them, but their worry faded as I entered the room and began to sing along with their cacophony. Noisy it was, but it was definitely joyful. I'm sure it was the best the Lord heard all day!

PRAYER:

Make sure that I take time out of this day to lift my voice to You in praise and worship. Fill my heart with songs to Your glory. Remind me of all I should be thankful for. Amen.

By the word of the LORD were the heavens made; and all the host of them by the breath of his mouth.
PSALM 33:6

With a simple breath—inhale and exhale—the Lord brought magnificence into creation. The stars and planets that revolve through space came forth on the breath of the Lord. The hosts, heavenly and earthly, sprang from His mouth. Our world and every last thing in it came into being by His Word. How can the splendor and mystery of our God ever be denied? Our Lord is above all things, and there is nothing that is beyond His control. His breath is within us: the breath of all life. Rejoice!

Budget

PRAYER: Creator, Your imagination has yielded wonders beyond comprehension. We stand in awe before Your mighty power. Thank You for finding a place in all of this for me. Your love shines forth throughout all of Your creation. Praise be unto You! Amen.

*The young lions do lack, and suffer hunger:
but they that seek the LORD shall not
want any good thing.*

PSALM 34:10

Remember the prodigal son? He thought he was ready to set out on his own, and it almost led to his ruin. He squandered all his wealth and found he really couldn't make it by himself. He had to humble himself and return home, where his father awaited him with open arms.

We need to learn that being mature and independent does not mean breaking our ties with other people. God did not create us to live apart from others. He gave us each other in order to make our lives more enjoyable. We never need lack for anything, because we are to take care of one another. The Lord provides for us through the love of our sons and daughters and other family members. Growing up doesn't mean learning to do everything by yourself, but realizing how wonderful it is to need other people.

PRAYER: I think I am strong and self-sufficient when I am not. I sometimes act as if I don't need anyone else, but deep inside, I know that I do. Put me in community with others who love You, Lord. Make me stronger through the relationships I develop. Amen.

*Keep thy tongue from evil, and thy lips
from speaking guile.*
PSALM 34:13

critical fast

B efore she could stop herself, the words were out
of her mouth. She hadn't meant to say anything,
but all her friends were talking, so she put in her
thoughts. Trouble was, when she began speaking, the girl
they were bad-mouthing walked into the room. Actually,
she liked the girl, but now any chance they had of being
friends was ruined. All because she had been thoughtless
and cruel.

James says that our tongues are mighty rudders,
guiding the body where it will go. We should be very
careful of the words that come out of our mouths. We
can do the greatest good, and the most terrible evil, by
the use of our mouths. Christians should let the truth and
grace of Christ govern their language. Otherwise, terrible
problems can occur. Let our words reflect our commitment
to Christ, and God will bless us
and defend us.

*PRAYER: Watch
me, Lord, that I
don't use my gifts
for evil. Help me to
use my mouth only for
praise and encouragement, and
keep me from saying things that could
hurt someone or lessen their faith.
Amen.*

Depart from evil, and do good;
seek peace, and pursue it.
PSALM 34:14

Phil was the big practical joker. He would do anything for a laugh, usually at the expense of someone else. Often his jokes lacked good taste, and more than a few caused hurt feelings and pain. None of that fazed Phil. He pushed and teased until many people wanted to have nothing more to do with him. When people reacted in anger to his stupid tricks, he dismissed them as having no sense of humor.

Everyone likes to have fun, but fun should never hurt anyone. Fun at other people's expense is selfish and cruel. God wants us to reach out to one another in love, spreading happiness and joy through the good things we do, not the evil. If we will dedicate our lives to the happiness of others, then our fun will be fun that everyone can enjoy.

PRAYER:
Lord, too easily I laugh at things that might hurt someone else. There is no joy in other people's pain. Help me to be an ambassador of Your love and goodwill, making people happy in deep and lasting ways. Amen.

Many are the afflictions of the righteous:
but the LORD delivereth him out of them all.
PSALM 34:19

Carla couldn't believe how things were going in her life. She'd always thought Christians didn't have to face the same kinds of problems everyone else had. What good was being a Christian if your problems didn't let up? It seemed that since she became a Christian, everything had gotten worse. No matter how hard she prayed, she never felt God close at hand.

It is folly to believe that God liberates us from all discomfort and affliction. What He does do is give us the will and determination to go on, even in the face of tough times. He works within us to give us peace and strength and courage, those things necessary to get through life. We can be sure that our trials will not come to an end, but the love of God will see that we get through anything that comes our way.

faith

PRAYER:

Lord, I sometimes feel I just can't go on. Please fill me with the strength I need, both of body and of character. Don't let me give up, but deliver me. Amen.

*Plead my cause, O LORD, with them that
strive with me: fight against them that
fight against me.*
PSALM 35:1

We need friends and supporters. Jesus sent the disciples out two by two because He knew how important it was to have someone to share with and to support. Standing alone, we feel like our strength is limited, but with someone else by our side, new reserves of strength surface. Psychologically, we need confirmation that what we believe in is true. Just one other person can give us all the confirmation we need.

It is good to remember that our Lord strives along beside us, never leaving us, pleading our cause at every step. He understands us, loves us, and never turns away from us. Because of the mighty love of God, we can be assured that we are never alone.

*PRAYER:
Lord, be
with me this
day. Support
me in the things I
desire to do, and help
me to always follow the
right path. Amen.*

Let them be confounded and put to shame
that seek after my soul: let them be turned
back and brought to confusion that devise my hurt.
PSALM 35:4

Tommy was an angry young man. He took every opportunity to vent his anger at those around him. Anytime he felt the least bit put-upon, he would lash out, trying to make others feel pain the way he felt it. Usually people would fight back, but occasionally someone would merely take Tommy's assault. At those times, Tommy felt a little ashamed and sorry for his actions.

There are many unhappy people living in the world today. The saying goes, misery loves company. Miserable people spread their misery around. On the other hand, people who possess joy can also share it. Our God shines forth His blessed light in order to destroy the darkness of anger and shame. As Christians, we should reach out in love, not only to those who care for us and build us up, but also to those who devise our unhappiness. They are the ones who need it most.

PRAYER:
My Lord, You
have filled my
heart with Your love.
Whenever I see sadness, let
me try to meet it with a measure of
Your joy. Amen.

How excellent is thy lovingkindness,
O God! therefore the children of men
put their trust under the shadow of thy wings.
PSALM 36:7

The chicks scurried around as the rain began to fall. They had been out in the yard in front of the coop. When the storm hit, they flew into a panic. Carefully but quickly, the mother hen gathered her chicks to herself, enfolding them in her wings.

Jesus used the same image to show His disciples how God would save His children in time of distress. We have no need to fear, for the Lord is watching over us, and He will pull us toward Himself during bad times. The love of God is beyond human comprehension. We need not understand it, only accept it.

PRAYER:
Father of
all creation,
You care
for us in very
special ways.
We turn to You for
comfort and security in a
frightening time. Be with us
always. Amen.

*Delight thyself also in the LORD; and he
shall give thee the desires of thine heart.*
PSALM 37:4

When I first became a Christian, I remember thinking how wonderful prayer would be. All I would have to do was let God know what I wanted, and He promised that I would have it. I began searching my life for the true desires of my heart, and was surprised to find that they weren't cars, money, or houses, but love, peace of mind, and happiness. The more I prayed, the more I became aware that the true desires of my heart were the desires of Jesus' own heart. They had been there all along, but I had never recognized them before.

Prayer is not a way for us to make ourselves wealthy and prosperous. The Christian's mind should be set on higher things. When we pray to the Lord, always remembering to say, "Thy will be done," we will find the truth of Christ squarely centered in our lives.

PRAYER:
There are few
people I would
rather spend my
time with than You, Lord,
though often I don't spend
time with You as I should. Forgive me
when I forget to turn to You. Make Your
desires my desires. Amen.

Cease from anger, and forsake wrath:
fret not thyself in any wise to do evil.

PSALM 37:8

Gordon was still shaking. He had never meant to hit his son, not so hard, anyway. When his little boy looked back up at him, his nose was bleeding and his eye was swelling. The rage of moments before was completely gone. Spent was the anger that had caused the injury. In Gordon's heart a heavy shame rose up, along with a vow to put to rest the beast called anger that lurked within his heart.

We are all capable of great anger. The passion is within each of us. However, we must rule the passion instead of letting the passion rule us. God helps us control the beasts within. His is a power to set our hearts right and dispel our evil with His own goodness. Ask God's help, and He will help you to cease from anger and strife.

PRAYER:
Take
from me
the tendency
to anger and
harm, Almighty God.
Reshape me in the loving
image of Your Son. Reign in
my heart with peace and love.
Amen.

But the meek shall inherit the earth; and
shall delight themselves in the abundance of peace.
PSALM 37:11

Marchers circled in front of the atomic plant. Not everyone agreed with the sentiments of the protesters, but at least they were getting out and speaking their minds, which was more than most did. One woman was concerned for the future of her children, another worried about the effects on the ecology, and a man carried a petition with signatures of over nine thousand citizens from the area, voicing outrage at the sloppy safety standards. It did no good to sit idly by while others made all the decisions. Peace and safety were worth speaking out for.

What is worth defending, if not peace? We live in a world of war and fighting. Battlegrounds pop up in every nation of the world. Our Lord, however, is the Prince of Peace. How can we remain unconcerned about world harmony? We cannot. Our mission in this world is to spread the peace of Christ wherever we go. As we spread peace, we find comfort in facing the future, and we come to know the peace that passes all understanding: God's own peace.

PRAYER: Make me an instrument of Thy peace, O Lord. Where I find discord, let me bring harmony. Where there is hatred, bring love. As Saint Francis prayed long ago, so I pray today. Amen.

My heart panteth, my strength faileth me:
as for the light of mine eyes, it also
is gone from me.
PSALM 38:10

Emma was as old as the hills. She had mothered a dozen children, tended a hundred grandchildren, and no one knew how many great- and great-great-grandchildren. She worked nearly every day of the first ninety years of her life, then decided to rest. In her one hundred and third year, she lost her sight, and two years later she was confined to a wheelchair. For a while she was resentful of losing her faculties, but in time she accepted it. After all, hadn't she lived more than a full life? Hadn't God given her more family than any one woman had a right to have? When all was said and done, Emma had had a wonderful life, and a few inconveniences at the end certainly weren't going to get her down.

We have two simple options when afflictions strike. We can moan about our fate and give up, or we can face it boldly and make the best of it. God grants us the power to become more than conquerors, if we will only choose to use it.

PRAYER:
Lord,
I know
there will be
times when my
strength fails and my
will is drained. At those
times, fill my heart with Your
will and power. Make me a
fighter, Lord. Amen.

But I, as a deaf man, heard not; and I was as a dumb man that openeth not his mouth.
PSALM 38:13

Simon Peter became the cornerstone of the church, but only after facing some tremendous trials. Jesus walked with His disciples for almost three years, and during that time He taught them many things. Peter, who listened intently to all He said, never really understood what He meant until Jesus returned from the grave. When he was called upon to affirm his faith in Jesus, he denied Him three times.

We can be so much like Simon Peter. We listen, but we do not hear. We have opportunity to testify to the glory of the Lord, and we keep silent. The Lord wants us to know Him completely and share our faith with all those we meet. Hear what the Lord has to say, and proclaim it with your mouth and with your actions.

PRAYER: Break through the thick cloud of confusion that so often covers us, Lord, and speak through us when we have the opportunity to share Your Good News. Amen.

11

When thou with rebukes dost correct man for iniquity, thou makest his beauty to consume away like a moth: surely every man is vanity.

PSALM 39:11

Connie was driving everyone crazy. All four co-workers had taken on one aspect of the project, and Connie had finished her part first. Now she was delighting in harassing the others for their slowness. Her taunting came to an abrupt end when their boss marched in, threw the report at Connie, pronounced it "unusable trash," and ordered her to do it again. With a flush of embarrassment, Connie returned to her desk to start over.

Everyone needs to be reminded that he or she is no better than anyone else every now and then. Conceit is a killing vice in the Christian life. God created us all equal. His image rests equally with every human being. Sometimes God needs to bring us back to earth when we get too puffed up. Those who exalt themselves will be humbled, while those who humble themselves will be exalted (see Matthew 23:12).

*PRAYER:
O Lord, do not let me think too much of myself. When I turn my attention inward, I lose sight of who You want me to be. Let me be honest and open with myself, and help me to find new ways to grow. Amen.*

He brought me up also out of an horrible pit,
out of the miry clay, and set my feet upon a
rock, and established my goings.

PSALM 40:2

Gina held on to the branch for dear life. The floodwa-
ters swirled around her, pulling at her, threatening
to carry her off in the raging torrent. The pouring
rain blinded her, and large clumps of mud kept bumping into
her. Her arms ached and throbbed. The last of her strength
gave out, but as she let the branch slip through her fingers, a
strong hand gripped her wrist. Gina felt herself slide up onto
the bank of the swollen river, and she spread herself out to
feel the firm ground beneath her.

❧ There are many days that feel like a struggle for life.
How wonderful it would be to have someone come along
and lift us up out of the struggle. God can do that. His
Spirit renews and strengthens us. Through the loving
power of God, we are pulled out
of the darkest pit and set upon
solid ground.

PRAYER:

Lord, hear me
as I call out to
You. Whether my
problems are huge or
tiny, I find I need Your help to
get me through. Pull me up into Your
loving arms, and surround me in Your
love. Amen.

Get Out of
the Pit —

Beth
Moore

For innumerable evils have compassed me about: mine iniquities have taken hold upon me, so that I am not able to look up; they are more than the hairs of mine head: therefore my heart faileth me.

PSALM 40:12

Church made Sue feel uncomfortable. She wanted to be there, but she felt so unworthy. Just sitting in the church made her feel like a hypocrite. She asked forgiveness for her sins, and she believed that God gave it to her, but there was so much to forgive. All her life, she had been told that God was great and that human beings were unworthy of the attention He gave them. Sue figured she must be about the most unworthy of all.

Too often we come before the Lord with the feeling that we shouldn't be there. True, we have sinned, but God does not want us to dwell on the fact that we have sinned, but that we have been forgiven, and that we are His chosen people. The love of God is greater than any sin we might commit. God makes us able to look up, because He lifts the burden of guilt from our shoulders.

out of the pit

PRAYER: Your grace has made me worthy, Lord. What I could not do on my own, You have done for me. Thank you, Father, from the depths of my soul. Amen.

Blessed is he that considereth the poor: the
LORD will deliver him in time of trouble.
PSALM 41:1

Curse the beggars! It was impossible to go anywhere without seeing someone with his hand
out. Ted refused to look into their faces. He de-
spised people who were always looking for a handout. He
worked hard for what he got; why couldn't they? It made
him so mad. He rounded the corner and abruptly stopped
in front of a young boy cradling the head of his mother in
his lap. The woman was obviously very ill. The boy looked
up into Ted's face and sobbed one word: "Please?"

All the excuses, all the anger, all the contempt melted
away. Ted's eyes were opened for the first time. These
people really needed help, and he had the power to make
a difference. Perhaps he couldn't solve the whole problem,
or even a big part, but he could help the boy and his
mother. With new resolve, Ted
swore to open his eyes to the
less fortunate and give as much
as he could.

PRAYER:

Father, am I doing
all I can? In my
times of need, I cry
out for someone to help me.
Make me sensitive to others as they
cry out. Amen.

As the hart panteth after the water brooks,
so panteth my soul after thee, O God.
PSALM 42:1

The male deer is a single-minded creature. Once its sights are set on its goal, nothing can dissuade it. It will battle opponents to the death in order to succeed. Even for a drink of water, the male deer will not be stopped.

Such single-mindedness is what the Lord desires of His children. The Lord loves to see real commitment that changes lives. To live for the Lord means to give oneself to Him: body, mind, and spirit. As the hart pursues the cooling brook with all that it has, so must we pursue our Lord.

PRAYER:

You are my goal, Lord. Keep my eyes focused on You. Make sure that I don't turn away. I can have no greater prize in sight, Father, than to spend eternity with You. Amen.

Why art thou cast down, O my soul? and why are thou disquieted in me? hope thou in God: for I shall yet praise him for the help of his countenance.

PSALM 42:5

P hilip fidgeted in the starting block. This was his race. Everyone said he was the favorite. He knew he could win, but something in him was causing quite a stir. His nerves were on fire. He tried to pray, but he felt like he was getting a busy signal. He knew that God was with him, but still he felt nervous. The starter was lifting his pistol. Soon it would be over, and the time for nervousness gone.

There are times when we feel anxiety that will not easily be gotten rid of. That's all right. Even in those times, God is with us. Trust in the Lord, and He will guide you. It is not so important that we *feel* His presence with us as it is that we have *faith* in His being with us always. Feelings come and go, but the presence of God in our lives never changes.

PRAYER:
Be with me, Father, in tense times as well as calm. Let me sense Your loving arms around me, but when I don't, help me to remember that You are there, anyway. Amen.

O send out thy light and thy truth:
let them lead me; let them bring me
unto thy holy hill, and to thy tabernacles.

PSALM 43:3

The tiny lighthouse sat out upon the rocky shore. Without fail, its bright beacon pierced the night, and its bellowing horn echoed from the rocks, warning ships of dangers and perils. Countless boats strayed off course in dense fog, to be steered from danger by the tiny lighthouse.

True light, sent out through the clouds and darkness, can save lives. A voice speaking the truth of Christ has real power behind it—the power of salvation. Be proud of who you are and all that Christ has done for you. It matters little whether you are big, strong, smart, or powerful. What matters is that you have the truth of Christ to share, and there is no greater force in all creation.

PRAYER:
Lord, may my light shine in the darkness until all darkness ceases to be. Let me reflect Your divine light, Lord, clearing away the fog and helping others come into the safety of Your love. Amen.

If we have forgotten the name of our God,
or stretched out our hands to a strange god;
shall not God search this out? for he knoweth
the secrets of the heart.

PSALM 44:20–21

Alan decided he would play it safe. Believe in everything; something had to be right. His home was cluttered with statues and pictures; incense burned in little tin pots. Bibles, writings of other faiths, prayer cards, and rosaries littered various tables. He told his friends he was Eastern Western Unorthodox. It worked for a while, but finally Alan realized that believing everything was the same as believing nothing. Gravity kept pushing him off the spiritual fence he was straddling. What he found was that he was afraid to commit to any one thing. In the end, he committed to nothing.

We need to be careful. Our spiritual lives are very fragile things. They need attention and care. We cannot toss our spiritual selves around too freely. The Lord gave us a need to search and question. He understands our doubts. Be patient. Ask the Lord to grant you understanding, and true wisdom will be yours.

PRAYER:
I stand at the crossroads of a thousand different paths. I get so confused, Lord. Each road has a sign marked Truth, and I know that can't be right. Lead me down the proper path, Lord. Take me where You want me to be. Amen.

I will make thy name to be remembered in all generations: therefore shall the people praise thee for ever and ever.

PSALM 45:17

The sculptor looked at the piece of stone and thought. His mind whirled at the possibilities the stone presented. He could make anything he wanted. He could carve out great beauty. He could create a monument to himself. He could immortalize a great figure from history. He could sculpt a statement of power and dignity. His mind danced with imagination. He began to dream of the ultimate statement he could make. He looked into the sky and saw the glories there. He looked at the trees and flowers. He watched people walking past. He thought of waterfalls and rainbows and beautiful music. His heart swelled full, then sank. What could he possibly carve into stone that would do justice to the world of wonder he lived in? He set about his carving, working with great care and determination. After days of labor and love, he unveiled the greatest work his life could offer. Three letters, finely shaped, lovingly created. The greatest legacy the artist could give. The name was GOD.

PRAYER: Make my life a symbol of Your love and a sign of Your grace. I live my life in Your will, trying to be the best person I can be. Accept my life as an offering of love. Amen.

God is our refuge and strength, a very present help in trouble.
PSALM 46:1

The cross I wear around my neck is not there for show, nor is it the object of my worship. I would not be lost without it, though I do like it. I do not believe it has some mystical power, nor does it protect me. The cross that I wear reminds me of the great love that God has for me. Christ's gift of eternal life is made real to me each time I look down at the cross or feel it lightly resting on my chest. In difficult times, I look at the cross and feel warmth and comfort. From its gentle reminder I draw strength when I am weary, refuge when I need to rest. Whether I wear my cross or not, God is with me, but sometimes it is nice to have a small reminder.

PRAYER: I run to You when I need rest, Lord. You take me in Your arms and protect me from the pressures of the day. In every time of trial, You are the source of my help. Thank You. Amen.

There is a river, the streams whereof shall
make glad the city of God, the holy place
of the tabernacles of the most High.
PSALM 46:4

In the woods of Maine, not too far from the eastern coast, there is a river that flows clear and cool. It winds through some of the most gorgeous scenery imaginable and carries with it a beauty that is unsurpassed. To see such sights convinces a person of the reality of God. God gives us glimpses of heaven here on earth, so that we might long for such a place from the deepest reaches of our hearts. That part of us that carries the seed of God responds to His beauty in creation. If we will look at the world with our spiritual eyes rather than our physical eyes, we will begin to see God's glories in many new ways. The gifts of God are indeed abundant. Open your eyes and enjoy them all.

PRAYER:
I stand in awe of the wonder of Your creation, God. Help me to see beauty wherever I look. Don't let me waste time on ugliness, but turn my attention to what is good. Amen.

Be still, and know that I am God: I will be exalted among the heathen, I will be exalted in the earth.

PSALM 46:10

The city was roaring with noise. Car horns blasted, construction noise filled the air, radios blared, people shouted. As the day wore on, the noise steadily increased. After awhile, you adjusted. It wasn't until you were able to move into a quiet place that you realized how loud the noise had been. In the silence, everything seemed to change. Waves of calm and quiet rolled in. The silence was a little alarming and unsettling. In the silence, thoughts could creep out and be heard.

God comes to us in silence. We have lost the art of being still. Everything is rush, rush, rush; and few people take time to be still. Noise provides us with a place to hide, where we don't have to face ourselves. Heavy schedules block honest reflection and renewal. Only through the still times in our lives can we hope for God to break through to help us make sense of our lives. Be still, and know that God is there.

PRAYER:
The day closes in on me, Lord, and I feel myself buried beneath a heavy layer of noise and activity. Break me free of the bondage of commotion. Bless me with quiet and peace. Amen.

O clap your hands, all ye people; shout unto God with the voice of triumph.

PSALM 47:1

What a wonderful feeling. Greg had wanted to tell his friends what he thought for a long time, but he had been afraid they would make fun of him. Drinking and driving was stupid, but he had always done it in the past so he could fit in. Finally, it just got to him. He didn't want to do it anymore. He told them how he felt, and instead of making fun of him, two of his friends agreed with him; and they had made a deal to not drink and drive anymore. His other friends had been as afraid as he was. Sure, some wouldn't ever understand, but that was their problem. Right now, Greg felt great that he had done something good and right. He wanted to shout about it.

When we do what is truly right, we need to rejoice. God celebrates with us, and He will honor our righteousness. To do right is to affirm who God wants us to be. The peace that comes from doing right is wonderful.

PRAYER: Lord, give me the courage I need to be the person I want to be. Let me know the triumph that comes from standing up for my values. Let me feel the power You share with those who strive for what is right. Amen.

Diane 4/25/12

Great is the LORD, and greatly to be praised in the city of our God, in the mountain of his holiness.

PSALM 48:1

Ajourney through the holy scriptures can be a thrilling experience. To hear the tales of God and His people is a joy. No one can deny the power of the scriptures. When we find our faith on the ebb, we need only turn to the Word of God in order to find renewal. The greatness of God has touched the lives of men and women throughout history. He still touches our lives today. Spend time with the Lord, and He will teach you amazing things.

PRAYER: Indeed, Lord, You are great. Teach me new things every day. Show me the glories of Your world. Help me to know You better this day. Amen.

Be not thou afraid when one is made rich,
when the glory of his house is increased;
for when he dieth he shall carry nothing
away: his glory shall not descend after him.
PSALM 49:16–17

Shield Industries was made great by one man: Grayson Shields. He devoted himself to his work and he made a fortune by his efforts. During his climb to the top, he experienced two divorces; lost both parents, but was unable to attend their funerals because of business conflicts; watched his health deteriorate; and was in part responsible for the suicide of one of his competitors. To his way of thinking, the benefits always outweighed the costs.

Men like Shields are not unusual in our world today. Nothing stands in the way of their climb to the top. Sadly, these men do not realize they have set an inferior goal for themselves. The top of the corporate ladder is far short of the top of the spiritual ladder that God has set before us. What does it profit a man to save his life if he forfeits his soul? Men and women who have sacrificed themselves totally to earthly gain can carry nothing with them beyond the grave. There they will stand naked to face judgment for a life poorly lived. Is it worth the price?

PRAYER: Make my life worthwhile, Lord. Set my sights on treasures that never fade away. Get my mind off earthly blessings and onto the blessings that come from above. Amen.

*Offer unto God thanksgiving; and pay thy
vows unto the most High.*
PSALM 50:14

Early Christians suffered terrible persecution, even
death, for refusing to bow down to idols. Images
of Caesar were prominent throughout the Roman Empire, and all were expected to pay tribute to these
graven images. The Christians refused, and so they were
thrown into jail, and sometimes they were thrown to wild
beasts. God was so important to these early Christians
that they could not offer tribute to anyone less worthy.

Only God is worthy to be praised. In all we do and
all we are, our lives should pay tribute to God.
Nothing else is good enough.
Offer to God thanksgiving and
praise, for He alone is deserving.

*PRAYER:
Thank You for
the gifts You give,
Almighty God. From
the rise of the sun to its
setting in the night, I will praise
You for all that You have done. Glory is
Yours, Father. Amen.*

Against thee, thee only, have I sinned, and done this evil in thy sight: that thou mightest be justified when thou speakest, and be clear when thou judgest.

PSALM 51:4

S in is not merely doing what is wrong, but doing what is wrong in the sight of the Lord. God has offered us suggestions for living full and happy lives. Our being disobedient to those suggestions doesn't hurt God; it hurts us. God is saddened by our refusal to be obedient, but He is always willing to hear our petition for forgiveness, and He will show us His mercy. When we sin, it is a private matter between God and ourselves. Take your sins before God, repent for each one, and glory in the grace of God, by which we receive full pardon for all we do wrong.

PRAYER:

Forgive me, Lord. Make a new creation out of this old soul. Prepare me for the kingdom to come each day of my life. Amen.

*Create in me a clean heart, O God; and
renew a right spirit within me.*
PSALM 51:10

I remember seeing a healthy heart and a diseased heart
side by side in one of my college classes. The healthy
heart looked strong and fit. The diseased heart was a
sickly color and looked bloated and spongy. That image
sticks in my mind. The diseased heart symbolizes for me
the sin-sick heart, discolored by evil emotions and intentions, bloated by selfishness, and spongy through lack of
love, giving, and compassion. The only solution for a sin-
sick heart is a transplant by the giver of all new life. God
can take a diseased heart and make
it new, fresh, and alive. Pray for
God to remove the disease of
sin, and He will heal you.

*PRAYER: Lord, I
want to be made
new and alive.
Remove the dead
tissue caused by sin and
replace it with tissue that is strong
and healthy. Create in me a new heart,
and renew my spirit within me.
Amen.*

The sacrifices of God are a broken spirit:
a broken and a contrite heart, O God,
thou wilt not despise.

PSALM 51:17

Thomas was a proud man. He had never liked admitting that he might need help from someone else. His daddy had taught him that the only way a man was worth his salt was to stand on his own two feet. Thomas had always tried to live by that rule, but now he was at a loss. His wife was sick, and he didn't know where to turn. The doctors were doing all they could, but Thomas felt helpless. Though it felt strange to him, Thomas got down on his knees to pray. Self-consciously, Thomas asked the Lord's help, and in his hour of quiet desperation, he was answered.

God wants us to need Him. He made us to need help, not to try to do everything on our own. When times get tough, God wants us to open our hearts to Him, that He might be made real to us. Call upon God from your brokenness, and He will be faithful to answer.

PRAYER: When all else fails, I turn to You, Lord. I should not wait until situations get bad, but I do. Be with me to help me in the hardest of times, and stay with me in all times, that I might know You better. Amen.

Thy tongue deviseth mischiefs; like a sharp razor, working deceitfully.
PSALM 52:2

Ed ran the blade along the cardboard cartons with speed and skill. He broke down the boxes and stuffed them in a crate. He had done the job a thousand times before, and it had become second nature to him. Often he let his mind wander. On this occasion, it was a poor idea. With lightning speed, the blade ran across the back of Ed's hand, cutting deep and wounding him severely.

Just as a blade cuts deep into flesh, unkind words cut into the heart. A sacred trust has been given to Christians. That trust is the dignity and feelings of the rest of God's children. We become our neighbors' keeper. It is our duty to love and defend them. The tongue has enormous power to build up or to tear down. How will we choose to use it?

PRAYER: May every word out of my mouth be one that encourages, builds up, or praises. Remove from my heart the desire to hurt others by my words. Fill my mouth with Your thoughts and words, Lord. Amen.

Lo, this is the man that made not God his strength; but trusted in the abundance of his riches, and strengthened himself in his wickedness.

PSALM 52:7

Lee couldn't understand any person who would put their faith in something you couldn't get your hands on. Spirits and angels and super beings in the sky were all fantasy. Now, money, there was something that was real. You could measure the benefits of money, not like God. You never knew what you would come up with, with God. Till his dying day, Lee believed that only fools followed God.

The wise man understands that the wealth of this age is inferior to the wealth God grants us through eternal life in His Kingdom. Money has its uses, but as a god it is a poor substitute for the real thing.

PRAYER: Do not let me be distracted by lesser gods, O Lord. There is nothing in this world that can take Your place. You are the greatest riches I can ever hope to find. Amen.

God looked down from heaven upon the children of men, to see if there were any that did understand, that did seek God.
PSALM 53:2

Mabel never walked alone. In her hand was an old leather Bible, which she read from all the time. It was bulging with papers and sayings and handcrafted bookmarks, and all her favorite passages were underlined in red pencil. She delighted in sitting down with someone and showing him all the history she had tucked away in her Holy Book. Mabel was never without her Holy Book, never without her smile. Mabel loved the Lord, and nothing gave her more pleasure than sharing Him with the people she met.

PRAYER:

Help me to seek after You, Lord. In the morning and throughout the day, give me reminders that You are with me. Remind me to tell others of Your love, that I might share the great gift I have been given. Amen.

Fearfulness and trembling are come upon me, and horror hath overwhelmed me.

PSALM 55:5

Liz sat crying in the small café. It looked as though she might be pregnant, and she was terrified. Her parents would yell at her, her boyfriend would probably leave her, and everyone would think she was somehow cheap and dirty; at least, that was how they would make her feel. This wasn't something she wanted or was proud of. She had made a terrible mistake. She had given in to sin. Now she was a very scared young girl, with nowhere to turn.

Sin makes us a prisoner. It takes away our freedom, and it controls us with fear and guilt. Thankfully, we have a Savior who crushes the power of sin and sets us free. Jesus Christ died to let us know we are loved, and God forgives us when we fall. Nothing we can do separates us from that love, so we have nothing to fear at all.

PRAYER:
Lift me from the horrors of sin, Lord. Set my feet upon right paths, and lead me away from things that will harm me. Give me courage in the face of frightening situations. Amen.

And I said, Oh that I had wings like a dove!
for then would I fly away, and be at rest.
PSALM 55:6

The boat took off at a high speed, and the towline lifted with a jerk. Jeff's arms strained to hold on, but he held the bar tightly in his hands. As the wind filled the parasail behind him, he felt himself rise up into the air. He was flying! The water rushed by beneath him, and he could see for miles. He let go of the bar and grabbed two steering guides dangling in front of him. He felt the freedom and joy of taking wing. His spirit swelled within him. He'd never felt a joy like this before in his life.

There are many breathtaking experiences in this life that God has given to us. He has reserved some special things for each of us. These experiences help us touch the wonder of God. They involve us in His mystery, and they remind us just how great He is. Embrace life fully. Try new things. The Lord is offering you new excitement and opportunity every day of your life.

PRAYER:
Grant me wings
to soar, Father. Set
me upon high places,
and show me the wonders
of Your love. Open my heart to new
things, and watch me grow. Amen.

*Evening, and morning, and at noon, will I
pray, and cry aloud: and he shall hear my voice.*

PSALM 55:17

Table grace was originally intended to help people turn their attention to God. The meals we share are a gift from God, and He is to be thanked, but we are also to reflect on the many other good things we are given. By praying morning and noon and night, we cover our day with a knowledge of God's presence and abiding love. We should take every opportunity to sing praises to God for all that He has done. Take time to pray. Make time to share your life with God.

*PRAYER:
Father,
I get so
busy that
I sometimes
forget to be as
appreciative as I ought
to be. Help me to be
thankful and attentive to the
many gifts You have given
me. All through the day,
I will praise You.
Amen.*

The words of his mouth were smoother than butter, but war was in his heart: his words were softer than oil, yet were they drawn swords.
PSALM 55:21

Carrie couldn't believe that she had been taken in so completely. The man had talked of love and peace and equality, and it had all sounded so right. Then he began teaching that the only way to achieve peace was through violence. She had gone along with it for a while because she really wanted to believe the man was good. What he really was was a terrorist, using young people to wage his war for him. Why did people have to live by a lie?

We live in a world dominated by smooth talkers who proclaim goodness but are corrupt to the core. Jesus warned that many false prophets would come preaching harmony and love, but that they were wolves in sheeps' clothing. Ask God's wisdom and guidance as you make choices in your life. He will expose the darkness of lies and deceit through His holy light.

PRAYER: Grant me a careful and discerning spirit, Lord. Make sure that I use the common sense You have given me. Protect me from those who would try to take advantage of me. Amen.

In God have I put my trust: I will not be afraid what man can do unto me.

PSALM 56:11

Eleanor looked one last time out of the airplane window. Though she couldn't make out individual faces, she knew her family was there somewhere. It was just really beginning to sink in that she wouldn't see them for a long time. The decision to go into missionary service had been difficult, but she was still certain it was the right thing to do. That didn't make leaving any easier. The only thing to do was put her trust in God and see where He would lead.

Trust is a tricky thing. It is difficult to put our trust in others, because we can't be sure whether they will value it or not. That fear should not apply when it comes to putting our trust in God. He will guard it even better than we do ourselves. No one can hurt us once we put our trust in God. He will follow us to the ends of the earth to make sure we know of His great love.

PRAYER: Wherever I go, Lord, I need to know that You are with me. I will put my trust in You, knowing that You will always do what is best for me. Help me to trust You more each day. Amen.

My soul is among lions: and I lie even
among them that are set on fire, even the
sons of men, whose teeth are spears and arrows,
and their tongue a sharp sword.

PSALM 57:4

Kevin thought that joining the fraternity would solve all his problems. Everybody seemed to look up to the fraternities. Ever since he came to college, Kevin felt a little left out and lonely. His loneliness only increased after he was initiated. None of the other guys in the frat thought or felt anything like he did. Most of them were shallow. Sure, there were a lot of great people in the fraternities, but it wasn't what Kevin was looking for. He felt so out of place. What he needed was someplace where he could be himself, and not always put on an act.

We are experts at wearing masks. We do the acceptable things so we don't feel strange or uncomfortable. We get thrown into the lions' den, and it feels like the only way we can hope to avoid being eaten is to become a lion ourselves. Take heart. God has seen our problems, and He is willing to help us stand firm for what we believe. There is a place for us. In time, God will lead us all to a place where we feel accepted and loved for who we are.

PRAYER:
There are many
temptations
before me that
threaten to make me less
than You want me to be, Lord.
Save me from my own weaknesses,
and make me strong in my beliefs and
convictions. Amen.

*The wicked are estranged from the womb:
they go astray as soon as they be
born, speaking lies.*

PSALM 58:3

Larry had developed quite a reputation over the years. Most people in his life said he couldn't be trusted. If there was a way for Larry to rip them off, he would do it. It had been Larry's nature from the time he was very small. As a child, he had told lies with unbelievable ease. He bullied other children without the least bit of guilt or remorse. In school he had cheated his way to the top of his class. He bought answers to tests in college and entered the business world believing that anything he wanted could be gotten by means both legal and illegal. It was all the same to Larry.

There are people in our world who have lived their entire lives by selfish and evil means. It's as if something good was left out of them, and they are incapable of doing what is good. The way we deal with people like that is to forgive them and vow we will never be like them. Evil people are not to be hated, but pitied. They are our mission in life. Lives devoid of the Good News are lives not worth living. Reach out to people who do wrong through your prayers. They need them most of all.

PRAYER: Lord, show me how to love even the most unlovable people. Instead of showing anger, let me show compassion, and grant me a deeper understanding of why people can be so bad. Fill my heart with Your love to share. Amen.

Because of his strength will I wait upon thee: for God is my defence.
PSALM 59:9

The young man sat quietly in the courtroom. He trembled as he waited for the hearing to begin. He had never been to court before. His parents had rarely even taken him into town. The Amish kept pretty much to themselves. He was being asked to fight in an army that he did not believe in, and that was something he could not do. They would ask him all kinds of hard questions, but all he knew was that war and killing were wrong, and he would have no part of it, even if it meant sitting in a jail for the rest of his life. They would want excuses, but all he could say was no. God was his only defense. Nothing more was needed.

PRAYER:
People do not always understand why I feel the way I do or believe the things I do. Help me to accept that, Father. Help me to be secure in my faith. Let me be an example of faith in a world full of doubt. Amen.

*Thou hast made the earth to tremble;
thou hast broken it: heal the breaches
thereof; for it shaketh.*

PSALM 60:2

B ombs burst, shaking the walls of the nearby houses. Villagers huddled inside, wondering when the thundering blasts would end. Finally, the assault slacked off, and quiet replaced the horrendous noise. Cautiously, people made their way from their homes to view the devastation that lay around them. Their once-scenic village lay mostly in ruin, the bombs having torn apart the beauty that had existed before.

Wars come and go, and always God has slowly and carefully covered the scars of battle with beauty once more. His great power stands against the worst that humankind can do. So far we have not done irreparable damage, and by God's grace we never will; but it is good to know that the Lord is with us, to heal all wounds and make all things new.

*PRAYER:
The
power of
humankind
does not even
compare with Your
might, Lord. Save us from
our own destructiveness, and
renew Your creation, which
we carelessly destroy.
Amen.*

From the end of the earth will I cry unto
thee, when my heart is overwhelmed:
lead me to the rock that is higher than I.
PSALM 61:2

E ric ran back and forth behind the crowd. The parade was coming, and he really wanted to have
a good spot to watch it from. Everyone was so
much taller than he was. Wherever he went, somebody
was standing in front of him. In frustration, he began to
cry. Suddenly, two strong hands lifted Eric up and placed
him on shoulders high up above the mass of people. From
the vantage point of the stranger's shoulders, the entire
parade was easy to see.

Sometimes we need a boost. Problems loom too large,
and we can't see our way around them. Pressures build
up, and we don't feel big enough to cope with them. God
sees all that, and He is ready to lift
us up—to give us a new vantage
point. Reach up to the Lord,
and He will lead you to Himself,
a rock that is higher than any
problem we might have.

PRAYER: Pick
me up, Lord, and
hold me in Your
loving arms. Protect
me from the pressures
of the day, and remove the
heaviness from my heart. Inspire
me with the knowledge that You and I
together can handle anything. Amen.

13

Trust not in oppression, and become not vain in robbery: if riches increase, set not your heart upon them.

PSALM 62:10

Glenn prayed for things to get easier. Every day he lifted his concerns to the Lord. Each day he faithfully read the Bible and thought about the Lord's loving works. Finally, his financial woes began to turn around. He thanked God for hearing him and helping him. His wealth began to increase, but as it did, Glenn turned less and less to God. He rarely prayed, almost never did he turn to God's Word, and he spent his time thinking of all the wonderful things he could do with his newfound wealth. Glenn attained a level where he could have been called a rich man. At the same time, Glenn attained a level of spiritual bankruptcy. The cost of wealth is often our very faith. Let not the wealth of the world turn you from God. That is the devil's finest work.

PRAYER: Forgive me when I let things come between us, Lord. Material wealth is nice, but not if it means that I lose my relationship with You. Help me be satisfied with what I have, and keep my mind and my heart on You. Amen.

O God, thou art my God; early will I seek
thee: my soul thirsteth for thee, my flesh
longeth for thee in a dry and thirsty land, where no water is.
PSALM 63:1

The rock face extended straight up. Terry was half-way up, and his arms ached. From the ground it hadn't looked nearly so great a distance. The sun was scorching, and all Terry could think of was a cool drink of water. He would give anything to be able to stop and drink, but there was no safe place to even think of do-ing it. The more he thought of water, the worse his thirst got. He comforted himself by thinking the next drink he took would be the best he'd ever had.

We often don't appreciate the simple things in life until we are unable to enjoy them. Taking God's gifts for granted is easy to do. Clean air, water to drink, food on the table; these things come easily to most of us, and so we are not as thankful as we might be if we didn't have them. Many in our world have to do without. Remember that even the most basic of our needs is met by the loving grace of God. Thank Him for everything He has given you.

PRAYER: For the air that I breathe, the warmth of the springtime sun, the food that nourishes me, and for so much more, I lift my voice in thanks and praise to You, Lord. Amen.

But those that seek my soul, to destroy it,
shall go into the lower parts of the earth.
They shall fall by the sword: they shall be a portion for foxes.

PSALM 63:9–10

Tracy couldn't believe the girls at school would be so cruel. She never did anything to any of them, but they were always finding some way to hurt her. It was all she could do to keep from telling them all off. Her mother told her to ignore them, but that was hard to do. Her mother also said that they would eventually have to pay for all the nasty things they did, but Tracy wished that day would come soon.

No one likes to be picked on. Some people love to spend their time making others unhappy. These people will have to answer to God for their actions. We are called to love one another and to look for ways to give one another encouragement. While the nasty people will answer in shame for their deeds, the kind will rejoice with Christ in heaven.

PRAYER: Lord, help me to shrug off the unkind words and actions of the people around me. Lift me above the hurts that come from unthinking and cruel people. Teach me to respond in love, no matter how I am treated. Amen.

Hide me from the secret counsel of the wicked; from the insurrection of the workers of iniquity.
PSALM 64:2

The charges were ridiculous. Didn't people have anything better to do than create perverse fantasies about other people? Cliff had been helping Judy through a really tough time in her life. The two had spent many long hours together, often sitting up through the night in Cliff's apartment, talking. Now a select committee from the school was calling into question Cliff's fitness to teach "young, impressionable minds." Important matters would take a backseat to an imagined scandal. It was ironic that when a person tried his hardest to do something good, his motives were most suspect.

Doing what is right and good is sometimes risky. There is always someone who will question our motives and try to undermine the good we hope to accomplish. Be assured that God sees all things, and He will richly reward those who continue to do right, even in the face of stiff opposition.

PRAYER:
Lord, I need to know that You are on my side and that You will not leave me to fight on my own. I am constantly made aware of how hard it is to do good things. Fill me with perseverance, Lord. Amen.

But God shall shoot at them with an arrow;
suddenly shall they be wounded.

PSALM 64:7

Jesus stood with a group of His followers. In the distance, a crowd appeared, pushing a woman along in front of them. They cast her down at the Lord's feet and said, "What should we do with this adulteress?" They hoped to trap Jesus into condoning sin.

Aware of the trap, Jesus gazed deeply into the eyes of the people. He stooped down and scribbled in the dust. Abruptly, He stood back up and said, "The one among you who is without sin, let him cast the first stone." (See John 8:3-11.)

His answer struck like a bolt of lightning. Words of pure love and power exploded their conceit, and they were forced to look at the truth of God openly and honestly. The sin was not at issue. What mattered was forgiveness. The hateful crowd was shot through the heart by an arrow of God's goodness. Killed was the sin of unrighteous judging. Whenever we present sin as righteousness, God will expose it for what it is.

PRAYER:

Turn my darkness into light, O Lord, and guide me away from things that are sinful and wrong. Teach me to love my neighbors rather than judge them. Let me cast love and peace, instead of stones. Amen.

Which by his strength setteth fast the
mountains; being girded with power.
PSALM 65:6

Todd's teacher talked about the mountains he had visited just the summer before. The teacher said that thousands of years ago, the mountains weren't nearly so high. With each passing year, they jutted higher and higher. Amazing power pushed them skyward. Todd had walked along the ridge of one mountain, taking for granted that it had always been there. The world was a really fascinating place.

It is wonderful to think of our God as the Creator of all that is. There is so much that truly is fascinating, and we cannot begin to understand it all. God set the mountains in their places, and He changes them ever so slightly all the time. A God powerful enough to do all that is a God worthy of our praise and devotion. Put your faith in God, and you will be moved no more easily than a mountain can be.

PRAYER: Lord, You have done so many wonderful things. Your power is beyond imagining. Send that power to me, that I might stand fast in my faith and be unmoved in a world full of temptation. Amen.

Which stilleth the noise of the seas, the noise of their waves, and the tumult of the people.
PSALM 65:7

The two boys stood out on the rocks, looking at the crashing waves. They tried to shout above the roar of the surf, but finally gave up. The water thundered as it hit the rocks. Both boys were a little frightened and a little thrilled by the deafening sound.

When we get a little cocky and conceited, a trip to the ocean can bring us back to reality really fast. The water rolls onto the shore in great, whitecapped waves, hits the rocks, sending spray high into the air, and creates a noise that obliterates every other sound. The sound of the water on the rocks is the voice of God thundering out through creation, "It is good!" Human beings in all their wisdom and genius have created nothing to compare with the least of God's creations. His power, might, and majesty humble us and help us to remember that He alone is God.

PRAYER: Show forth Your might through Your creation, O Lord. Remind me of Your greatness and power throughout the day. You are wonderful, Lord, and I thank You that I can worship You. Amen.

Thou crownest the year with thy goodness;
and thy paths drop fatness.
PSALM 65:11

Dick was thankful. The year had been a good one. He wasn't a wealthy store owner. He lived from week to week, and it was vitally important to him that things work out well. He watched friends of his go under all the time. There was no such thing as a sure thing in business anymore. The Lord had been good to Dick, and he was indeed grateful.

Not everything in life goes the way we would like it. Sometimes we make out okay; other times things just don't seem to work out. In both cases, the Lord is with us, and He wants to help us make the best of things. God has given good things to His children, and when one thing doesn't work out, we can rest assured that something else is soon to come along. When things do work out, we need to remember to give thanks to the One who made it all possible.

PRAYER:
You give so many good things, Lord. Help me to see past the things that are wrong in my life and see all the things that are so right. Thank You for all the blessings You have given me. Amen.

The pastures are clothed with flocks; the valleys also are covered over with corn; they shout for joy, they also sing.

PSALM 65:13

Each year the rice paddies were laid out and the tender plants were planted. Each year the people of the village waited with anxious hope, looking to see whether the storms would come and wash the fields away. Many times, the people would watch as their hard labor was destroyed, but other times they rejoiced to see their crops full and bountiful. After each harvest, the village offered a portion of their harvest to God, thanking Him for His mercy and grace.

What do we offer to God when we are blessed with good things? Do we even remember to say thank You? The Lord has given us so much, and we should always and everywhere give Him thanks and praise.

PRAYER:
In bad times, please be my strength; in good times, celebrate with me, Lord. Thanks for being with me, doing so much for me, and giving so much to me. Amen.

Come and see the works of God: he is terrible in his doing toward the children of men.
PSALM 66:5

In the days of Jesus, a common usage of the word *terrible* meant to be beyond belief. God truly is beyond belief. We cannot begin to understand all He has done and all He continues to do in our world. A walk through the country will expose us to more miracles than we can count. A look at the night sky will fill us with wonder to the core of our being. God has offered us untold questions to explore and contemplate. Come and see the works of the Lord. They are incredible!

PRAYER: Lord, I do not pretend to understand You, but I do surely love You. Show me new wonders and teach me new questions, that I might come to know You better each day. Amen.

He turned the sea into dry land: they went
through the flood on foot: there did
we rejoice in him.

PSALM 66:6

Professor Marsh shook his head emphatically. He maintained that the story of the Red Sea was phony. Dr. Reed proposed that maybe they crossed somewhere else. Brother Allwell said true believers knew it happened just as it was written. For hours the men argued and fought. No one changed his mind, nothing was gained, faith was never spoken of, and the promoters of the debate thought that, all in all, it was a great success.

What is the big idea? The fact is, the Hebrew people escaped the finest fighting force of its day by crossing a body of water that stopped the Egyptian army. A miracle is a miracle is a miracle. The *how* is not nearly as important as the fact that it *did* happen. Our God is a God of miracles and wonders. Praise Him for what He does, rather than for how He does it; and you will find your faith grows by leaps and bounds.

PRAYER:
When Your miracles get reduced to topics for debate, I find I lose interest, Father. Refresh me with the strangeness and awe of Your power, Lord. Amen.

Deane May 30, 2012

*Blessed be God, which hath not turned
away my prayer, nor his mercy from me.*
PSALM 66:20

Think of it! God is actually waiting to hear from us. It's not that God doesn't have other things to do, but there is nothing He'd rather do than spend time with the children He loves. It boggles the mind to realize that God loves us that much. He has made us to be like Him, and He anxiously awaits our call. Offer your prayers to God. He will hear them, and He will send His mercy upon you.

PRAYER:

*Hear me, O God.
Though I may
have nothing of
much importance to say
to You, I need to know that
You will listen to me and respond. I
love You, Lord. Amen.*

As smoke is driven away, so drive them away: as wax melteth before the fire, so let the wicked perish at the presence of God.

PSALM 68:2

The conference room was a fog of cigarette smoke. Everyone sat red-eyed, both smokers and non-smokers alike. It was hard to utter a sentence without choking. Finally, someone discovered switches that turned on exhaust fans. The room cleared, and breathing was possible once more.

Evil is as oppressive as a thick cloud of smoke. It envelops people and chokes them, making it impossible for them to function. One day the Lord will dispel all evil as a fan dispels smoke. On that day, all God's people will breathe richly of the fragrance of God, and no more will we be covered by the haze of sin.

PRAYER: Lord, send the breath of Your Spirit to cleanse me of all sin. Free me from the oppression of all that I have done wrong, through Your blessed forgiveness. Amen.

A father of the fatherless, and a judge of the widows, is God in his holy habitation.
PSALM 68:5

Andy was a saint. It wasn't enough that he had a wife and a large family to take care of. He chose to adopt every person he met who was in need. He befriended a young boy in the neighborhood who had no father, and spent precious time with him. He sought out the widows and single women on the block and offered to do whatever they needed done around their houses. He never took payment for what he did. Instead, he shared a Christlike love and spirit, and served everyone unselfishly.

The Andys of the world are those rare individuals who take seriously their call to be perfect as God is perfect. They strive to be the best people they can be, and they do this by exemplifying love and sacrifice. God gives us the Andys to prove that it can be done. We, too, can walk in the steps of Christ, if we will only give ourselves totally to God. It means nothing more than giving to God what He has given to us.

PRAYER: I want to talk in Your footsteps, Lord. Help me to be willing to share with others what I have been given. Teach me to use my time, my talents, my gifts, and my service to show Your glory. Amen.

*Blessed be the Lord, who daily loadeth us
with benefits, even the God of our salvation.*
PSALM 68:19

When we ask God for our daily bread, what do we mean? Is it merely food to nourish our bodies? Is it all the basic necessities of life? Does it include the bread Jesus spoke of: the Word of God? It is all these things and more. Our heavenly Father wants us to have everything we need to affirm His image within us. God never calls His children to tasks they are not ready for, and He will not abandon us without the resources we need to succeed. Our God provides us with everything we need to be the best people we can be. Call upon the Lord to load you daily with benefits. He will do even more than you expect.

PRAYER:
Lord, I
do not
even know
what I need
to be better than
I am today, but in Your
wisdom, You see my every
need. Give me what You will,
in order that I might honor
and glorify You. Amen.

Save me, O God; for the waters are come in unto my soul.
PSALM 69:1

The canoe creaked once, twice, then a seam began to split. Water rushed in through the gap and filled the bottom of the small boat. The nearest bank was hundreds of feet away, and the current was swift. Jill and Ann began to scream and bail water as fast as they could. Trying to fight panic, they grabbed hold of their life jackets and plunged into the river. Their counselor saw their plight and acted. She moved up on them quickly and fished them out of the strong current.

As we fight to stay afloat in life, it seems like new leaks spring up every day. Thankfully, the Lord of the fleet is watching over us, and He will never let the water rise above our heads. His loving-kindness keeps us afloat and rescues us when troubled waters threaten us.

PRAYER:
I'm trying to keep my head above water, Lord. Thank You for being an island in the stream, where I can climb out of the water, rest from the struggle, and renew myself for the swim ahead.
Amen.

*I am weary of my crying: my throat is dried:
mine eyes fail while I wait for my God.*

PSALM 69:3

There comes a point where there are no more tears to cry. The sadness remains, but the waters dry up. It is in this calm after the storm that we can make sense of things. David cried unto the Lord often. He needed to vent the emotions and pressures that built up inside him. Being the king of a headstrong people was not easy. David experienced periods of intense joy, but also of excruciating heartache. He learned the value of a purging cry. In moments of desperation, David let down all his defenses to stand exposed before God. In those times, God was sure to come to him and offer David all the comfort he needed. In our times of desperation, the Lord will give us comfort, too.

*PRAYER:
When
there are
no more tears
to cry, Lord, fill
me with Your peace
and consolation. Heal my
wounded emotions, Father.
Amen.*

They that hate me without a cause are more than the hairs of mine head: they that would destroy me, being mine enemies wrongfully, are mighty: then I restored that which I took not away.
PSALM 69:4

Being king isn't easy. Either people love you or they hate you. The same is true of every position of power and authority. Presidents, deans, prime ministers—the list can go on and on—all these people have to face the passions of the people they lead. Even God Himself has to face such problems. God is not loved by everyone. There are those who, for whatever reason, have chosen to reject God. There are those who curse Him as regularly as we praise Him. We are the subjects of the greatest sovereign in creation. Our Lord rules with justice and love. We might not agree with everything He does or everything He calls us to do, but we owe Him our allegiance and loyalty. Be loyal to the Lord, and He will rule over you justly and with compassion.

PRAYER: It is easy to bow down before a ruler of such love and grace, Lord. In every age, You have ruled fairly. I pray for all those who do not know Your greatness and Your goodness. Break through with Your light into their lives. Amen.

*They gave me also gall for my meat; and
in my thirst they gave me vinegar to drink.*

PSALM 69:21

Sometimes we think things are going really bad in our lives. It's easy to fall into the trap of thinking we're worse off than anyone else. When we feel sorry for ourselves, all we need to do is turn to the story of Jesus' last few hours on earth. There the man who knew no sin became sin for us, so we might have eternal life. He was stripped, beaten, spit upon; and when, as His dying request, He asked for a drink to wet His lips, they put vinegar before Him instead of water. No kindness was shown to the Prince of Peace, the One who had done nothing in His life to warrant such cruel mistreatment. Compared with the trial and misfortune of our Lord, we have very little to complain about. To even compare ourselves to Him is to open ourselves to shame. Christ endured torment and death upon a cross for our sakes. Now He abides with us to help us endure every trial.

*PRAYER:
I can hardly
believe all
that You did
for me, Lord.
You walked this
earth so that I might one
day walk with You in heaven.
Thank You for giving me so
much. Amen.*

Make haste, O God, to deliver me;
make haste to help me, O Lord.
PSALM 70:1

Kathy thought she was going to scream. The man came into the office and paced back and forth until she had gotten off the phone and was able to ask him what he wanted. He fidgeted at the desk, telling her that he was a very busy man and didn't have time to wait around. She told him to have a seat. In the next five minutes he sat drumming his fingers on a table, looked at his watch a dozen times, asked twice whether it would be much longer, and intermittently sighed heavily. Kathy had no patience with people who lacked patience themselves.

Patience is not a strong virtue in the twenty-first century. We are people who want instant gratification. We want what we want when we want it. We don't like to wait. Unfortunately, we worship a God of eternity who chooses to operate on His time schedule, not ours. Therefore, patience is a vital component of the happy Christian life. Ask the Lord for patience. You'll need it.

PRAYER: Father, I need to learn to wait graciously and patiently. Fill my heart with peace and give me a spirit of acceptance, that I might know happiness even when things don't happen fast enough to suit me. Amen.

*Cast me not off in the time of old age;
forsake me not when my strength faileth.*
PSALM 71:9

Once, older people were revered for the wealth of knowledge and wisdom they possessed. Today they are often treated as inconveniences. They are shoved aside and ignored. Certainly, this is not true in every case, but that it happens at all is a tragedy. Older men and women are gifts from God. They are the conquerors in this life. They have fought the spiritual battles, and they have war stories to tell that can benefit us all. To have lived a full and fruitful life should be a joy, not a burden. In a society gone youth crazy, the need for the elderly is greater than ever. They provide the balance we need. Theirs is the voice of reason and experience. Theirs are the spirits of perseverance and triumph. They have walked our roads before us, and they can guide us when times get rough. Reach out to the older branch of God's family. Reach out and grasp the treasure.

PRAYER:

As I grow older, Lord, let me not worry whether or not I will be welcome. Open my heart to older people, and have me treat them as I will one day want to be treated. Amen.

Thou, which hast shewed me great and sore troubles, shalt quicken me again, and shalt bring me up again from the depths of the earth.
PSALM 71:20

The Indian boy shivered in the night, his third since he had been let go. He had one week to kill a wild animal with his bare hands and find his way back to his home camp. If he succeeded, he would be considered a man. This was the most important rite of passage of his entire life. He was afraid to be alone, and he had failed to catch an animal yet, but he had learned much; he was sure things would work out by the end of the week.

Many times we must go through adversity and hard times in order to learn and grow. The lessons we learn are invaluable, even though we would often rather learn them some other way. The Lord allows us to meet adversity because He knows we must endure in order to be better people. He does not allow adversity because He is cruel, but because He is kind and wants the best for His children.

*PRAYER:
I know that I will face many challenges and ordeals, Father, and I will try to accept them. Help me to be strong for those times, and to bring honor and glory to You. Amen.*

He shall judge the poor of the people, he shall save the children of the needy, and shall break in pieces the oppressor.

PSALM 72:4

A man of humble means walked along a road and encountered Jesus seated on a rock with a thin child on His lap. The man looked at Jesus, threw himself down before Him, and worshipped Him. Jesus sat, unmoved. The man praised Jesus, and still Jesus was impassive. In frustration, the man asked Jesus what was wrong. Jesus looked down at the child in his lap. The child had grown thinner and was on the verge of starving to death. The man turned away from Jesus in disgust and walked on his way.

While we worship Jesus, people are dying. Jesus holds those dying children in His arms. To come before Jesus means to come before the needy of this world. Jesus said unless you do good unto your brothers and sisters, you have not done good unto Him. We cannot expect Jesus to pay attention to us unless we're willing to pay attention to the things that matter to Him. Let us join with our Lord in being saviors to a world in need.

PRAYER:

Forgive me for wrong priorities, Lord. I worship often in word, but not in deed. Let my actions reinforce the faith I confess with my heart. Amen.

He shall come down like rain upon the
mown grass: as showers that water the earth.
PSALM 72:6

B ud looked out on soil with cracks so wide you could
put your hand in them. The summer had been bru-
tal. Weeks ago, Bud had given up any hope of a
harvest, but now he wondered whether he would even
have a farm much longer. The sky remained cloudless. So
many people cursed the rain because it spoiled picnics and
closed parks. It was foolish to curse the rain. It was the
lifeblood of all that lived. Bud wondered what he would
do if the drought lasted much longer.

Many of us have experienced spiritual droughts. We
find ourselves in a desert of doubt and apathy. Nothing
seems to be the way we want it to be, and frankly, we really
don't care. We wonder if God is listening; all we hear is the
echo of our own voices. God's loving touch is so necessary
in our lives. We cannot live without the water that Jesus
offered the woman at the well. This living water quenches
our spiritual thirst and brings our drought to
an end. Ask God for the living
water. He will issue forth a flood
to wash you and refresh you.

PRAYER:
I am waiting, Lord,
for Your Spirit
to rain down upon
me and soak me with Your
loving-kindness. Drench me in the
waters of love and life. Amen.

Yea, all kings shall fall down before him:
all nations shall serve him.

PSALM 72:11

Imagine a world where everyone acknowledged God and promised to try to live by His will. Imagine leaders who were committed to love and peace and justice. Imagine a world where people forgave one another instead of living for revenge. Imagine a world where no one felt the need for bombs and guns and wars. Imagine. God gave us a beautiful world and gave the choice of what it would become to us. He said, "Imagine!" Is this the best we could do?

PRAYER: Lord, where have we failed to be Your people on earth? Guide me as I try to be the person I think You want me to be. Help me to strive for the world I imagine this one could be with Your aid. Amen.

Verily I have cleansed my heart in vain, and washed my hands in innocency.
PSALM 73:13

Lisa tried so hard to be a good girl. She did what she knew was right. Many of her friends were immoral and wild, but she had always been quiet and sweet. For what? Every time she came home, her parents interrogated her, trying to find out if she had done something she shouldn't have done. She had never given her parents any reason to mistrust her, and yet they treated her like a dangerous criminal. It wasn't worth it. Sometimes she felt like going out and doing something wrong just to justify her parents' suspicions.

Our world is upside down. We reward the wrongdoer and we chastise the righteous. To be good is equal to being somehow deficient. Words like virtue, purity, and sweetness have taken on negative connotations. To be good is foreign or alien to the majority. The key is not to give up. The Lord will reward those who persevere in the face of persecution and frustration. God loves the pure in heart, and it is well worth it to hold on for His sake.

PRAYER:
Be with me, Lord,
to cleanse me, to
strengthen me, and
to help me deal with people
who think wrong is right. I want
to be Your child, not a child of the
world. Amen.

JUNE

8

My flesh and my heart faileth: but God is the strength of my heart, and my portion for ever.

PSALM 73:26

Pete faced the idea of death with calm. In his day, Pete had been a strong, good-looking man. He had watched himself grow old, but that was okay. He had lived a wonderful life. Sometimes he wished he were young again, but mostly he was happy with where he was in life. Even though his flesh grew wrinkled and his heart didn't pump quite as well as it had before, his mind was still sharp and his spirit was good. To live was wonderful, but dying would be okay, too. He'd done well on earth; maybe it was time to see how he'd fare in heaven.

Christ makes us strangers to the earth. His home is in heaven, and when He dwells within us, He prepares us for our true, eternal home. The longer Christ is with us, the more He readies us to leave this place and to enter into heaven. Death need hold no fear. On the other side waits God and an eternity spent in His loving care.

PRAYER:
With Paul,
I can claim
that to live
is Christ and to
die is gain. Whatever
Your will for my life, Lord,
whether it will be long or
short, help me to accept it.
Amen.

Thine enemies roar in the midst of thy congregations; they set up their ensigns for signs.
PSALM 74:4

The pastor felt the focus of the church year should be missions. Definitely missions. The head of the church school wanted education to be the main concern. Finance felt that stewardship was the ticket. Each committee of the church had its own banner to wave. The conflicts that arose over the issue left deep wounds, and some left the church. The different groups sat together on Sunday mornings, but they left the sanctuary engaged in bitter arguments.

What kind of behavior is that for Christians? We are supposed to rise above the pettiness that rules the outside world. If we cannot learn to deal with one another in love, what business have we calling ourselves Christ's church? Our Lord is a Lord of compromise, sacrifice, and caring. No Christian should be our enemy. We are all members of the same body, and Christ blesses those who strive to live in peace and harmony with one another.

PRAYER: Remind me, Lord, that I am a Christian first and foremost. The causes I support are second to the fact that I follow Jesus Christ. Let Him rule in my heart, and lead me in the ways I should walk. Amen.

We see not our signs: there is no more any prophet: neither is there among us any that knoweth how long.

PSALM 74:9

A friend lamented to me, "Our problem today is that the voice of God is silent. We have no prophets. What we need is a good Jeremiah or Isaiah."

The crowd that listened to Jeremiah and Isaiah lamented to their contemporaries that what they needed was a good prophet like Elijah. In every age, the people long for a different voice than the one they are hearing. God speaks to us in many different ways. The trick is to be open to His call. We often don't see signs because they are not the signs we hope to see. Almost everything that God communicates to us means that we must be willing to give and to serve. The only communication that God has made with no duty involved on our part was sending His Son, Jesus Christ. All we have to do is accept Jesus as our Savior. Looking for signs and longing for prophets does us no good. God has made known what He wants us to do. The job is before us. Let's do it.

PRAYER:

Lord, I am not even doing the things I already know I should do. Why then do I look for something more? Help me to do what I can now, and make me open to Your messages as they come in this age.

Amen.

Have respect unto the covenant: for the dark places of the earth are full of the habitations of cruelty.
PSALM 74:20

A new government had seemed the best solution. The overthrow had taken place, a new government was installed, and then something had gone wrong. The new president sat enthroned in a palatial estate, where no one could get in to see him. The proposals of the new majority went unheeded. The oppressors had not been eradicated; they had merely changed faces and places. The people were betrayed, and the cruelty continued.

Broken promises. They litter the land of most countries. Trust is offered; then it is trampled on. A man's or woman's word is only as good as the individual chooses to make it. Thank God that He is constant and true. His covenants are eternal. God never turns from His people, and they never need to fear that they will be forgotten. Let us work in our lives to copy God's commitment to covenant in the promises that we make.

PRAYER:
Make my word as good as the finest gold, dear Lord. Help me to accept the fact that I am lied to each day, and to forgive those who offer up the lies. Amen.

O let not the oppressed return ashamed:
let the poor and needy praise thy name.

PSALM 74:21

A government official was asked why more wasn't being done for the poor and starving. He answered, "We have no right to impose our culture on their chosen lifestyle. These people do nothing to better themselves, so they must want to live as they do. What should we be expected to do in a case like that?"

Why do we look for ways to shame the poor and destitute? Of course, there are a few who are poor because they choose nothing better for their lives, but they are a distinct minority. All too often, poor people are made out to be lazy, evil, and greedy, when nothing could be further from the truth. The poor are our brothers and sisters, and they are worthy of our help, just because Christ said so. God blesses the poor and those who help them. Take hold of your blessing. Help someone in need.

PRAYER: Lord, all your children deserve dignity and respect. Let me give all people the respect that I would give You, Lord. Humble my heart when I feel myself looking down on those around me. Amen.

For promotion cometh neither from the east,
nor from the west, nor from the south. But
God is the judge: he putteth down one, and setteth up another.
PSALM 75:6–7

Evelyn came from Charity Hill, the most expensive section of town. She had always received everything her heart desired, and she considered herself to be one of the finest people she knew. Jane came from Cheesebox, the poor side of town, so named because all the houses there looked like cardboard cheese boxes. She had never had much of anything special, and felt she really didn't deserve better, anyway. Both women worked for an ad agency that wanted a new production designer. Evelyn knew she would do well in the position. To her dismay, Jane did even better.

Things don't always work so well in real life. The rich often get richer while the poor sink lower. And yet God has promised that in the end, justice will always carry the day. God knows every heart and every situation. He will set all things right if we will only trust in His wisdom.

PRAYER:
Nothing I do,
Lord, will increase
Your love for me,
but still I want to do all
that I can. Search my heart and
know that I do truly love You. Help
me to show Your love to others. Amen.

14

The stouthearted are spoiled, they have slept their sleep: and none of the men of might have found their hands.

PSALM 76:5

Bob didn't need anybody. He had always done things on his own. He thought he would do well in sports, but he couldn't play as part of a team. He thought he would settle down and have a happy marriage, but he couldn't stand having to answer to another person. He couldn't hold a job because he could neither take nor give orders graciously. No, Bob didn't need anyone, which was a lucky thing. No one needed Bob.

We were created to live with and for one another. When we think the universe revolves around us, we upset God's intended order. Our goal in life should be to reach out to as many of God's children as we possibly can. When we learn to walk with others, we have learned to walk with God.

PRAYER: Lord, do not let me become spoiled and conceited. I want to share my life and to share the lives of others. Help me to know others better, and in so doing, know You better, too. Amen.

Vow, and pay unto the LORD your God: let all that be round about him bring presents unto him that ought to be feared.
PSALM 76:11

O*h, no,* thought Kent, *here comes the old pitch.* We don't have enough money. We can't keep the doors open. Give till it hurts. On and on and on and on. He gave five bucks a week. That was enough. He didn't see others beating him out of the way to give more. Hey, a movie cost about five bucks, and you got two hours of entertainment. For the same price he only got an hour's worth at church. Get real. Sometimes it annoyed him enough to make him put his wallet back in his coat without taking anything out. This morning? What the heck—he was in a generous mood.

People forget where their financial support originates. Without the Lord, no one would receive anything. The Bible says that 10 percent off the top should go to the Lord. This isn't charity on our part, but a return to God of what is really His, anyway. We tithe out of gratitude for what God has given. The Lord teaches us to give so we will not think too highly of material wealth, and instead will remain committed to the wealth that cannot be destroyed. God's wealth endures forever.

PRAYER: O Lord, I possess more than I really need. There is something that I could do without. Help me to learn to give as You Yourself have given: freely, joyfully, and completely. Amen.

In the day of my trouble I sought the Lord:
my sore ran in the night, and ceased not:
my soul refused to be comforted.

PSALM 77:2

The sharp ache kept bringing Fran fully awake. The tooth was bad, but there was nothing she could do about it until the next day. She wanted to slip into blessed sleep to escape the pain, but the tooth wouldn't let her. She prayed continually for God to ease her suffering enough for her to fall asleep. She was on the verge of tears when she felt He wasn't listening. He wasn't doing anything to help her.

Too often we want God to make it all better, when that just simply isn't the way He operates. Sometimes we have to endure pain or suffering, and God isn't going to make it go away. When our pain threatens our very being, then He will intercede for us, but when we experience the pain of normal everyday living, God allows us to endure it. Endurance builds us up and helps us grow. We can seek the Lord, and He will be with us, but He may not take away the irritation we suffer from.

PRAYER:
Lord, I'm sorry that I often ask You to deal with things that I should deal with myself. I am lazy, and sometimes I refuse to face everyday life. Help me get over my selfishness.
Amen.

Hath God forgotten to be gracious? hath he in anger shut up his tender mercies?
PSALM 77:9

Liz lay on her back, looking up at the stars. She and Jim had watched the stars together a thousand times. She still couldn't figure out why he'd broken up with her. She thought they were perfect together. She had thanked God a million times for Jim. Now she wondered whether God even cared about her at all. Why would He break up such a great relationship?

Perhaps we give God too much credit for being active in our lives. There are some things He wants us to handle on our own. Christ works inside of us to make us kingdom people, but we have to make choices on our own. We need to take the things Christ teaches and use them in our relationships, our actions, our lives. God is with us to comfort us when we fail and to celebrate with us when we triumph, but He still allows us to make our own choices. It's not always what we want, but our God is the God of freedom of will. He will not make the world work our way just because we think He should.

*PRAYER:
Lord, I want many things. I have asked You to make me happy, but I need to take some responsibility for my own happiness. Grant me the encouragement and wisdom I need to make the right decisions. Amen.*

The voice of thy thunder was in the heaven:
the lightnings lightened the world: the
earth trembled and shook.

PSALM 77:18

The little airplane bobbed and weaved. The storm was playing havoc with its small engines. Arthur looked out of the cabin windows. His gaze was met with pitch blackness, but he continued to look out, anyway. He said a short prayer to God for safety, and as he finished, a bolt of lightning lit up the entire sky. Down below, a town was exposed by the flash, and Arthur was struck by the calm beauty and peace of the village. The plane was closer to the ground than he had realized, and he was suddenly convinced that everything would be perfectly all right. A strange peace filled his heart, and he sat back and relaxed for the rest of the flight.

The fury of a storm can be frightening, but the hand of God is mightier, and His hand is ever upon our lives. Though we might feel tossed around, we are in God's care, and nothing can happen to us that with God's help we can't handle.

PRAYER:
O Lord,
I do not
know what
Your will is for
me this day, but I
do know that whatever
happens to me, it will be the
best possible thing. Your love
rules my life, and I trust You
completely. Amen.

I will open my mouth in a parable: I will utter dark sayings of old.
PSALM 78:2

Sarah, the old woman with mysteries to tell. The whole town buzzed around Sarah's house. Sarah had lived in the same house in the same town for seventy years. She was a throwback to an earlier time. She dressed in fashions of the twenties, and she talked a language that sounded foreign to young ears. Sarah was a walking cliché. She remembered the stories and sayings of old, and so she was a treasure chest of days gone by. Everyone loved Sarah, for Sarah was history come to life.

Life is a story. It is a parable we live through day by day. Just as a parable has a hidden meaning, so, too, the events of our daily living have significance and deeper meanings. Our present and our past are important components of who we are. We like to hold on to the past, and we strive to make the present the best it can be. God, the greatest storyteller of all, is a part of our past and our present. He can shape our parable for us, if we will let Him. When we do so, we can be confident that our story has a happy ending.

PRAYER: I don't have any idea what the outcome of my story will be, Lord, but I thank You for giving my life an interesting and unique plot. Go with me through the chapters of my life, Lord. Amen.

That the generation to come might know them, even the children which should be born; who should arise and declare them to their children.

PSALM 78:6

There is a wall in Washington, D.C., which has engraved on it the names of all the men and women who gave their lives in active service during the war in Vietnam. It stands as a testimonial to their courage. To remember them and what they did is important. We need reminders of where we have been and what we have done. The monument should make us both proud and ashamed. It should swell our hearts with joy that the war is at an end, and sorrow that it cost so much to attain so little. We need to know these things. God wants us to know these things, and He wants our children to know them after us. Perhaps one day we will learn enough so that such monuments are no longer necessary, and we can get on with being God's people. Let us hope so.

PRAYER: Let me remember not only the good things in life, but also the bad. The good helps me to rejoice, the bad helps me avoid making the same mistakes again. Lord, let me learn from my mistakes. Amen.

In the daytime also he led them with a cloud,
and all the night with a light of fire.
PSALM 78:14

The chosen people were afraid. They had to cross a barren wasteland, a desert, with no provisions and no definite sense of where they would end up. The scorching sun frightened them. The dark, cold nights frightened them. They were a people afraid. But the Lord saw their fear, and He sent a cloud to block the scorching sun, and He placed a bright fireball in the sky at night to light their way. The people of God came through the desert safe and sound.

God brings us through the wastelands of our lives in the same way. He will not allow us to be tested beyond our strength and endurance. Trust in God's mercy and love, and He will bring you through any situation.

PRAYER:
Lord, I am
sometimes
frightened by the
challenges I am called on
to face. Be with me, and let me
lean upon Your strength for support.
Amen.

Behold, he smote the rock, that the waters gushed out, and the streams overflowed; can he give bread also? can he provide flesh for his people?
PSALM 78:20

Brittany wanted a car, and she got a car. She wanted to go to an expensive college. She wanted her own apartment, and Daddy came through with the money. She wanted nice clothes, a stereo, a microwave, a television. There was no end to Brittany's wants. Nothing satisfied her. No matter how much she was given, she wanted more.

We need to be careful that we don't approach God that way. God wants us to truly appreciate what we have before we start asking for more. He gives good things to His children, and He is willing to give abundantly, but He desires us to learn the real meaning of thankfulness.

PRAYER:
Dear God,
make me
appreciative
of all the
wonderful gifts You
give. When I take things
for granted, show me the
error of my ways. Fill my
mind and heart with
gratitude for the many
blessings I have.
Amen.

How oft did they provoke him in the wilderness, and grieve him in the desert!
PSALM 78:40

Brad knew that if he was good, his father would take him out for ice cream. It was up to him. Brad knew he could only push his luck so far. His father was a patient man, but even he had his limits. If Brad acted up, he could kiss his ice cream good-bye. It was worth being good for.

Conditions. There always seem to be conditions on everything. Little strings attached. How wonderful it is when we find relationships with no strings attached. Our relationship with God is like that: no conditions, no strings. He loves us even when we are unlovable. We can misbehave, and we can sin, but God welcomes us back whenever we repent and return to Him. He doesn't ever withhold His favor from those who reach out to Him.

PRAYER: I'm not always as good as I know I should be, Father. I act terrible at times. Please forgive and accept me, Lord. I love You, and I want to make You proud of me. Amen.

He sent divers sorts of flies among them,
which devoured them; and frogs, which
destroyed them. He gave also their increase
unto the caterpillar, and their labour unto the locust.

PSALM 78:45–46

God sent plagues upon the Egyptians, who perse-cuted the Hebrew people. Through these afflic-tions, God sent the message that no one could do evil for long and get away unpunished. Our Lord doesn't supersede the laws of nature often; but when He does, it is with good cause. And yet, even in the face of the terrible plagues, the Egyptian pharaoh refused to believe. People who lack the love of God in their lives so often refuse to admit they might be wrong. It is easier to deny God than to do what is necessary to please Him. The Christian re-fuses to deny her heart, and she continually acknowledges God's great works for what they really are. In our own day, the Lord does not send many plagues to afflict us, but there are definitely enough hardships to make us want to reach out to Him. We need God, and thankfully we have Him every step of the way.

PRAYER:
My eyes
are blind to
many of Your
great works, Lord.
I miss so much of Your
greatness and love. Help
me to see You in new ways
each day. Amen.

Pour out thy wrath upon the heathen that have not known thee, and upon the kingdoms that have not called upon thy name.
PSALM 79:6

It's not easy loving unlovable people. Some people do such terrible things. King David looked at evil men and felt nothing but contempt. Why should evil men prosper while good men struggled just to get by? Why should hateful women get their hearts' desires while virtuous women could hardly lift their heads? David wrestled with God's justice throughout his lifetime.

It is difficult to remember that God's justice plays itself out in eternity, not just in our lifetime. In the end times, righteous people will prevail, while the evildoers are left out in the cold. The Lord has little desire to reward only good people and punish those who are bad. If He did that, people would follow Him for the wrong reason. God wants His children to come to Him because they love Him, not because they think it will bring them good things.

PRAYER:
Lord, help me
to accept the
fact that bad
things happen to
good people, and that bad
people are often prosperous.
I may not like it now, but I need to
keep in mind that one day each of us will
receive exactly what he deserves.
Amen.

Let the sighing of the prisoner come before thee; according to the greatness of thy power preserve thou those that are appointed to die.

PSALM 79:11

Jack sat with his head hanging, hands dangling between his knees. Just over a year had gone by since he was convicted of murdering his girlfriend. He didn't do it, but no one believed him. Within hours, his life would be at an end, and the truth would never be known. What had his life really been for? He closed his eyes and prayed to God. Sometime during his prayer, a stay of execution came through. New evidence would reopen a case almost permanently closed.

When we despair of life itself, the Lord comes to us gently and with love. He stays beside us, bringing us comfort when we need it most. Through Jesus Christ, we have received the reprieve from death. Our prayers are heard, and the Lord will be faithful to answer every one.

PRAYER: Sometimes I feel like my life is hopeless, Lord. It seems that I am serving out some kind of sentence. Lift that burden from me and let me experience life the way You meant for it to be. Amen.

Turn us again, O God, and cause thy face to shine; and we shall be saved.
PSALM 80:3

The silly-looking little clown wobbled back and forth across the tabletop. He would jerk along in a funny walk, then, as his foot cleared the edge of the table, he would rock back, spin, and head off in a new direction, barely averting disaster.

We are a lot like that clown. We head off in wrong directions and then have to change our ways time and time again in order to avoid bad consequences. The word *repent* means to turn away from or toward. God wants us to turn from the things that are wrong in our lives and to turn toward Him. If we will always try to do just that, the Lord's face will shine upon us, and we shall be saved.

PRAYER:
Be patient with
me, Lord. I run
off in so many wrong
directions, but I want always
to come back to You. Thank You for
not giving up on me. Amen.

*The boar out of the wood doth waste it, and
the wild beast of the field doth devour it.*

PSALM 80:13

Betty loved her flowers and plants. She spent hours pruning, planting, and paring. Her garden was her pride and joy. Betty invested so much of herself into her plants. For that reason, Betty was at war with the woodland animals that made their way into her yard. They would always get through the fences somehow and mutilate her beautiful garden. To Betty, the plants were beauty and joy, but to the animals, they were nothing more than lunch.

We have the capacity to truly appreciate the beauty and splendor of God's creation. Why, then, do so many people trash God's gift as blindly as animals destroy a beautiful garden? Why don't we appreciate and respect nature more? The Lord gave us His ability to see the beauty in things. Let us use that gift, and protect and defend the wonders of the world in which we live.

*PRAYER:
Do not let
me stomp
through life
like some wild
animal. Help me to see
all creation as You see it.
Fill me with the beauty of this
world. Amen.*

Take a psalm, and bring hither the timbrel,
the pleasant harp with the psaltery.
PSALM 81:2

Beth was different when she was singing. Somehow the pressures of the world disappeared when the music filled her head and heart. Her whole life felt somehow lighter, brighter, when she lifted her voice in praise through song. Music was the best expression of who she was and what she believed. Music made God real to Beth.

Music is a universal language. Every culture has its music, and it is revered as one of the finest arts. Music brings people together and can move us closer to God. God loves music and the spirit from which music springs. The quality is not nearly as important as the intention of the heart. Sing out to God, and He will bless you richly.

PRAYER:
Music touches my
heart in a special
way, Lord. Speak to
me through the beauty of
music. Touch me day by day. Amen.

30

There shall no strange god be in thee;
neither shalt thou worship any strange god.
PSALM 81:9

Chrissy was a smart girl. It was hard to understand why she would want to run off to some strange communal religious group. She had been active at church all her young life. Then, out of the blue, she started hanging around with a bunch of college students who belonged to a commune called Light of Life. One day her parents came home to find a note. All of Chrissy's things were gone; she was now a member of Light of Life.

Thousands of people turn to cults and sects, hoping to find something Christianity can't give them. Usually, they don't want to take the responsibility Christ gives to live a holy and upright life. It is easier to run away to somewhere where the self doesn't matter so much, than to face the problems right in front of us. Sadly, there is no place to run. Jesus is the only true answer to a life that is empty and void. Strange gods come and go. They have no staying power. They may be attractive for awhile, but only God endures forever.

PRAYER:
When I get discouraged in my faith, Lord, turn me back to You, that I might know Your truth. Do not let me be swayed by false teachings that sound so appealing. Protect me with Your love. Amen.

The haters of the LORD should have submitted themselves unto him: but their time should have endured for ever.

PSALM 81:15

Water stretched out in every direction, as far as the man could see. He didn't know what direction would lead him most quickly to safety. He kept swimming, not knowing whether the shore was any closer or not. Each direction he tried seemed as hard as the last. The current was against him, no matter which way he turned. He was so tired. Every muscle ached. His heart filled with fear and anxiety. He wondered if the nightmare would ever end.

Such is the fate of one who realizes too late that God is who He says He is. All the futility of life comes crashing in. Sadness and frustration will reign. God wants us to turn to Him so we never have to face such despair. Christ is the life jacket that keeps us afloat when life becomes too much for us. Nothing else will suffice.

PRAYER:
The waters are rough sometimes, and I need something to keep me from sinking. Thank You for throwing me a lifeline: Jesus Christ the Lord. Amen.

*I have said, Ye are gods; and all of you
are children of the most High.*
PSALM 82:6

The wood-carver who made himself a son out of a stump of a tree did so out of love. He wanted someone to love and care for, to teach and to guide, to spend time with and to share with. Pinocchio was the answer to the prayers of a lonely old man. In the end, the old man's love brought the boy made of wood to life.

God carved for Himself men and women to be with Him forever. He filled them with good things. He made them to love, and care, and learn, and grow. He fashioned them out of clay; then He made them as He was. He made us just less than Himself. He calls us gods and children, the greatest of all His creation. In God's eyes, we are sacred and good. Let us do everything we can to live up to His holy expectations.

PRAYER:
Make me worthy,
Lord, of
the great love
that You have given
to me. Turn me from
my woodenness to true
life—life that comes from Your
indwelling Spirit. Amen.

Yea, the sparrow hath found an house, and
the swallow a nest for herself, where she may
lay her young, even thine altars, O LORD of
hosts, my King, and my God.
PSALM 84:3

Rosa had no place left to turn. She was in the country illegally, but for her children's sake, she had to try to stay. She found herself with her two boys on the steps of a New Mexico church. Inside, she hoped to find the sanctuary she needed. There was no hope if the church turned her away.

Many people in this country are in deep trouble for offering sanctuary to illegal immigrants. These men and women have taken seriously God's charge to care for all His children, even at the risk of personal safety and security. Some have gone to jail, so strongly do they believe.

The church should be a place where people find hope and safety. If it does not provide these things, it is not really the church. We need to reach out to those who reach out to us. Only by doing so can we stand proud, calling Jesus Christ our Lord and Savior.

PRAYER: Let the feelings of my heart be made real through my actions, Lord. Help me to live out the things that I believe.

Amen.

As the fire burneth a wood, and as the flame setteth the mountains on fire; so persecute them with thy tempest, and make them afraid with thy storm.

PSALM 83:14–15

The fireworks lit up the Independence Day night sky. Children watched wide-eyed, and parents exclaimed appropriately at each burst. The town echoed with the booming blasts of each rocket. The show was spectacular, and everyone had a good time. A few even remembered why the celebration took place. Some remembered that the fireworks represented all the bombs that had burst for freedom. A handful walked away from the celebration with hope beating in their breasts. The hope was that there would come a time when no more bombs would burst, where no one would have to live in fear for their lives. Some hoped for a day when peace would rule the land.

Some fear is healthy. It brings us to our senses and forces us to look at things with a level head. War is a terrible thing. It breaks down and destroys. God wants us to consider well the consequences of war. What we do to one another, He will not undo. Perhaps a fear of the Lord would bring us to our senses. Maybe we would then realize where we stand, and we would choose to stand closer to God.

PRAYER:

I pray for independence and freedom for all of creation, Lord. While we celebrate and laugh at the bursting bombs, some cower in fear and trembling. Be with them, Father. Amen.

For a day in thy courts is better than a thousand. I had rather be a doorkeeper in the house of my God, than to dwell in the tents of wickedness.
PSALM 84:10

Mike had seen pictures of most of the places he visited before he went. Even so, he was not prepared for the beauty he found. Pictures lost the magnitude somehow. Traveling across the country brought everything into sharp focus. Being in it was a thousand times better than just seeing pictures of it.

Nothing beats the real thing. Once we are touched by the grace of God, nothing else compares. What this world has to offer us is but a snapshot of what we can really have. The real thing is best. Embrace God, and all that He is, and all that He does. You'll never need anything else.

PRAYER:
Lord, nothing can compare with You. In my life I have experienced wonderful things, but none so wonderful as Your love. Thank You. Amen.

For the LORD God is a sun and shield; the LORD will give grace and glory: no good thing will he withhold from them that walk uprightly.

PSALM 84:11

Loren worked on his tan all summer. He wanted that "ruddy, healthy look." All his efforts went into the pursuit of the perfect tan. By fall, he knew he'd be the envy of all his friends and the object of desire of all the ladies.

A suntan is an outward sign. Everyone who looks sees that the person has been changed in some way. The same is true of our Son tan, the spiritual bathing we take in Christ. Do people notice a difference in our lives just by looking at us? If we have been touched by the light of Christ, people should be able to tell. When we walk upright, God shines forth through us. Let us work as hard on our spiritual image as we do on our physical one.

PRAYER:

Shine Your light on, in, and through me, Lord, that I might fight against darkness wherever I go. Amen.

*Surely his salvation is nigh them that fear
him; that glory may dwell in our land.*
PSALM 85:9

Roger was the best cop in the precinct. His record
was sparkling clean, and he was the model for
most rookies to follow. His most frequent piece of
advice was simple: Pay attention. Roger had watched a lot
of his friends blow it just because they got careless. Police
work was not for careless people. Bad things happened to
careless people, things that couldn't be undone. The best
way was to be careful. The last thing Roger wanted to have
happen was for his career, or his life, to come to an end
over some stupid mistake.

One of the best ways we can honor our Lord is to pay
attention and be careful. Other people see the way we live
our lives, and if we are sloppy and sinful, we can hardly
hope to make others see the benefits of being a Christian.
Once we have been touched by the
saving grace of God, we need to
pay attention and live as careful
and wise a life as possible.

*PRAYER:
Make me a good
example, Lord,
of a life made new
through Your love. Help
others to see in me that Your way is
the best way. Amen.*

Truth shall spring out of the earth; and
righteousness shall look down from heaven.

PSALM 85:11

Marge had denied God's existence for years. She had grown up in a huge city, and she rarely got out of it. Her argument against God was that a loving being wouldn't allow people to live in such terrible conditions as existed in so much of the city. Arguments did nothing to persuade her. Marge's mind was made up.

When she was twenty-six, she went with friends into the mountains of Vermont. Like a wide-eyed child, she soaked in the awesome beauty of the hills. One evening, at sunset, her heart was filled with an unbelievable joy, and she somehow knew that God did exist. Cities weren't God's fault; they were the creation of men and women. Nature was God's expression of reality, and that reality was too good to deny. The truth rose up out of God's green earth to convince her. Never again would she say God did not exist.

PRAYER:
What a wonderful world we live in, Lord. You give us happiness, and yet we create sorrow. Turn our tears into laughter, God, that we may enjoy this blessed gift of life we have been given.
Amen.

*But thou, O Lord, art a God full of
compassion, and gracious, longsuffering,
and plenteous in mercy and truth.*
PSALM 86:15

Erin thought the minister would be more understanding. She had gone to him with her problems
because she thought he would be forgiving and
loving. Instead, he made her feel dirty and sinful. There
was no love in what he told her. He just said that what she
had done was evil, and she had to ask God's forgiveness
and hope He would hear her. How could he call himself a
Christian, let alone a minister? Erin left the church feeling worse than when she went in.

Pastors are people, too. They make mistakes, and just
because they choose to serve God does not mean they will
do everything the way God would do it. Too many people
place pastors high up on pedestals, only to watch them
come tumbling down. Only God is capable of total love
and care. His forgiveness is what really matters. Often
pastors can help us find God's will
for our lives, but in those cases
where they do not, God will
still reach down to us, lifting us
in love, sharing with us His
mercy and truth.

*PRAYER: Lord,
when people let
me down, be
with me to help me
understand them. Shower
Your love upon me, and deal with
me with compassion. I need to feel Your
love. Amen.*

Shew me a token for good; that they which
hate me may see it, and be ashamed: because
thou, LORD, hast holpen me, and comforted me.

PSALM 86:17

During high school Chris had been a total loser. He had partied heavily and bullied other kids, forcing them to give up their lunch money in order to avoid a beating. Everyone walked in fear of Chris. Ten years was a long time, but no one expected such a great change from Chris. At the reunion, Chris came into a room that was still somewhat fearful of the old bully. What the people found was a man of grace and charm, who extended a warm hand to everyone he saw. In a few cases, Chris apologized for his behavior ten years before. When asked what had made the difference in his life, Chris replied simply, "I'm a Christian now."

Christ is the changer of lives. He will give us a token that will attract people's attention. When others see the miracles of God in our lives, they cannot help but be touched themselves. God works through us to touch others. Open yourself to His guidance, and He will use you greatly.

PRAYER:
Take my life
and use it
for Your will,
Father. If I can
be the instrument
that leads someone to
You, then don't hesitate to
bring me into service. Let me
give to others a portion of
what You have given to
me. Amen.

I am counted with them that go down into the pit: I am as a man that hath no strength: free among the dead, like the slain that lie in the grave, whom thou rememberest no more: and they are cut off from thy hand.

PSALM 88:4–5

Annette sat with red-rimmed eyes. She had been crying for quite some time. Everything in her life felt like it was going wrong. She called herself a Christian, but she kept doing things she knew were wrong. She asked forgiveness, but she felt like a liar and a hypocrite. She wanted God to love her, but she kept being so unlovable. One of her friends told her that she was going to hell, because God would judge her for all the lies she told and all the sins she committed. Now she sat sobbing, not knowing what to do.

It is hard to be good when we are so weak. Even the great apostle Paul spoke of doing things he knew he should not do. No one ever rises completely above sin. God wants people who will try and who will strive to do better, even when they know they can't be perfect. God will judge us on the intentions of our hearts to be reconciled to Him. He loves us that much.

PRAYER:

Lord, forgive my weakness, fill me with strength, and continually remind me of Your great mercy. Though I am not worthy, I am loved, and therefore I am saved. Hallelujah! Amen.

Thou hast put away mine acquaintance far from me; thou hast made me an abomination unto them: I am shut up, and I cannot come forth.

PSALM 88:8

Fritz had read the horrible stories about AIDS but had never given it much thought. Now his doctor was telling him that he had the disease. Fritz didn't want to die, especially all alone, but he knew that many of his friends would make themselves scarce as soon as they found out what he had. He had become a leper, an outcast, with nowhere to turn. Facing death was only a part of it. Facing life would be even harder.

We do terrible things to some people in our society. People who suffer greatly need our compassion and love, but instead they receive our judgment and condemnation. Christ does not ask us to accept sin, or the results of sin, but He commands us to love the one who sins. One thing we may never do is cast aside another of God's children. We do not have that right. The Lord loves all His children, and we need to learn to love all our sisters and brothers. No one need ever be alone, if we will extend our hands in love to the sick, the lonely, and the poor.

PRAYER: My God, there are so many suffering people in this world. Lead me to where they are, that I might give them something of myself, that together we may become the family You made us to be. Amen.

Shall thy wonders be known in the dark?
and thy righteousness in the land of
forgetfulness?
PSALM 88:12

The man fell in love with the painting. Its beauty was beyond words. He would give anything to own the painting—to possess its beauty for himself. He bought the painting and took it home with him. Immediately, he began to worry that it might get damaged. He packed the painting in a crate and locked it in an airtight vault, away from seeking eyes, where no one could benefit from its loveliness.

We have received a treasure of great value: Jesus Christ. Should we hold Him in our hearts, never letting Him be seen, or should we expose Him to the view of all who would look? We are to be the city on the hill, the light shining in the darkness, the salt of the earth. No one has the option to call himself a Christian and then keep it selfishly inside. Our faith is intensely personal, but it is never private. We possess a pearl of great price. Be proud of it and let the whole world see it.

PRAYER: Make my life a picture of Your love, Lord. I want to be one more example of Your greatness and glory on this earth. Be with me to guide my steps. Amen.

And the heavens shall praise thy wonders,
O LORD: thy faithfulness also in the
congregation of the saints.
PSALM 89:5

The rainstorm had been terrific. Torrents of rain had fallen, drenching everything. Now the clouds began to part. Shafts of bright sunlight stretched to the earth, causing all foliage to sparkle with droplets of water. On the horizon, a rainbow stretched from earth to earth. The clouds climbed high into the sky, turning rosy pink with the sunlight.

God's creation gives testimony to His truth all the time. All His wonders unfold through the course of one day. From the sunrise through nighttime starshine, God's glories unfold. Take time to view God's handiwork. Search the daytime skies and see the majesty of the Almighty. His hand is ever upon His creation.

PRAYER:

All praise
and honor
belongs to
You, Lord, for the
magnificent works of
Your hands. You have made
such beauty, and You have
loved us enough to share it.
Thank You, Father. Amen.

Justice and judgment are the habitation of
thy throne; mercy and truth shall go before thy face.
PSALM 89:14

"What's He going to do to me? He loves everybody. He's got to take me to heaven, or He wouldn't be God."

Jeff's statement left Cathy stunned. Was it true? It certainly made sense. What kind of loving God could send someone to hell? Maybe Jeff knew what he was talking about. Maybe it didn't really matter what a person does on earth.

Don't kid yourself. God cares very deeply about how we choose to live our lives, and as far as hell goes, only people who choose to go there make it. God has given us free will. He will not force any of us to spend eternity with Him if we don't want to. If we decide, however, that we do want to spend our eternity in heaven, then it is our responsibility to prepare ourselves, body, mind, and spirit. Our earthly existence becomes boot camp for the kingdom. We train for the world that is to come. God is just and merciful, but He will indeed judge. It is the innocent who will stand beside Him.

PRAYER: Let me not tempt Your mercy, Lord, but help me do everything in my power to act as I think You want me to act. Train me to be a kingdom person, worthy to enter Your presence when I am ready. Amen.

Blessed is the people that know the joyful
sound: they shall walk, O LORD,
in the light of thy countenance.
PSALM 89:15

Magic! No matter where the children were, they heard it. It called them from their homework, their play, their naps, their chores. In an instant, heads came up, slightly cocked, in order to hear the delicate chimes. The ice cream man! No greater sound could be found. From every corner of the neighborhood, children with beaming faces were drawn magically to the little white cart with its row of silver bells.

When the voice of the Lord calls out to us, may we respond to it with the same childlike glee that our youngsters demonstrate at the approach of the ice cream man. May the name of the Lord bring joy to our hearts and smiles to our faces.

PRAYER:
Fill me
with a joy
that remains
untouched by
the trials of the day.
When I hear Your name,
Lord, let me respond in
jubilation. Be the source of
my comfort and peace.
Amen.

Nevertheless my lovingkindness will I not utterly take from him, nor suffer my faithfulness to fail.
PSALM 89:33

Amy tried everything she could to get the little boy to learn to tie his shoes. She had sat with him for hours. There was nothing she could do to make him understand. Finally, she lost all patience and walked off angrily. His shoe-tying education would have to come from someone else with a lot more patience and endurance!

We may give up on each other, but it is comforting to know that God never gives up on us. His offer of forgiveness is open to us today and every day to come. Even though we reject the offer or do things that are frustrating and displeasing to Him, He never gives up. He asks us daily to follow Him, until the day we finally do. Thank goodness His patience is without bounds.

PRAYER:

Though I push the patience of others to the limits, I am glad to know that I have not pushed Yours, Lord. Continue to forgive me, Lord. I am weak and foolish, and only Your great love keeps me going. Amen.

*So teach us to number our days, that
we may apply our hearts unto wisdom.*

PSALM 90:12

S helley had a dream. In it she was told she had only one week to live. The dream haunted her throughout the day. Every time she did something, she asked herself, "Is this really important?" She found that there were so many things she did that wasted precious time. People became more important to her than things. She wanted to go for a walk rather than sit in front of the television set. Time became more valuable, and it caused her to realign her priorities. Shelley found her life completely changed.

God wants us to value the time we have on earth. We take time for granted, acting as though our earthly life will go on forever. Time on earth is too short to waste. Number your days, and God will fill you with a special wisdom.

PRAYER:
Don't let
me waste
time, but let
me use every
moment to the fullest.
Help me to appreciate my
life, and teach me new ways
to use my time. Thank You for
all my blessings. Amen.

And let the beauty of the LORD our God be
upon us: and establish thou the work of our
hands upon us; yea, the work of our hands establish thou it.
PSALM 90:17

Cheryl loved her artwork. She could express so many things with canvas and paint that she couldn't express any other way. She showed the depths of her soul. All her work had a spiritual sense to it. It came from a deep and beautiful place inside her own soul. Cheryl felt that the image of God in her was best displayed through the works of her hands and heart.

Within each of us is a wellspring of beauty that comes from God above. How we express it varies from person to person, but it is there, nonetheless. Reach deep into your soul and share the wealth of beauty buried there. To do so is to share God.

PRAYER:
Enter into my life,
O Lord, and make
it something beautiful
and special. Whatever talents
I have are Yours. Bless them, that
they might produce much, Father.
Amen.

Surely he shall deliver thee from the snare of the fowler, and from the noisome pestilence.

PSALM 91:3

Mr. Frederickson stormed into the dean's office with Carol in tow. He shoved her down into the seat and said, "She's the one! I caught her this time. She's the one who keeps letting the animals go."

"I'm sorry," Carol began, "but I can't stand to see the animals treated the way they are. They shouldn't be used for experiments. They have a right to live, and I just couldn't watch them suffer."

The dean worked to settle Mr. Frederickson down and to explain why Carol couldn't do what she'd done, though deep down inside he was on her side. It was nice to see a young person care so much about something other than herself. It was good that the animals had a champion.

We have a champion in Jesus Christ. Held captive to sin, trapped with no way out, we could only wait to see what would happen. What happened was the saving love of Christ, which set us free from the trap and continues to protect us every day.

PRAYER: Thank You for rescuing me from the snare of sin. On my own, I get so tangled in sin, but with You to guide me, I can avoid the traps and remain free for a life of joy and love. Amen.

*For he shall give his angels charge over
thee, to keep thee in all thy ways.*
PSALM 91:11

Louise had an angel. She felt the presence of her guardian angel wherever she was. She didn't even tell most people about her angel, because they looked at her like she was crazy. She wasn't. God had sent her an angel to keep her company and to remind her that she was loved. There was nothing crazy about that. Sometimes, in the still of the night, she thought she could hear angel songs, and they comforted her. She loved her angel, and she thanked God for it daily.

Who's to say where God's angels are? Perhaps we each have an angel who watches us and guides us. God, in His love for us, has set the angels over us. They are His ambassadors of goodwill in this world. Though angels have been shoved aside to the category of myth by many, we know that there is another realm where everything doesn't always make sense to us. Rest secure. The angels are watching.

*PRAYER:
Help me to
believe in the
angels that You send,
Lord. I need watching over. I
need You to be with me. I thank You
for guiding me in all my ways. Amen.*

With long life will I satisfy him,
and shew him my salvation.

PSALM 91:16

Chuck was in no big hurry to die. He was eighty-five, alive and kicking. He had no intention of cashing in his chips. He still had work to do. Every day, Chuck went down to the mission to pass out food and Bibles and sit with the men and women and tell them about Jesus. He wasn't pushy or anything; he just let them know he was there to talk. He'd been there almost every day for twenty-one years. The Lord willing, he would be there twenty-one more.

It's wonderful to see people so in love with life and with Christ that they make the two things one. A long life well lived is a powerful testimony to the goodness of God. Use your life to glorify God, and share the Good News of your salvation with everyone you meet.

PRAYER:
Make all
my days
productive
ones, Lord.
Show me what my
ministry is. Open doors
so that I might serve You in
new ways. Look kindly on my
efforts to glorify You, Lord.
Amen.

Upon an instrument of ten strings, and upon the psaltery; upon the harp with a solemn sound.
PSALM 92:3

Dana's fingers lovingly flew across the strings. The guitar took on life beneath his fingertips. As his eyes closed and his head tilted back, the man and the guitar became one. The music that came forth was not from the fingers or the instrument, but from the heart. The music was the rhythm of creation. The beauty and majesty of God's love flowed through the air. When the music played, God's presence was not to be denied.

The book of Psalms is full of musical imagery. Throughout time, music has been used to express the divine. God loves harmony and purity of tone. Together, we can become a melody of beauty and praise. We can become the rhythm of creation by affirming who God created us to be. Let the music of the Lord fill your heart, and get carried away in its beauty and power.

PRAYER:

If there is any discordance in my life, Lord, remove it from me. I want my life to be harmonious and beautiful, reflecting the divine music that You alone compose. Play me, Lord, that I might be Your song.

Amen.

The LORD reigneth, he is clothed with majesty; the LORD is clothed with strength, wherewith he hath girded himself: the world also is stablished, that it cannot be moved.

PSALM 93:1

The commander stood a head above the rest of the soldiers. He was dressed in finest battle attire, head aloft and proud, sword drawn. To see the man was to be filled with the confidence that everything would work out. He exuded the sense of triumph and victory. Everything about him claimed victory before the battle was even begun.

Our Lord is like that. He is the source of all power and might. His wisdom is matched by none. As we fight our daily battles, it is good for us to keep in mind that the Lord is on our side, and He leads the charge. There is no retreat for God. He is with us every step of the way. Trust in Him, for He is the commander who cannot fail.

PRAYER: In Your power, and strength, and courage, and wisdom, and patience, I take my refuge. You are the fortress that protects me, and in Your love, I have no fear of anything. I will always praise You. Amen.

LORD, how long shall the wicked, how long shall the wicked triumph?
PSALM 94:3

G inelli hated to see the boys come. They tore up his store, threatened his customers, and called him dirty names. They'd never hurt anyone—yet. All he wanted was for the police to come, but they never bothered. It seemed the boys were just his cross to bear. No one would help him, so he just had to tolerate it.

Why do the evil people in this world get away with so much? Because it's their world. God gave this world over to Satan long ago, and it has been downhill ever since. Our realm is that of heaven. We are kingdom people now, and so we have to put up with all kinds of bad and terrible things while we wait. Thankfully, we don't have to fight alone. The Lord is with us, giving us His strength and encouragement. Take heart, the Lord is on our side.

PRAYER:

Be with me, Lord,
as I stand alone in
a world gone crazy.
There are times when I can
find no one who seems to care, no
one willing to help. In those times, reach
down to give me aid. Amen.

Understand, ye brutish among the people:
and ye fools, when will ye be wise? He that
planteth the ear, shall he not hear? he that formed
the eye, shall he not see?

PSALM 94:8–9

There's no fooling God. There is no place we can go where He does not see our every move. Those people who think they have God fooled are only fooling themselves. God sees all things, He hears all things, and nothing escapes His attention. For those who live in sin, that is a very frightening thought. For those who walk in righteousness, there is no problem. Let the Lord watch. It is good to know that He is here.

PRAYER:
Lord, be
with me
this day.
Search my
life, and help me to
correct the wrong things
that I do. Keep me walking
in the light, and prevent
me from straying into
darkness. Amen.

Shall the throne of iniquity have fellowship with thee, which frameth mischief by a law?
PSALM 94:20

What a minister does on his day off is his business. Reverend Gray was fuming. Members of his church had seen him go into a casino and bar on his day off, and now the entire congregation was in an uproar. He liked to fraternize with some regulars at the casino, old friends from college days. There was nothing wrong with getting together with old friends, and if a couple of coins hit the slots, what was the harm? It was nobody's business but his own.

We need to be careful how we walk in our Christian lives. We are examples to others of how Christ wants His people to be. That is a big responsibility, and one that we must take very seriously. Our business becomes the business of other people when it could possibly affect their faith. Who we associate with matters very much to who we want to be. It is good to remember that not only God watches the faithful.

PRAYER:
If I am to be an example of what it means to follow Christ, then help me to be the best example I can be. Guide me by Your Spirit. Amen.

O come, let us sing unto the LORD: let
us make a joyful noise to the rock
of our salvation.

PSALM 95:1

The children lined up on the steps to the altar. Their fresh-scrubbed faces shone in the morning light. Nervously, they swayed, twitched, and squirmed. The music began, and each child in turn joined in at a point of his or her own choosing. Some sang out boldly, others mouthed the words, while a few ignored the songs altogether and just waved and smiled at Mommy and Daddy. To call the presentation "music" was stretching the point, but to call it a joyful noise was right on target. The spirit of the children was joy and love, and the hearts of all present were captured quickly. The sound rose to the rafters, and beyond. The Lord heard that special choir, smiled, and said, "It is good!"

PRAYER:
Let the
words of
my mouth
produce a joyful
noise, acceptable to
the Lord and glorifying to
Him in all ways. Amen.

Harden not your heart, as in the provocation,
and as in the day of temptation in the wilderness.
PSALM 95:8

Edgar was being a brat. Whenever Edgar didn't get his way, he was a brat. As if a secret button had been pushed, the minute Edgar heard the word *no*, he began to whine, kick, scream, stomp, pout, throw things, and cry. After that, he would do nothing that was asked of him. He became stubborn and rebellious. At those times, everyone just backed off and left Edgar alone. Who wants to be too close to a brat?

Sometimes we're brats. We don't get things the way we want them, so we pout and harden our hearts toward God. God is patient with us, but sometimes He has to put some distance between us until we settle down. God doesn't want to deal with our brattiness any more than we want to deal with the brattiness of children. In time, we learn to deal with our disappointments; and like children, we finally learn that pouting gets us nowhere.

PRAYER:
Lord, help me to
grow up, to be
a mature Christian,
one who has learned to
accept disappointment and adversity.
Strengthen my heart, and give me
patience. Amen.

Honour and majesty are before him:
strength and beauty are in his sanctuary.
PSALM 96:6

Take time to be quiet and think about the good things God has done for you. Look at both the good times and the bad times in proper perspective. We are loved by a God of all creation, the Master of all eternity. He has made us important by His love for us. Think of how wonderful this love is. We have no way to comprehend this kind of love and attention. It is well that we take time to contemplate all these things. All honor and glory belongs to the Lord, who loves us so much. By entering into His presence, we come to know just how very blessed we are.

PRAYER:
Who am I,
Lord, that
You take
notice of me?
I cannot believe
that You love me
the way You do. Though
I don't understand, I do
accept Your gracious love,
and I am thankful from the
depths of my soul. Amen.

*Say among the heathen that the LORD
reigneth: the world also shall be established
that it shall not be moved: he shall judge
the people righteously.*
PSALM 96:10

The concrete mixers rolled in and out of the lot throughout the day. Each deposited its load into the foundation of the new office building, then departed. Dozens of men worked to shape and structure the foundation. Finally, the huge concrete slab was in place. Tons of concrete provided the base for what would become a huge office complex. With a firm foundation in place, construction could begin.

We need to have a firm foundation before we structure our lives. If we set our hearts and minds upon God, He will give us His strength, a strength that cannot be moved. God is the only real foundation. Anything else is a poor substitute.

*PRAYER:
Lord, be my
anchor and
support. When the
day gets too rough, help
me to remember that I am firmly
established in Your Spirit and in Your
love. Amen.*

Ye that love the LORD, hate evil: be
preserveth the souls of his saints; he
delivereth them out of the hand of the wicked.

PSALM 97:10

Sarah sat by herself, wondering if it was really worth it to try to live a clean, Christian life. Everyone thought she was so old-fashioned and prudish. She wouldn't drink, hated dirty jokes, refused to gossip, and had no desire to engage in sex before marriage. She didn't like going to parties with her friends, but she hated to be alone all the time. Every once in a while, Sarah felt like just giving in and doing what all her peers were doing. Those feelings passed, though, and Sarah felt a special peace and comfort in refusing to give in.

Being different is difficult. To say no to wrongdoing and evil can be excruciatingly hard. Yet our Lord calls us to be different—to stand apart from the crowd. If we will continue to say no to evil, while saying yes to God, He will preserve and strengthen us. We are never truly alone if we will only love the Lord.

PRAYER:
Father, I
want to do
what is right,
but sometimes
to do wrong is very
tempting and appealing.
Please grant me strength to
resist and hold on to what I
know is right. Amen.

Let the sea roar, and the fulness thereof;
the world, and they that dwell therein.
PSALM 98:7

P aul's nerves were shot. Everywhere he turned there were crowds of people. Cars sped by on all the streets, and the noise of the city was deafening. He was beginning to feel like there was nowhere to go to find peace and quiet. A little silence was all he was looking for. Nothing more.

In this world of noise and confusion, where can we find a place of peace and tranquillity? If Christ is the Lord of our hearts, then we can turn inward. Christ is the giver of peace. He transforms our hearts into refuges, where the clamor of the outside world cannot enter in. Call upon the Lord, and He will surely grant you peace.

PRAYER:
Father, I am tired
of the furious
pace of the world.
Sometimes I just want to run
and hide. Allow me to run to You. Be
the source of my peace, Lord. Amen.

Exalt the LORD our God, and worship at his holy hill; for the LORD our God is holy.

PSALM 99:9

Betty loved the old church. She had come to its sanctuary since she had been a young girl, and that was a long time gone, indeed. The place was special. Betty had always been filled with awe whenever she stood in the church. From the moment she entered the door, she felt God's presence. This church was a holy place. She felt closest to God when she felt the special magic of the old church. It was easy to worship God there.

We need reminders to help us understand God's holiness. Truly, only He is worthy to be praised, and yet we so often act as if there's nothing special about God at all. There is no life in our prayers, we decide to skip church, or we ignore opportunities to share Christ with those around us. Our actions say, "No big deal." It is a big deal. God is the biggest deal of our lives. Everything we do should exalt the Lord and show others just how important He is to us. Anytime we can experience the holiness and majesty of the Lord, we should jump at the chance. Nothing pleases God more.

PRAYER: You are so important to me, Lord. Help me to prove, through the living of my life, how much You mean to me. Inspire me with Your holiness, and let me worship You always. Amen.

*Know ye that the LORD he is God: it is he
that hath made us, and not we ourselves;
we are his people, and the sheep of his pasture.*
PSALM 100:3

Jeff loved spending his days out on horseback, checking the livestock around the ranch. The animals were undisturbed by Jeff's approach, and he often thought that they must look forward to his arrival. Many of the animals rushed out to meet him whenever he appeared. They sensed in him a friend and protector. Indeed, on those rare occasions when he found the animals threatened by wild creatures, Jeff had not hesitated to do what was necessary to protect the stock.

Our Lord watches over us carefully and lovingly. He wants us to look forward to the times we spend with Him. He also wants us to be assured that He will take care of us and protect us. As a shepherd gives everything possible to protect his flock, so God gives everything He can to guard His followers. Trust in Him, and He will watch over you.

*PRAYER:
Lord, I need to
know that You
are watching me.
You are the source of my
confidence and security. Lead
me to spend all of my time pursuing
Your love and protection. Amen.*

I will behave myself wisely in a perfect way.
O when wilt thou come unto me? I will walk
within my house with a perfect heart.

PSALM 101:2

G wen couldn't help remembering how her grandmother used to tell her, "Act like a perfect little
lady." She had hated to have her grandmother
constantly nagging at her to sit properly, speak properly,
walk, chew, and sneeze properly. However, the lessons she
had been taught had stayed with her, and they had helped
her many times. She had gotten the job at the gallery because they had been impressed by her manner and poise.
Perhaps she wasn't a "perfect little lady," but she made a
good showing, nonetheless.

Our behavior is important. People see us in many
situations at many different times, and the
way we act can be a powerful witness to the
power of Christ in our lives. Christ calls us
to a perfection that we cannot achieve on
our own. Rely upon the Lord, and He
will give you the capacity to live an
upright, holy, and pleasing life.

PRAYER:
Lord, You
are the
author of
perfection.
You have created
me to be an example
of Your image, the Light of
the World. Fill me with the
brilliance of Your holy light,
that I might shine forth in
beauty and power. Amen.

Whoso privily slandereth his neighbour, him will I cut off: him that hath an high look and a proud heart will not I suffer.
PSALM 101:5

Bess was the blight of the bridge club. For some unknown reason, she had taken it upon herself to be judge and jury over the actions of her friends. Whenever the women got together for cards, they were treated to Bess's opinion of what everyone else was doing wrong. When anyone got tired of hearing what Bess had to say and tried to back away, she became Bess's next target of attack. People were afraid to be friends with her, and they were even more afraid to not be friends with her.

No one likes to hear gossip and criticism all the time. Gossips are usually avoided, and thus they become outcasts from the rest of the world. God will cast out the gossip. There is no room in His kingdom for those who delight in the shortcomings of others. Christ within us should build up, not tear down. If we give our hearts over to Christ, then we will never say damaging things against our neighbors. Speak only with the tongue of Christ, and you will be a blessing to everyone you meet.

PRAYER: Remove from me a malicious and gossiping nature, Lord. Fill me with praise and joy and spiritual thoughts. Let my words bless others with kindness and love. Amen.

I will early destroy all the wicked of the land;
that I may cut off all wicked doers from
the city of the LORD.

PSALM 101:8

No one mourned when the old skinflint died. He had held the future of hundreds of people in his hand during the course of his life, and he had never missed an opportunity to hurt them whenever he could. He loved to wield his power mercilessly. His every thought had been of himself. Now, at the day of his death, it seemed like a black, noisome cloud had finally been lifted. New hope dawned in the lives of so many who had been oppressed for so long.

The dawn of a new day will one day come for all of God's people. Evil will have no place in the kingdom of God. It will be wiped away, dissipated like a storm cloud after it is spent. While we live in the storm, we find it hard to see the future, which will be brighter. Trust God. His light conquers the blackest clouds, and once conquered they will never come again.

PRAYER:
The days are certainly dark, Lord. The clouds are closing in, and there are times when no light can be seen at all. Help me to remember that You are here, O God, and that the light that never fails will one day shine forth. Amen.

My heart is smitten, and withered like grass;
so that I forget to eat my bread.
PSALM 102:4

Sarah couldn't eat. She couldn't sleep. She hadn't ever meant to hurt anyone, but now there was a little girl in the hospital because of an accident she was responsible for. The guilt that raged within her made it impossible to get on with normal, everyday life. No matter how much she wrestled with herself, there was no peace. She had prayed to God for forgiveness, but even that felt empty. Sarah could remember no time in her life when she had felt so horrible.

There will be times in our lives when we find ourselves unable to function normally because of our emotional upheaval. When we are sensitive to what is right and good, we instinctively rebel against wrong and evil. The Psalms are full of David's own struggles with times when he felt alone and wretched. Those times were necessary for David to grow and mature. He learned to accept guilt and go on, knowing that God's love for him endured and that His forgiveness was without bounds. God loves us just as much. He suffers when we suffer, and He stands with us, even in our darkest hours.

PRAYER: Lord, be with me when I am so low that I don't even feel like eating or sleeping. Grant me peace and comfort in Your love, and if that is slow in coming, help me to learn all I can from my despair.

Amen.

I said, O my God, take me not away in the
midst of my days: thy years are
throughout all generations.

PSALM 102:24

Everyone said it was such a tragedy. Doug was a funny, bright young man, and he had so much to look forward to. He wasn't even through college yet. The accident had been senseless, and so had his death. Why would God allow such a thing to happen?

We ask ourselves that question a lot. Why does God allow some things to happen? We always look at the question from our own earthly, human perspective. We forget that death is a part of life and that it is a necessary passage in existence. To God, death is not a bad thing, but merely a part of the way things are. Death isn't a cruelty or a punishment. Our days on earth are a gift, and we should live them as fully as we can. If we die, we are in the Lord's hands, and everything will work out just fine. Faith is the key. We must learn to know that God has everything under control, and that He will turn all situations to good. Even death is a wonderful thing in the hands of God.

PRAYER:
Lord, I do not understand the way things work sometimes, and I do not like to experience pain and suffering. Help me to see Your hand in all things. Grant me understanding. Amen.

Bless the LORD, O my soul, and forget not all his benefits.
PSALM 103:2

C larence sat on his bed, pouting. His parents wouldn't let him go to the rock concert on a school night. He hated them sometimes for being so unfair. He hardly ever got what he wanted. He'd had to beg for his computer, and they had waited a whole year from the time he asked for his own DVD player until they gave it to him. They made him come home from tennis camp a week early to go on a family vacation to Europe. Now the skis he bought last year had scratches on them, and his parents didn't act all that interested in replacing them. It just wasn't fair. Clarence wished he could have his own way at least some of the time.

Are we more thankful for what we have than we are bitter for what we don't have? God has given us so much. Remember to praise Him for all He has done. Set aside the Clarence inside, and appreciate all that has been given. It is given in love.

PRAYER:

Forgive me when I don't appreciate all that I have. Too often I look at the things I don't have, rather than at the things I do have. Thank You, Lord, for all the blessings You shower upon me.

Amen.

The LORD is merciful and gracious,
slow to anger, and plenteous in mercy.
PSALM 103:8

Mara welcomed her sister and did everything in her power to make her feel at home. In return, Dani complained about everything and tried to take over. She bossed Mara around, arranged the house to her own liking, and imposed her opinion on everyone. Mara raised her two boys. Mara took it in stride, with a smile on her face. No matter how grave the insult, Mara never wavered in her hospitality. The bonds of sisterhood overcame even the hardest of times, and love gave her the strength of character she needed.

God puts up with a great deal from His creation. We turn ungrateful hands toward the Lord, always expecting more. We often insult Him by the way we regard His world and all the wonderful things in it. Thankfully, He is slow to anger and plenteous in mercy, for we test Him constantly. We can learn from God's long-suffering patience with His children, and in turn we can share the same compassion and caring with those around us.

PRAYER: Make me merciful and caring, Lord. Help me to improve my attitude toward others and You. Do not allow me to take for granted the great gifts You give. Amen.

He hath not dealt with us after our sins;
nor rewarded us according to our iniquities.
PSALM 103:10

Karl sat outside the principal's office feeling the sweat begin to trickle down his back. Mr. Creed was notorious for dealing out harsh punishments. "Crusher" Creed was what the older kids called him. Karl had never been to him before; but he didn't like it, that was for sure. Minutes dragged by, feeling like hours, and Karl began to tremble. It was all he could do to keep from crying. When the door finally opened, Karl sobbed, "I'll never do it again." The principal comforted the boy and told him why what he had done was unacceptable. Karl left the office still shaken, but not so much that he couldn't dream up a juicy story of the tortures he'd suffered at the hand of "Crusher" Creed.

God deals with His children with love and forgiveness. Often, we are much harder on ourselves than God will ever be. Many times we feel alone in our trials because we need to realize what is wrong with what we do. Our sins can be a great learning ground, and though God waits willingly to forgive us, He wants us to benefit from our errors as much as we can. God will deal with us not according to what we have done wrong, but according to our desire to make things right through our repentance.

PRAYER:

My mind runs wild with worries and fears, Lord. I have done wrong, and I need Your forgiveness. Accept my apologies, God, and create in me a new heart. Amen.

As far as the east is from the west, so far hath he removed our transgressions from us.

PSALM 103:12

A woman asked God for forgiveness for a sin she had committed. He granted her pardon, but she had a tough time forgetting what she had done. She just couldn't let go of her guilt. In desperation she returned to God to ask His forgiveness once more. When she asked Him to remember what she had done, He said, "I can't remember what you're talking about. It never happened. Once sin is forgiven, it is dropped into the sea of forgetfulness, and it is no more. Go your way. No one condemns you, not even I."

It is not that God has a bad memory, but that His love is so complete and boundless that He will not retain the memory of something we ask to be forgiven for. He erases the sin from our slate, and we start fresh. As far as the east is from the west, that is how far God removes our sin from us.

PRAYER: Though I don't deserve Your loving care and forgiveness, Lord, I continually thank You that You give it to me so freely. Help me to accept it graciously, and to know that You hold nothing against me once I ask Your pardon. Amen.

*As for man, his days are as grass: as a flower
of the field, so be flourisheth.*
PSALM 103:15

Deanna built up a career on her looks. She had
been the dream girl of Hollywood and had loved
living the fast life. Now her looks were fading
and Deanna had nothing to fall back on. She had believed
her charmed life would never end, but the hard reality was
that she no longer could bank on her beauty.

We are given each day as a gift. Once a day is gone,
it can never be recaptured. Too often we live our lives as
if they are going to go on forever just as they are. Lives
change, and we need to be ready to change with them.
God helps us to accept where we are and to grow to new
levels of maturity. Before this day passes and is gone, call
upon the Lord to help you make
the most of it. Then, when the
new day dawns, be ready for the
challenges it brings.

PRAYER: Help
me to live for
what is important
this day, so that
I might truly be ready
for all the days to come. Your
gifts are so wonderful, Lord. Please
don't allow me to take them for granted.
Amen.

But the mercy of the LORD is from everlasting to everlasting upon them that fear him, and his righteousness unto children's children.

PSALM 103:17

Some people can't understand how the raging, harsh God of the Old Testament can be the same God of love in the New Testament. Has God really changed? Of course not. God is the same in all times and in all places. What has changed is people's views of God. It is difficult to make sense of all that God does. However, we all must do our best to know Him. From the beginning of time until this day, God is the same. The righteousness He held forth for the children of Israel is the same righteousness He holds forth for us today. In a world where all else changes so quickly, we can find great security in knowing that our Lord never changes.

PRAYER: Be the anchor in my life, O Lord, so that I might not be tossed around by all the winds of change in my world. Make my faith constant so I will remain true to You. Amen.

*Bless the LORD, O my soul. O LORD my God,
thou art very great; thou art clothed with
honour and majesty. Who coverest thyself with light as with
a garment: who stretchest out the heavens like a curtain.*
PSALM 104:1–2

As the car crested the hill, the entire family drew in
their breath. The sky was painted with a hundred
different colors and hues. Pinks, reds, oranges,
blues, lavenders, and golds blended into a canvas of glory
and light. God in His awesome beauty once again presented the proof of His existence. Only a blind fool would
deny God in the face of such splendor.

Time and again, God offers us signs of His power
and wonder. If we will just keep our eyes open, the truth
of God's existence will present itself over and over. God
gives graciously to His children. Relax and enjoy
the show that God puts on. It is
nothing less than perfection.

*PRAYER: Do
not let me turn
blind eyes to
the beauty of Your
world, Lord. Throughout
Your creation is Your signature.
I cannot doubt Your existence in a
world of such amazing splendor.
Amen.*

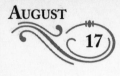
He watereth the hills from his chambers: the earth is satisfied with the fruit of thy works.

PSALM 104:13

Emily sat patiently explaining the way of the world to Jeffrey. "The sun shines when God is happy, and it rains when He is sad. Rain is God's tears."

"Why would God cry? Isn't He happy all the time?"

"Goodness, no. Would you be happy if you and I were your children?"

Children have a way of cutting through a lot of confusion to the heart of the matter. Though God doesn't cry because of us, He often cries with us when we suffer. Many people perceive God to be so detached and above us all that He never relates to what we go through. Nothing could be further from the truth. The reason that God sent His only Son to be our Savior was so that He could reach out to us in our struggles and say, "I struggle with you." Perhaps the rain is not actually God's own tears, but let it be a reminder to us that God does indeed cry for His children in their times of need.

PRAYER:

Lord, thank You for sending Jesus into the world to relate to me on terms that I understand. I need to know that Your love for me is emotional and passionate. Teach me to love others as You love me. Amen.

O LORD, how manifold are thy works! in wisdom hast thou made them all: the earth is full of thy riches.
PSALM 104:24

Timmy did not want to go on the science field trip. Science was so boring. They were going to climb around on rocks and look for fossils of animals that died half a million years. Big deal! Nothing could interest Timmy less.

Then, an amazing thing happened. Timmy was one of the first to find fossilized remains. He held the rock in his hands and traced the fragile trilobite fossil with his finger. He was enthralled by the sight, and a new love was born in Timmy's heart. Timmy saw the earth as a treasure house of wonders too magnificent to understand.

We ought to take time to study this wonderful world of ours. There is so much to behold. God has done so many wonderful things, and He has given them over to us to enjoy. Search out the riches of God's world, and you will never be poor.

PRAYER:
Have I lost the capacity to believe in miracles, O Lord? Show me the wonders of Your creation. Let me take nothing for granted. Indeed, Lord, make all things new in my eyes.
Amen.

He looketh on the earth, and it trembleth:
he toucheth the hills, and they smoke.

PSALM 104:32

The volcano rumbled, then fell silent. Clouds of smoke billowed from its crown, and the people in the towns surrounding it made hasty plans to leave. Experts were assuring people that there was no immediate danger, but when the old mountain began to grumble, the people tended to listen to it rather than the experts. Wisdom being the better part of valor, the neighboring residents departed until the danger was clearly over.

In nature there is mighty destructive power. This world of God's contains forces beyond our wildest dreams. It is wise to respect the forces of nature, and it is wise to respect the forces of our Lord. No one can challenge the Lord as to truth and justice. God wields the true power, and He does so with perfect love and compassion. God has made His desires known to His children. To ignore the rumble is foolishness.

PRAYER:
Lord, make me an obedient child and a willing follower. Break my willful nature, and help me to see the wisdom of Your ways. Amen.

Remember his marvellous works that he hath done; his wonders, and the judgments of his mouth.

PSALM 105:5

The old pastor was only a few months out of the church, and it seemed like everyone took glee in recalling his faults and shortcomings. The problems of the church were all attributed in some form to the inadequacies of the pastor who had just left. It was the rare individual who stopped to recall all the wonderful qualities the former pastor had possessed. In his time he had served with love and affection, and the glories of his love far exceeded any shortcomings he displayed.

Do we spend much time glorying in all that the Lord has done for us, or do we lament over what has yet to occur? So often we can find ourselves blaming God when things don't go right. The Hebrew people did it. The kings did it. Even the early Christians did it. We should be careful to learn from their mistakes and fill our hearts and mouths with the praise that God deserves.

PRAYER:
Remove from my mouth any curse, Lord. Fill me with praise and thanksgiving for all that I have and all that I am.
Amen.

Our fathers understood not thy wonders in Egypt; they remembered not the multitude of thy mercies; but provoked him at the sea, even at the Red sea.

PSALM 106:7

I want it!" Becky screamed.

Her father turned to where the little girl stood red-faced and defiant. He looked at her and said, "I don't want to hear another word. I bought you a toy last week, and I told you not to ask for anything else. You've had ice cream, and I took you to see the pets; now you straighten up. Do you understand?"

Whether Becky understood or not may still be in question, but her behavior is all too familiar. Some of us want what we want when we want it, and we really don't care whether we're being ungrateful or not. God has showered us with blessings, and sometimes we stand defiantly demanding more. God is willing to give us many good things, but not when we refuse to value what we've got. Christian maturity requires that we learn to be satisfied with what we have. It is pleasing to God when His children say "thank You" instead of "more."

PRAYER: I forget how gracious and giving You have been, O Lord. Forgive my lack of gratitude and appreciation. I have no reason to desire more. I have more than I truly need already. Help me to use my abundance for the sake of others. Amen.

Many times did he deliver them; but they provoked him with their counsel, and were brought low for their iniquity.
PSALM 106:43

The agent folded his arms and shook his head. The offer was totally unacceptable. He wanted his ballplayer to receive top dollar. The team owners conferred and made another offer substantially higher than their previous one. Still the agent held out. To his dismay, the owners threw up their hands in disgust and closed the talks. The ballplayer would not play; the owners would look elsewhere.

Greed causes so many problems. We only want a little more, but each time we take a little, we leave less for others. God gives great things to His people, but when they continually look for ways to get more, He is not so free to give. There are too many people who will appreciate what the Lord has to give. God will bring low those who try to take more than their share. His love is freely given, but it is given to be shared, not taken advantage of.

PRAYER: Do I provoke You, Lord, through my many sins, both large and small? Help me to do what is pleasing in Your sight, and to use the gifts You have given me to spread Your Good News. Amen.

Save us, O LORD our God, and gather us from among the heathen, to give thanks unto thy holy name, and to triumph in thy praise.

PSALM 106:47

Mary knew she was in trouble when the bus entered unfamiliar territory. When it finally pulled up to the last stop, she wasn't sure what to do. The driver hardly spoke English, and Mary began to panic. She rushed to the phone through a crowd of vagrants and drunks. In tears, she called her sister, pleading for her to come rescue her from her trial. When her sister's car pulled up outside the terminal, tears of joy and relief flowed freely down Mary's face.

Often we need to have a terrible trial in order to remember what it means to be truly thankful. Our praise is from the heart when we have been in danger or discomfort. Bad situations help us to appreciate how good our lives can be. Even in our trials, God reaches through to help us to a deeper understanding of ourselves. Praise the Lord for all the good things He has given, and know that He will rescue you from all perils.

PRAYER: In times of darkness, help me not to dwell on what is wrong, but turn my mind to all I have to be thankful for. Amen.

*Let the redeemed of the LORD say so, whom
he hath redeemed from the hand of the enemy;
and gathered them out of the lands, from the east,
and from the west, from the north, and from the south.*
PSALM 107:2–3

The missionaries were prepared to share the Word
of God with the natives of the small isle off the
North African coast. They were well stocked with
crosses and Bibles, and they had become well versed in the
native tongue. Nothing, however, prepared them for the
shock when they deplaned and were greeted by a band of
natives singing out, "God bless you; Jesus loves you!"

The reality of God has spread to the four corners of
our globe. Voices sing out His praises continually, and it
is often true that our poorer brothers and sisters have the
clearest and loudest voices. We can learn a great deal from
those people who live day to day in the shadow of poverty,
who truly understand how fortunate they are to be
alive. Let every woman, man, and
child sing forth in praise to God.
He has been good to us all.

*PRAYER:
I have been
transformed by
a love far beyond
my understanding.
Thank You, Lord, for taking my
life and making it something holy
and special. Make my life a glory to Your
name. Amen.*

He brought them out of darkness and the shadow of death, and brake their bands in sunder.

PSALM 107:14

Mabel made sure that children in her neighborhood got a better start than she had. Each day she would invite children into her home, and she would help them with their reading. She would labor long and hard with some, but she was determined that they would never have to face a life lived in darkness and ignorance. Illiteracy was a terrible kind of slavery that no one should suffer under. Mabel's special ministry of love helped children in her area break free from the bonds of ignorance and led them into a bright and exciting light.

God has given us minds to use and wonderful technologies. There is no excuse for living in fear and darkness in our world today. He has liberated us from ignorance and has granted us knowledge and wisdom beyond measure. Take hold of the great gift of the mind, and thank God daily for it.

PRAYER: Shed Your light upon my heart and mind, Father, that I might know all that I can about You, Your creation, and Your will. Be the source of my understanding and my liberation. Amen.

Oh that men would praise the LORD for his goodness, and for his wonderful works to the children of men!
PSALM 107:21

J ay was one of the most unpopular men in the office. He never had a good word to say to anyone. He was critical, snide, self-centered, and jealous. People simply got tired of hearing all the negative comments coming from his mouth. Just once they wanted to hear something good come from his lips.

Negative people get on our nerves quickly. They get on God's nerves, too. He calls us to praise Him and lift our voices in positive ways. If only more people would praise the Lord for His goodness, what a wonderful place our world would become. We need to occupy our thoughts with what is good, and turn away from what is bad. Praise God throughout the day, and see what wonderful feelings you find along the way.

PRAYER:

Erase from my vocabulary all negative words and from my mind all negative thoughts, Lord. Create in me a fountain of positive feeling and goodwill. Share Your grace through my witness. Amen.

*They mount up to the heaven, they go down
again to the depths: their soul is melted
because of trouble.*

PSALM 107:26

The waves were rolling and crashing, and the luxury liner was pitching with each and every one. It would ride high upon the crest of one wave, then plummet to the trough of the next. The passengers were despairing of life itself. Even the most stouthearted grew uneasy in the rolling sea.

Our lives are like tempest-tossed boat rides sometimes. We climb to breathtaking heights and fall to desperate lows, and there are times when we feel as though we just can't go on. The Lord understands these feelings. He was exalted on Sunday and nailed to a cross just five days later. He has experienced the highest of highs and the lowest of lows; and He, too, felt Himself melt in the face of distress. It is well to remember that the Lord is with us, and He can truly be of help to us because He has walked our path before us. When the storms of life toss us the hardest, that is when we can count on the Lord to be closest.

PRAYER: In both good times and bad, Lord, be close by me to help me keep my head about me. Do not let me be swept up in temporary situations, losing sight of Your hand on my life, but let me always feel Your guiding presence. Amen.

He poureth contempt upon princes, and causeth them to wander in the wilderness, where there is no way.
PSALM 107:40

I don't need any help. I can do everything just fine on my own!"

Randy shouldered his pack and headed off down the path. Jerry and Tom shook their heads and followed along. Before long, Randy was out of sight, and his two friends gave up trying to follow. As evening set in, they made camp and waited for their friend to return. While they sat by a warm and inviting fire, Randy stumbled through dense forest, lost, alone, and afraid.

We were created for one another. There is no sense in trying to deny it. Those who attempt to stand on their own two feet find that they tire before long, and they wish they had someone to lean on. God created us equal, so that we can adequately fill one another's needs. He hopes we will share our lives with one another and with Him. People who feel they are above needing others will be shown the error of their ways in due time. It is better to admit our need and wander this wilderness with companions who make the journey a lot more enjoyable.

PRAYER: Father, I thank You that I never have to walk alone. You are by my side, and I have opportunities to share my life journey with so many others. Bless my path, O Lord. Amen.

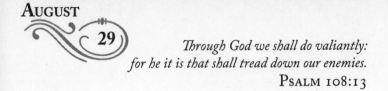
Through God we shall do valiantly:
for he it is that shall tread down our enemies.
PSALM 108:13

Dan could think of nothing he would want to do less than speak in front of an audience. And yet, here he was preparing to speak to a conference of young men and women on the importance of Christ in his life. If not for the transforming power of Christ in his life, Dan knew he would never be able to get up in front of that crowd to speak. Through Christ, all things really were possible. Miracles could still happen, and Dan could break his bonds of shyness to spread the gospel word.

God allows us to do valiantly. Things we never thought possible become almost commonplace. God will enable us to do things we never even dreamed of. Rely upon the Lord, and He will help you conquer the enemies of your heart and mind that threaten to make you less than He wants you to be.

PRAYER:
I can be
my own
worst enemy,
Lord. Help me to
overcome the things
in my life that make me
less than I can be. Use me in
whatever way You can. Amen.

And they have rewarded me evil for good, and hatred for my love.

PSALM 109:5

The old man loved to sit in the park. He had come to the same bench each day for over fifteen years. In that time he had spent many hours talking with children, teaching them games, and telling them stories. In simpler times, they had adored the old man. Now it seemed they treated him with contempt and made fun of him. They no longer flocked to sit at his feet, and he was lonely for bygone times. Each time a young boy or girl hurled an insult, he closed his eyes and asked God to forgive him or her. No matter how they chose to treat him, he would always love the children.

There are many kind and loving people in our world who are treated terribly. They offer nothing but goodness, and they receive evil in return. Our elderly population has much to offer us, and we need to reach out to receive the treasures they hold. To ignore them is the worst kind of cruelty. To a group who has worked long and hard to provide what is good and lasting, we need to extend the hand of fellowship and love. God rejoices when we repay good for good and love with love.

PRAYER: If I have hurt anyone this day, Lord, help me to make amends and to do better in the future. Let me repay no one evil for good, or evil for evil, either. Let my response always be one of love.

Amen.

*As he loved cursing, so let it come unto him;
as he delighted not in blessing, so let it be
far from him.*

PSALM 109:17

The young tennis star was known for both his fiery play and his fiery language. Whereas he excelled in the mastery of the game, he had not yet matured in the art of sportsmanlike conduct. His wrath was vented each time he disagreed with the umpire's call. He cursed, stomped, screamed, and kicked. Never was he known to back down and admit his own fault. In time, he lost even his own following of fans, because they tired of his childish outbursts.

People who live by selfish emotions find themselves empty and alone most of the time. Their bitterness causes them to curse their life, their friends, their God. Finally, they find it nearly impossible to utter any kind words at all. Those people will not find blessings in their own lives, because they refuse to bring it to others' lives. It is a fact that the blessing we share is the blessing that comes back to us. Likewise, the curse we impart comes back on us, to make us unhappy and guilty.

PRAYER: Though things don't always go the way I would like, Lord, help me to accept all that happens with grace and peace. Amen.

I am gone like the shadow when it declineth:
I am tossed up and down as the locust.
PSALM 109:23

Doug was bullied by all the other children. Some days he would dream of being bigger than everyone else; then he would show them. In the morning he would walk to school, watching his shadow loom out large before him. Oh, if only he were as big as his shadow. Then the other children would run! But each day by noontime, Doug's shadow had dwindled in size and he had to turn his dreams to other solutions.

Often we try to put our hopes in solutions that just aren't real. We kid ourselves into thinking that maybe our problems will take care of themselves and will require little effort on our part. Earthly, easy solutions fade away like shadows in the daylight. We shouldn't look to shadows for answers, but to the light. God is the source of all our solutions. Unlike the shadows, nothing causes God to fade into nothingness. His solutions are forever.

PRAYER:
Shine the light of
Your truth into
my life, and help
me to see that there is no
situation too large for Your love to
handle. Reassure me in times of doubt,
O Lord. Amen.

*Let mine adversaries be clothed with shame,
and let them cover themselves with their
own confusions, as with a mantle.*

PSALM 109:29

The executive was beginning to sweat. He thought he'd covered his tracks fairly well, but now the tangled web he had woven was collapsing around him as his double-dealings were uncovered. The questions came at him fast and furious, and he had little time to make sure he wasn't contradicting himself. By the time the hearing ended, all his dealings were in ruin, and he had no one to blame but himself.

Let the conniving and deceitful people be warned: The time will come when you will be called to account before God. He is watching each of us, to see how we handle our lives. Those of us who entangle ourselves in less than honest practices will one day have to pay. The Lord wants us to deal with our earthly affairs with the same purity and honesty we use in our relationship with Him. Anything less is not good enough. If we will deal with others as if they are our Lord Jesus Christ, then we will never suffer the confusion of the deceitful.

PRAYER: Lord, the only way to avoid the traps of subterfuge is to avoid evil dealings altogether. Make me to walk in the way of righteousness, always acting toward others as I try to act toward You. Amen.

The LORD said unto my Lord, Sit thou at my right hand, until I make thine enemies thy footstool.

PSALM 110:1

Ben was a diligent worker in his firm. He put forth his best effort in all he did, but unfortunately he lacked the assertive personality so many of his coworkers possessed. Promotions came and went, always passing Ben by, falling to the men and women whose personalities caused them to be noticed. After thirty years of service, Ben struck out on his own, forming a new company. Within months the new company rose to the top of the field, and many of Ben's former coworkers came to work for him.

It is easy to begrudge others their fortune when they are no more deserving of them than we are. Yet God calls us to rejoice in the triumphs of others, and to await His justice rather than seeking our own. Often we must wait a long time, but the justice of the Lord will prevail, and those who once kept us down will be made a footstool for our feet. Have faith in the Lord, and He will set all things right.

PRAYER: Fill me with Your patience, Lord. When I see others receive rewards, help me to rejoice in their benefit rather than be bitter that I did not receive it.

Amen.

Thy people shall be willing in the day of thy power, in the beauties of holiness from the womb of the morning: thou hast the dew of thy youth.

PSALM 110:3

Sylvia often lamented over the fact that she became a Christian so late in life. Her teenage years had been such a lonely time. College had not been much better. If only she had felt the need for God in her life then. She would have had so many opportunities to spend time with other people. Now her youth was gone, and she had only regrets of what might have been.

When we feel we have all the time in the world, there is no urgency to make decisions right now. Yet if we put off our decision for Christ, we hurt no one but ourselves. We should be willing to follow Christ today, not sometime in the future. We miss so much when we are not in fellowship with other believers. Praise the Lord that He has seen fit to offer us the blessed community of the church.

PRAYER: Help me to make the most of each day, Father. When I feel the urge to put off my commitment to You, fill me with the urgency and the joy of being in fellowship with You immediately. Amen.

Praise ye the LORD. I will praise the LORD with my whole heart, in the assembly of the upright, and in the congregation.
PSALM 111:1

I n one church, we had things called "Say-sos." These were times for members of the church to stand up in front of the rest of the congregation to share their personal faith testimonies. The power of the stories of people's lives is immense. We are walking through this life together. Others share our experiences and pains and joys, but most of the time we are totally unaware of them. Proclaim your faith and the power of Jesus Christ in your life. Share your story. Praise the Lord with your whole heart in the assembly of the upright. You will find new unity through the grace of Jesus Christ.

PRAYER:
Father, give me the courage to share my faith and proclaim Your transforming power in my life. Bring to me others who have been touched by Your great love. Help me praise You every day. Amen.

The fear of the LORD is the beginning of wisdom: a good understanding have all they that do his commandments: his praise endureth for ever.

PSALM 111:10

Brian had been told time after time to stay away from the neighbors' dog. Still, he didn't look too ferocious, and Brian wanted to pet him. While no one looked, Brian crept over to the fence and stuck his hand through to pet the dog. Cries of terror and pain brought the adults running, and Brian learned a lesson he would never forget.

God gives us His laws and commandments for our own good. He is not controlling or domineering. He simply knows what is best for His children, and He tries to instruct them in the ways that will make them happiest. If we decide to violate God's will, then we have to pay the consequences. Once we suffer the costs, we learn what is involved, and a deep wisdom begins to set in. Our lessons may often be difficult and painful, but in all ways, they will help us to be better than we have been before.

PRAYER: Forgive me when I go my own way, O God. I do not mean to be disobedient, but there are times when I just need to experience things for myself. Be patient while I learn my lessons, and protect me from lasting harm, I pray. Amen.

Unto the upright there ariseth light in the darkness: he is gracious, and full of compassion, and righteous.

PSALM 112:4

Jerry and Ed were different as night and day, though they were the best of friends. Jerry loved fun and games, and it was difficult for him to be serious about anything for very long. Ed was studious and hardworking, and nothing swayed him from his course once his mind was made up. The two boys decided they were going to enter a ten-mile run sponsored by their school. Ed practiced every day, exercising and running and eating foods that would get him in shape. Jerry exercised occasionally, ran a few times, and paid little attention to his diet. When the race came and went, Ed was leading the pack and Jerry couldn't even finish.

Leading an upright life prepares us for the race that God has waiting for us. Our spiritual fitness puts us in shape to run that race of life. Without a healthy spirit, we cannot hope to finish. Life without God beats us down and defeats us. Life in the Spirit lifts us before any obstacle and empowers us to meet every challenge.

PRAYER: Like Paul the apostle, I want to run the good race and fight the good fight. Make me fit to be a member of Your team, Lord. Inspire me to prepare my spirit to meet all the challenges that might come my way. Amen.

A good man sheweth favour, and lendeth:
he will guide his affairs with discretion.

PSALM 112:5

Pops always had people coming to him for help. Whenever there was a real need, you could count on Pops to be there, ready to pitch in. Pops had worked construction for about thirty years, and there were few fix-up jobs that anyone could do better than he could. He loved to help people in need, and he loved to feel needed.

Our God is much the same way. He loves to assist us when we need help, and He loves to be needed. No one possesses more knowledge or experience than God does, so He is the perfect source to turn to when we need help. His willingness to give knows no bounds, so there is never a time when He will be unavailable. Turn to God in time of need. He will always help those who love Him.

PRAYER:

Let me follow the giving example of Christ. Make me ready to serve, sharing time, talents, and gifts whenever possible. Amen.

Blessed be the name of the LORD from this time forth and for evermore.

PSALM 113:2

Jimmy had heard it all before, but this time there was something different. Though he couldn't quite put his finger on it, suddenly the idea of a relationship with Jesus Christ made perfect sense. Before, he had missed the logic, somehow. It had never made sense, but now it did. The image of being born again was so appropriate. A part of Jimmy felt like it had never lived. From this day forward, his life was going to be different. He wasn't sure how it would change; he simply knew nothing would ever really be the same again.

At various times in our lives, the reality of Christ will come crashing through the ordinariness of our days. From those times we face life anew, changed at the very core of our being. We move forward in a new, deeper, strengthened relationship with the Lord.

PRAYER: From this day forward, Lord, help me to praise You in new ways. Lead me to a deeper relationship with You through Christ Jesus. Shed Your light upon me, that I might know You better. Amen.

Who is like unto the LORD our God,
who dwelleth on high.
PSALM 113:5

The entire campus was caught up in the Supreme Light movement. Two men claimed to be privy to special insights, and they had developed an amazing following in a very short time. Kevin couldn't believe so many of his friends had bought into it so completely. As far as he could see, neither one of the men had that much to give. All they preached was instant gratification and total forgiveness for all sin, whether repented of or not. For Kevin's money, Jesus Christ would suffice. Long after these two jokers were gone, Christ would still be around. New ideologies pop up all the time, but none offer as much as Christ offers. There was absolutely nothing to be gained by settling for less than Jesus. Nothing to gain, but everything to lose.

PRAYER: Lord, I hear of new answers to life's problems all the time, and some are quite tempting. Help me to remember that I have all the answers I need in You. Amen.

*He raiseth up the poor out of the dust, and
lifteth the needy out of the dunghill.*
PSALM 113:7

A woman sat begging alongside a dirt road. Dozens of people passed her by without even affording her a glance. No one cared to see that she wasn't begging for herself, but for the child she held tightly in her arms. At last, a young boy passed by and saw the woman. He journeyed home, gathered some food and a blanket, and then he returned to the woman and her child.

Selfless acts of kindness are the true signs of a Spirit-filled life. We can call ourselves Christians, but our actions must verify the claim. Mary and Joseph begged for help once in Bethlehem. How would we have responded if they had come to us to beg? How we treat people who are in need is Christ's criterion for judging how much we love Him. In all ways, we should strive to serve the poor and needy.

PRAYER:
Lord, remind me
that I actually
serve Christ when
I serve others. Let
me serve gladly, without
expectation of reward. Teach me
to give to others as You give to me.
Amen.

Not unto us, O LORD, not unto us, but
unto thy name give glory, for thy mercy,
and for thy truth's sake.

PSALM 115:1

Max had worked at the mission for over forty years. There had been weeks on end when he hadn't even gotten to go home. He lived to serve the poor and homeless in his area. When he finally decided to retire, the entire city pitched in to pay him tribute. Throughout the proceedings, Max seemed uncomfortable, and finally he stood to speak.

"I don't want to seem ungrateful, but all this really isn't necessary; and besides, I don't really deserve it. God is the One who needs to be honored. I have just been fortunate enough that He has used me all these years. I really haven't done anything special; I just did what God wanted me to."

It is difficult to set aside our own egos in order to serve God freely. When all is said and done, however, all that we are able to do is made possible by God's grace. Our triumphs are God's triumphs. Like Max, we should feel privileged that God has chosen to work with and through us.

PRAYER:
Use me,
Lord. With
the gifts
and talents You
bestowed upon me,
enable me to spread Your
Good News to everyone I
meet. Amen.

The heaven, even the heavens, are the LORD's:
but the earth hath he given to the children of men.
PSALM 115:16

Joey tossed his candy paper on the playground. Patty ran over from where she was playing with her friends and said, "You pick that up!"

"I don't have to. Who made you boss?"

"It's not nice to throw trash on the ground."

"It's okay. I learned in Sunday school that God gave the earth to us, and we can do anything we want to with it."

Indeed, God has given the world into our hands, but His deepest hope is that we will care for it and protect it. Like careless children, we allow the earth to be mistreated. Like a fragile toy, the earth can only take so much. One day the earth will be damaged beyond repair. What we will do then, God only knows, but for now we must learn to treat God's creation as God Himself would. Otherwise, how will He ever trust us to share eternity with Him in heaven?

PRAYER: Do not let me be careless with Your creation, Lord. I love the beauty of this world, but I am not always quick to protect it. Help me to value our planet more dearly. Amen.

The sorrows of death compassed me, and the pains of hell gat hold upon me: I found trouble and sorrow.

PSALM 116:3

Julie didn't want to think about dying, but ever since her third heart attack, she could think of little else. She was so afraid of dying, and she simply hated the hospital. Worrying was the worst thing she could do. She needed a positive frame of mind, but try as she might, her thoughts always turned to gloom and despair.

It is unfortunate that so many people are ignorant of the everlasting life that can follow this one. Through God's promise of glory in eternity, we no longer have anything to fear from death. Whatever befalls us in this lifetime, it is nothing in relation to the eternal home that awaits us. We need to focus on the life to come in times of trial and sorrow. In the face of death we can feel secure that everything will be just fine.

PRAYER:

In times of fear, dread, and sorrow, shine Your light of love upon me, God. Help me to remember that I have life everlasting, and nothing that occurs now can keep me from it. Amen.

I said in my haste, All men are liars.
PSALM 116:11

Craig trusted no one. He had counted on friends to help him a number of times before, but they all disappointed him. The lesson: Never put your trust in others; trust only in yourself. Now Craig looked to no one for help, and he offered no help to others.

Many people in our world feel that way. They have been burned in their relationships, so they pull in and break off relations altogether. What a shame. If we cut ourselves off from others, we deprive ourselves of a lot of wonderful experiences. This is why God places such emphasis on forgiveness. If we will learn to forgive others when they wrong us, we can remain open to the possibility of relationships in which we won't be disappointed. If we have no forgiveness, we will miss out on the blessings of good relationships. Ask God for the ability to forgive, and He will bless your life.

PRAYER:

Lord, I want to share my life with others. Prevent me from being too hasty in my judgments of others. Help me to be open to new relationships whenever they might occur. Amen.

I will pay my vows unto the LORD
now in the presence of all his people.
PSALM 116:14

The teacher asked the class if anyone went to church. At first, no one raised his hand. Greg went every week, but he wasn't sure he wanted the rest of his class to know. There were some people who might laugh. Then someone raised his hand. Others followed, and soon Greg was surprised to see that over half his class attended church regularly. He raised his hand, a little ashamed that he hadn't had the nerve to raise it earlier.

We need to be proud of our faith. What God has done for us is a miracle, and we should want the whole world to know. Take every opportunity to let others know what you believe. Pay your vows to the Lord in front of other people, and be amazed at how much good it does.

PRAYER:

Forgive me when I keep my faith to myself, Lord. You have given me so much, and I waste it when I refuse to share it with others. Teach me to proudly honor You. Amen.

For his merciful kindness is great toward us:
and the truth of the LORD endureth for ever.
Praise ye the LORD.
PSALM 117:2

Some people think that God kicked Adam and Eve out of the garden as a punishment. I think not. There were two trees of special note in the garden. One was the tree of the knowledge of good and evil, which the duo ate from, and the other was the tree of eternal life. What could have been more cruel than to allow Adam and Eve access to the tree of eternal life after they had chosen to experience evil? God wanted our eternal existence to be sin free, and so He removed the temptation from the midst of men and women. In His great mercy, He made certain that there was an escape from evil for those who wanted it. God's merciful kindness is truly great toward us. Praise Him always.

PRAYER:
Thank You for
making possible
an eternity of peace
and joy, free from sin and
sorrow. Prepare my heart for my
heavenly home. Amen.

The LORD is on my side; I will not fear:
what can man do unto me?
PSALM 118:6

Scott was a natural. He moved like a fox, had a sharp eye and a sharp mind, and believed that teamwork was the only way to win. He also stood just shy of seven feet four inches tall. In all of basketball there was not a more mature, competent player. Under his expert captaincy, the team was unstoppable.

Everyone likes a sure thing. We all look for that person or thing that will give us an edge and make us unstoppable. God is that Someone. Nothing can compare with the power of God. When He is on our side, we have absolutely nothing to fear. In this lifetime, many unfortunate things might occur, but through the grace of God, we will conquer them all.

PRAYER:

Make me a conqueror, Lord. Please allow me to join Your team, to count You as my ally. Be with me all of my days. Amen.

I shall not die, but live, and declare the works of the LORD.
PSALM 118:17

It had been touch and go for a while, but Frank came through the surgery amazingly well. After he recovered, he shared with his friends his conviction that God had been with him throughout his surgery. He felt a deep calling to share what God had done for him with others, and he traveled to different groups to share his witness.

We are given so many opportunities to share our faith with others. How sad it is that often we have to nearly lose that life before we are motivated to do so. We never value things properly until they are gone. It is foolish to wait until then. God calls us to declare His works as often as we can. Sing forth praises to the Lord. He has given us so much.

PRAYER:

As long as I live, Lord, I want to point people in Your direction. Help me to witness to others and share the stories of all You have done in my life. Amen.

The stone which the builders refused is become the head stone of the corner.

PSALM 118:22

When Jesus walked upon the earth, it was not the common people who rejected Him but those who should have known better. The learned men of the day, who had studied long and hard, knew that the Messiah was to come, but they were unwilling to accept the carpenter's son from Galilee as the chosen One. They rejected Him and masterminded His death on a cross, but that was not enough to thwart the holy plans of God. Christ was, is, and always shall be the one true Son of God. Those who reject Him build their faith with faulty materials. Only Christ is the true cornerstone of faith. Upon that stone alone can true faith be built.

PRAYER: Provide the foundation for my faith, O God, and help me to construct a fortress that will withstand all assaults. Protect me with Your love. Amen.

This is the day which the LORD hath made;
we will rejoice and be glad in it.
PSALM 118:24

Rainy days are loved by farmers. Snowy days are loved by children who can stay home from school. Storms are loved by mystery fanatics. Gray days are loved by romantics. Sunny days are loved by picnickers. Warm days are loved by beachgoers. Cool days are loved by those who stroll. All days have their purposes under heaven. Enjoy the day that the Lord has made. He has many more to share.

PRAYER:
Let me appreciate
the gift of this day,
Lord, help me to use
my time wisely, teach me
to rejoice, and fill me with joy that
never ends. Amen.

Blessed are they that keep his testimonies,
and that seek him with the whole heart.

PSALM 119:2

I don't have time. I can slip in a prayer now and then, but I really can't commit to Bible study, or even church."

Terri was so busy that she didn't have time to spare for God. When times got tough, she couldn't understand why her faith didn't do her more good. Unfortunately, faith will not do more for a person than that person allows it to. We will benefit from our faith in proportion to how much time we are willing to put in. God is waiting to spend time with us, to help us develop our faith. Seek Him with your whole heart, and He will richly bless you.

PRAYER: Teach me new ways to seek You, Lord. Grant me special dedication to study Your Word, spend time with You in prayer, and grow in the community of faith and fellowship that is available to me. Amen.

Wherewithal shall a young man cleanse his way? by taking heed thereto according to thy word.

PSALM 119:9

It was a strange feeling to be back in control. The last few years were just a fog in Al's memory. He had spent them in a haze of drugs and alcohol. Thank God that Janet had come along. She had seen the trouble he was in and offered him a friendly hand. She had invited him to her church, and there he found a circle of friends that he'd decided could never exist. Miraculously, withdrawal had been easier than he dreamed. The church people rallied around him and gave him all the support he needed. Now he was clean, and he owed it all to God.

God is the great purifier. He will remove all that is impure in our lives and fill us with good things. We no longer need earthly crutches, because we have found total healing in the Lord. All that is required is a willingness to change. The Lord will help us do the rest.

PRAYER:

Make me a new person, Lord. I may not be hung up on drugs, but there is plenty in my life that should not be there. Help to wash it all away, and replace it with Your blessed love. Amen.

I will meditate in thy precepts, and have respect unto thy ways.

PSALM 119:15

Carol had never thought of meditation as a part of her Christian life. Meditation was something the Eastern faiths believed in, or so she'd always thought. But the speaker at the church had begun talking about Christian meditation, and it made a lot of sense. So often her prayer time was hurried, and she often didn't even stop to listen to see if God might be trying to get through to her. In the ensuing weeks, Carol began to meditate daily, and she felt a closeness to God that she'd never known before.

Meditation sets our whole mind and spirit in a proper mood for encountering God. We are made ready for hearing the Word of God in our hearts. It also makes it easier to spend time with God. Meditation opens doors to God that we might have missed before. Take time to quietly contemplate the glories of the Lord.

PRAYER: I need to be quiet and think of the many miracles that go on all around me. Come to me in my peace, O Lord, and share the blessings of the calm. Amen.

Open thou mine eyes, that I may behold
wondrous things out of thy law.
PSALM 119:18

G us had lived in the hills since his childhood. He
had only learned to read the simplest words, and
he could do little more than sign his name; but he
was a happy man and a hard worker. His niece brought him
to live with her in the city when his wife died, and it was
quickly discovered that Gus needed glasses. For the better part of his life, Gus had lived in nearsighted blindness.
Suddenly, the whole world was opened up to him, and he
viewed it with childlike awe.

Many of us live our lives in a kind of spiritual
nearsightedness. We refuse to experience the fullness
of our faith because it might cost too much, or it might
make us uncomfortable. God offers to let us see this
world through His eyes, and a more
beautiful sight does not exist.
Allow Him to give you second
sight, and behold the wonders of
the world.

PRAYER:
Remove the
blinders that I so
often place upon my
eyes. Expand my horizons
beyond the limits I place on
myself. Grant me vision through Your
eyes of love. Amen.

Remove from me the way of lying: and
grant me thy law graciously.
PSALM 119:29

It started with a few small fibs. Then a lie or two to take the heat off. Before long, Ralph had dug himself a hole he couldn't climb out of. Too many false stories had slipped from his mouth, and his friends were beginning to distrust him. He wasn't really a dishonest person, but a few lies had made him appear to be one.

Truth has no hidden traps in it. When we live in truth, we live above reproach. When we lie, even a little bit, we open ourselves to problems that are unnecessary. Walk in the ways of God, always holding to the truth, and you will find that there is nothing to fear.

PRAYER: Lord, remove any lie or deceit from my mouth. Let truth and tact rule my words. If I find no truth within me to share, then let me keep silent. Amen.

Turn away mine eyes from beholding vanity;
and quicken thou me in thy way.
PSALM 119:37

When the church caught fire, everyone turned out to offer assistance. Many members of the congregation were crushed by the loss of the building. To many, the church had been a showplace, and they wondered whether the church could ever recover. The pastor chastised those members, reminding them that a church is much more than the building that houses it. Whether services took place in an assembly hall or a church sanctuary made no difference. What was important was that people stuck together and worshipped as a church family.

We cannot allow ourselves to lose sight of what is really important in our churches and in our Christian lives. Certainly, our church buildings are important, but the work of the church will go on regardless of the condition of the buildings that house them. Let not your eyes be turned from the way of the Lord. Focus always on Him.

PRAYER: I can get sidetracked from the really important things, Lord. Help me to remain steadfast concerning Your work and gospel. Set my priorities as You would have them. Amen.

The proud have had me greatly in derision:
yet have I not declined from thy law.

PSALM 119:51

Umpiring had its good points and its bad points. Being a part of the game of baseball had always been exciting to Harry, but sometimes it wasn't worth all the abuse. Harry always gave his best effort to be fair to everyone. Still, there was no pleasing some people. All he knew was that he was going to go by the rules, and if others didn't like it, that was their tough luck. At least Harry could sleep well at night knowing that he never compromised the game due to pressure. He might make an occasional bad call, but every call he made was done with integrity.

Sometimes standing up for what is right is the hardest thing we can do. Others will mock us for doing things by the book, but that should only confirm that we are on the right track. God rejoices when we do what we know is right, and He will strengthen us so we can rise above the derision.

PRAYER:
I find that I am too weak to stand up for what is right all the time. When I am weakest, Lord, fill me with Your divine strength. Do not let me shrink from doing what I know is right. Amen.

Horror hath taken hold upon me because of the wicked that forsake thy law.

PSALM 119:53

No one had seen Edna for weeks. They had talked to her on the phone, and she insisted that she was all right, but she had dropped her social life altogether. A group of her friends dropped by to see her and found her terribly distraught. Weeks before, Edna had been the victim of a purse snatcher, and ever since she was afraid to go out. Television and newspapers only fueled her fears. With the way the world was moving, Edna feared she would never leave her house again.

Our world is filled with horrors. Sometimes the answer seems to be to lock the doors and wait for all that is wrong to just go away. Unfortunately, that is no way to live. In such a horrifying time, we need to draw upon the courage of the Lord to meet the world head-on. God will instill in us the power to conquer our fears and enjoy this life as the gift it was meant to be. He will also lead us in the ways that we can work together to change this world for the better.

PRAYER: I cannot believe the things I see and hear in the world today. Everything is so crazy. Be the source of sanity in this mixed-up world, Lord. Set my feet upon the solid rock of Your salvation.

Amen.

Let the proud be ashamed; for they dealt
perversely with me without a cause: but
I will meditate in thy precepts.
PSALM 119:78

Paul did chores for his neighbor, Mrs. Bower, each Tuesday after school. He had done chores for her for three years, and no one had said much about it, but for some reason this year was different. All the kids at school had started making fun of him. He couldn't understand why other kids would laugh at him for trying to help someone else. It made him feel ashamed for no good reason. He'd almost gotten into a fight with one boy. Why couldn't people just leave him alone? It wasn't their business, anyway.

PRAYER:
Lord,
it is hard
enough
when people
find fault with me
for what I do wrong,
let alone when I am trying
to do what is right. Make
their insults bounce off me
like water off a duck's back.
Strengthen me in Your will
and way. Amen.

There is always someone who will find fault with us, no matter what we do. Some people just aren't happy unless they criticize. In times when we feel the most persecution, God waits for us with open arms. He understands well what it is like to be mistreated for no good reason. He went to the cross in just that way. When times get rough, turn to the One who understands best. God will comfort you and give you the strength you need to persevere.

*I have more understanding than all my
teachers: for thy testimonies are my meditation.*
PSALM 119:99

Jesus amazed the learned men in the temple when He was just twelve years old. He had never received professional schooling in the history and law of the Hebrew people, and yet He displayed an incredible insight into even the most complex meanings of holy scripture. His understanding far surpassed that of many of the elders present. Where did His incredible knowledge and wisdom come from? God, of course.

True knowledge is not found in books. God has granted us each a measure of common sense and logic. He is willing and able to instruct us in all His ways if we will take time to contemplate His mysteries. We, too, can amaze the learned of our age by speaking forth the truth of God, which surpasses even the most complex knowledge. Like Christ, we can know more than we ought, through the guidance and counsel of God Himself.

*PRAYER:
Instruct my mind,
heart, and soul
in all of Your ways,
O Lord. Teach me those
things that are truly important,
and enable me to spread what I learn to
others. Amen.*

I understand more than the ancients,
because I keep thy precepts.
PSALM 119:100

The counsel of elders had been the ruling voice of the tribe for centuries. In every decision of the tribe, the elders were consulted. Then came a young man who knew a better way. He told of a rule that would guide each individual to right action. It was the rule of love: the golden rule, which said to do only those things to others that you would have them do to you. The wisdom of the young man was beyond dispute. All the elders had tried to teach was summed up in the simple law. By grasping the full meaning of the rule, any person could obtain the wisdom of the elders. Even more wisdom would come to any and all who would put the rule to practice. The way of the Lord is to love. Higher wisdom does not exist than to live life in love.

PRAYER:
Guide me
by the law
of love, Father.
Show me new
ways to serve others
and to do to them the
things I would wish done to
myself. Grant me the highest
kind of wisdom. Amen.

How sweet are thy words unto my taste!
yea, sweeter than honey to my mouth!
PSALM 119:103

The singer spun a tale of joy and triumph. The audience sat enthralled by the young woman's voice. She painted a picture more lovely than words. The senses came alive as she performed her art. The sights, sounds, colors, smells, and tastes burst forth through her song. She sang from the heart, and her story was shared by many. Emotions connected, and the entire crowd—singer and audience—moved together in a spiritual harmony. The experience was electrifying.

When we are in the presence of truth and beauty, it is undeniable. There is a chord struck within us all. That chord is the image of God in each of us. We connect with the universal rhythm that God set in time long, long ago. The result is joy—a sensation and a feeling that defies explanation—but assures us of the reality of God. Open yourself to His truth.

PRAYER: There are times when I feel Your presence so strongly, Lord. I know that You have orchestrated a masterpiece of which I am a small but important part. Thank You for including me. Amen.

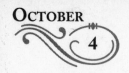

*Thy word is a lamp unto my feet,
and a light unto my path.*

PSALM 119:105

Nick and Davy thought it would be fun to explore deeper in the cave. When they saw their chance, they separated from the rest of their class and headed down a corridor that was roped off. They walked on through twisting and turning shafts until they were no longer sure how to get back. They stood in total darkness, feeling the cavern closing in around them. Just as they verged on panic, Davy looked down and noticed a fine, dim glow. Phosphorescent stone was embedded in the cave floor, and it cast off a dull shine. By following the path of light, the boys made it back to the safety of the well-lit shafts.

Darkness can close in around us quickly in this world today. It seems to be getting darker all the time. However, we are recipients of the light that cannot be put out and will never fade away. The Word of God will guide us through even the darkest times, and He will be close by to comfort us in times of trouble. Rely upon the light of the Lord.

PRAYER:
Light my way, dear God, and keep me from stumbling on the wrong path. Keep me from my own folly. Truly, save me from myself, Lord. Amen.

I have done judgment and justice: leave me not to mine oppressors.

PSALM 119:121

It was never easy giving an F to a student. In fact, if there were any way around it, Jill would have taken it. Most of the time, the student was willing to do anything to avoid the bad mark. Garrett was another case. She had offered to tutor him, she had given him extra-credit work to do, and she had taken all kinds of extra time with him. Through it all he had just blown her off, ignoring her attempts to help and mocking her to his friends. He had ripped up notes she had written to his parents, and he forged his parents' signature on his report cards. Jill had contacted Garrett's parents, but they were too busy to come in. Now, however, with an F in hand, the parents were coming, and they were looking to pick a fight.

Doing what is right is not all that easy. When we dedicate ourselves to justice, we must be ready to face the wrath of all those who don't see things the same way we do. God loves justice and righteousness, and we need to remember that He is ever on the side of what is right. He will be with us when we face persecution for righteousness' sake. Rely on Him.

PRAYER:
Whenever I try to do right, it seems like someone finds fault with me. Help me to ignore the insults and remain true to what I feel You want me to do. Protect me, Lord. Amen.

Rivers of waters run down mine eyes,
because they keep not thy law.
PSALM 119:136

Reverend Hawkins sat at his desk and cried. He had been a good shepherd for his church, and he had given everything he knew to give, but the members of the church had so far to go. In all his years, he had not asked anything special from his congregation, but now he wanted to open their doors as a shelter to vagrants in the area. He was committed to the project to the very depths of his soul, but the church had voted it down by a strong majority. All he had ever tried to teach them was lost. It made him heartsick to think that the gospel was just a story and not a way of life.

Christian growth comes slowly. Not all Christians operate at the same point at the same time. Very little that Jesus asks or commands in the New Testament is easy. It takes time to learn how to walk in the steps of Christ. We may lament that others are not committed in the same ways that we are, but if they are trying their best to follow Jesus, we need to rejoice at their progress and hope for continued growth in their lives and in our own.

PRAYER: I weep for those who have forgotten what it means to follow You, Lord, and I pray that You will help me to continue to grow, and that You might use me to help others in their growth. Amen.

I have gone astray like a lost sheep; seek thy servant; for I do not forget thy commandments.
PSALM 119:176

The shepherd will go looking for a lost sheep, no matter where it might have wandered. Regardless of ravine, cavern, raging river, or steep cliff, the shepherd will endeavor to save even the scrawniest, mangiest sheep. His devotion to his flock is total and absolute.

God's devotion to us is even greater. We can never be separated from the love and care of God. No matter how far we might stray from Him, He is continually on the lookout for us, and He will rescue us from whatever our peril might be. Rest sure and secure in the love of God. He will never give you up for lost.

PRAYER: Lord, I wander off sometimes, but I always want to be with You. Keep a watchful eye upon me, a foolish sheep. Herd me back to the fold, where I am always safe and warm. Amen.

I am for peace: but when I speak,
they are for war.
PSALM 120:7

C hip was in the fight before he knew what happened. He held up a hand to defend himself, and a crowd gathered, urging on a confrontation. Chip really didn't want to fight, but when he tried to make peace, the other boy called him a chicken and started hitting him all the more. Faced with a fight either way, Chip fought the boy down, and then walked away winner of the fight, but feeling like a loser inside.

It is hard to be a peace-loving person these days. It seems like someone is always trying to get us stirred up. Sometimes we have to defend ourselves. Other times, we must take a total stand for peace, no matter what may happen to us. In either case, we need the guidance and support of God in our lives. His wisdom is the only wisdom that will suffice. Our defense is in the Lord, and He will protect us in every situation.

PRAYER:
My heart is filled with thoughts of peace, while the world is filled with rumors of war. Guide me through such hard times, Lord. Teach me when to fight and when to resist. Amen.

I will lift up mine eyes unto the hills, from whence cometh my help.

PSALM 121:1

Bruce lay in the mud waiting for an enemy to pass by and put him out of his misery, or for an ally who would give him aid. The jungle sounds pounded in his ears, and the glare of the sun blinded him. Evening fell, turned to night, and all Bruce could do was wait. With the morning light, Bruce squinted to see if he could make out any landmarks to give him an idea of where he was. As he scanned the horizon, his heart leapt with joy. A familiar flag waved gently in the breeze as a battalion approached. The waiting was almost over, and the fear was gone.

We wait in this life, not sure of what is coming next. The options don't look promising, but we can rejoice in the fact that our Lord is coming to set all things right. His banner is ever out before Him, and as we look unto the hills of the new age to come, we cannot help but notice that God is there waiting for us. Where does our help come from? It comes from the Lord God, who created, who sustains, and who will redeem.

PRAYER:
Lord, make all things new. Usher in a new age: an age of love and caring, an age of compassion and equality. Thank You for granting me Your strength. Amen.

He will not suffer thy foot to be moved:
he that keepeth thee will not slumber.

PSALM 121:3

B enedict was the best butler the Trumbells had ever had. Never had they been treated with such care and concern. Benedict really seemed to care that they were comfortable. They never had to ring twice for his services. He was always right there when they wanted him. He prided himself on doing his job well, and it showed.

As absurd as it seems, God is willing to wait on us, to make sure that we have all we need. The Lord of all life came to earth, and in His time, He stooped to washing His friends' feet—a job usually reserved for the lowliest of slaves. God came to earth to serve us so that we might learn how to serve others. We are to be ready to serve whenever the occasion arises. When we serve untiringly, we show the world the glory of God and make His gospel a reality.

PRAYER: I fear that too often I am asleep at the switch, Lord. Make me ready to serve and to give. Teach me to think less of myself and more of others. Amen.

*The LORD is thy keeper: the LORD is thy shade
upon thy right hand.*

PSALM 121:5

Jeremy always took time out of his day to tend the little maple tree that grew on the east lot. Maintaining a cemetery was hard work, and there was always plenty to keep him busy, but Jeremy never forgot his tree. One of his coworkers asked him once why he doted over the tree so, and he said, "That little tree is the only shade in the east lot. When I'm out digging or mowing, I need to rest in some shade for a while. My tree out there is the best place I know to go. We've got a deal: I take care of it; it takes care of me."

When activities wear us down and we just can't go on, we need a port in the storm, a source of shade and comfort. The Lord is just that. He is the place where we can rest and be renewed. Turn to the Lord when you are weary, and He will rejuvenate you and set you back on your feet.

PRAYER:

*Let me find my
rest in You, Lord.
When the day gets
to be too much for me,
welcome me into Your presence,
where I find sanity and reason. Amen.*

The LORD shall preserve thy going out and thy coming in from this time forth, and even for evermore.

PSALM 121:8

Gene grabbed his poncho and headed for the door. Whenever there was a bad storm, the linemen got called out by the power company. Funny, but they were expected to work in the least safe conditions at a moment's notice, and nobody ever said please or thank you. Every time he headed out on a night like this one, Gene took time to say an extra prayer for protection.

The Lord watches over all His children. He is with us in safe times as well as the dangerous ones. He guards our steps from the day we are born until we are ushered into our heavenly home. Know that the Lord is with you. He will never leave you alone.

PRAYER: Guard me this day, Lord. Be with all the people who serve in dangerous positions, and keep them safe. Watch over us all. Amen.

I was glad when they said unto me, Let us go into the house of the LORD.
PSALM 122:1

Mike and Jerry were neighbors for about five months when one day Jerry asked Mike to play golf with him on a bright, beautiful Sunday morning. Mike graciously declined, asking for a raincheck. Jerry invited Mike on a couple more Sundays, but Mike always refused. Jerry asked him why, and Mike told him that he went to church. After that, Jerry didn't ask again, on Sunday or any other day of the week. Mike finally asked Jerry why, and he replied, "I asked you to go with me three times to do something that was important to me, but you never once asked me to go to church with you."

Mike never thought that Jerry might like to go to church. Too often we shy away from asking people because we don't want to seem pushy. But the Lord asks that we work diligently to bring people to Him. Often people do not go to church simply because they feel awkward and have never been asked. Share your faith. Ask someone to church with you. You never know what might happen.

PRAYER: Open my eyes to the needs of others, Lord. Help me to not think I know people's minds before I ask. Be patient with me as I learn to share my faith with others. Amen.

*Peace be within thy walls, and
prosperity within thy palaces.*

PSALM 122:7

Some people's homes are war zones. Families in conflict abound in our society. So much unhappiness comes from people who no longer knowing how to share and give. Too many people are looking out for themselves, and they aren't willing to look out for each other. Mothers fight with daughters, sons with fathers, husbands with wives, and brothers with sisters, each feeding the beast of hurt and discord. We are lost without a peacemaker—one who knows our hearts and can pave the way to reconciliation. Thankfully, Christians have such a peacemaker. Christ came to unite all of God's children as brothers and sisters in the faith. He works in the home to call us to a deep love that is consecrated in blood. If we strive for peace within our walls, then we are one step closer to peace between our nations. God will heal all our wounds, if we will only welcome Him in.

PRAYER: Christ, You have broken down the dividing walls of hostility, and You are waiting to build bridges of love. Begin with me, Lord, and move forth in love. Amen.

Behold, as the eyes of servants look unto the hand of their masters, and as the eyes of a maiden unto the hand of her mistress; so our eyes wait upon the LORD our God, until that he have mercy upon us.
PSALM 123:2

Ryan had trained dogs for almost thirty years. A lot of people didn't like his tactics, because he demanded that the animals learn respect fast. He never raised his voice, but he was quick to discipline with sharp, painful shots to the rump and muzzle. Within a few short days, his dogs knew what was expected of them and what they could expect if they disobeyed. By the turn of a hand, Ryan was able to make his dogs do almost anything.

As we wait upon the Lord, we should think about what is expected of us and how well we are doing what we should. We know what is expected of us, and we know what might befall us in our disobedience. We look expectantly to God, and it is right that we should, but we should also look at ourselves to see that we are doing all we know we ought to be.

PRAYER:
Have mercy upon me, Lord, in my disobedience. I am trying to learn Your will for my life. Help me to grow in all of Your ways. Amen.

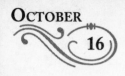
Have mercy upon us, O LORD, have mercy
upon us: for we are exceedingly
filled with contempt.

PSALM 123:3

The Greens couldn't tolerate the Reds, because the Reds read their Bibles out loud. The Reds couldn't stand the Blues, because they sang too many songs; and they didn't always sing words the Reds knew. The Blues didn't like the Golds, because the Golds never did any mission work. And the Golds didn't like anybody else, because no one else took in as much money on a Sunday morning.

The things we let divide us! God shakes His head in disbelief at the contempt we hold for others who don't quite agree with us. We live in a country where there are almost three hundred different denominations, all claiming to have a special understanding of the Christian gospel. What is more important than any point of doctrine is that we love one another, and that we treat one another accordingly. We need to ask God's forgiveness for our bent toward judging others. Each of us has enough to keep us busy with his own faith. When we start pointing fingers at others, that's when we prove positively that our own faith is in serious need of help.

PRAYER:
Have mercy upon me, Lord. I apologize for all the times I have judged another person's faith, when my own faith is in such need of help. Remove the enormous plank from my own eye, O God, that I might truly begin to see. Amen.

Our soul is escaped as a bird out of the snare
of the fowlers: the snare is broken,
and we are escaped.

PSALM 124:7

Clifford was a strange man. He served his country in Vietnam and spent three years as a prisoner of war. While a prisoner, he amazed his companions by never complaining about their situation. In fact, when questioned about it, he smiled and said, "I'm not really here, anyway." Once Cliff returned to the States, he shared what he had meant. Each day he sat against the stone wall and began listing in his mind all the places he had ever been that he loved. He pictured those places, and he selected a different one every day. In his mind he journeyed to the beloved spots, and he turned off the reality around him.

As Christians, we need to do the same thing. We're not from here. Our true home is with God in heaven. When the reality around us gets too intense and hard to handle, we should turn our thoughts to God. We can be liberated from the trap if we will only call upon the Lord. God offers us a way to escape the harshness of our earthly life by entering into quiet time with Him. Reach out. His peace awaits.

PRAYER:
Rescue me from
the craziness
around me. Be my
refuge when life gets too
hectic. Lift me out of the race, and
grant me rest. Amen.

*As the mountains are around about
Jerusalem, so the LORD is round about
his people from henceforth even for ever.*

PSALM 125:2

Peggy loved the island. Her grandfather had purchased the land and built a cottage on it before the First World War. Now it was hers, and she felt safe and surrounded and at home. Some of her friends thought it would be unpleasant to be completely surrounded by water, but she said it was just like having a private moat. To Peggy, this was paradise.

For some people, being surrounded is a great source of security. Our Lord waits to surround us in His love. From time immemorial, the Lord has gathered His children to Himself, encircling them in His protective care. We are held in that circle today. Rejoice that the Lord is near. He protects and defends us, and will continue to do so forever.

PRAYER:
Circle me in Your love, Lord. Surround me and keep me safe, I pray, and help me to draw others to You. Amen.

Do good, O LORD, unto those that be good,
and to them that are upright in their hearts.
PSALM 125:4

Mrs. Hendricks was the most popular music teacher around. Young and old alike hired her to teach them how to play and sing. Actually, the only thing Mrs. Hendricks did differently from other teachers was to make you feel good about what you were trying to do. She complimented, encouraged, and affirmed her students at every possible opportunity.

We like to be around people who make us feel good. We all need to be affirmed and supported. We look to the Lord for approval, because we want more than anything for Him to be proud of us. He is. When we try to live upright and holy lives, we are doing that which makes Him happiest. He will continually bless those who do good, for to them belongs the kingdom of God.

PRAYER:

Help me know
that I'm on the
right track, dear God.
Let me know that what I am
trying to do pleases You. Keep me
ever in Your care. Amen.

*Then was our mouth filled with laughter,
and our tongue with singing: then said they
among the heathen, The LORD hath done great
things for them.*

PSALM 126:2

Young people all seemed to think you had to get drunk to have a good time. Steve and Dan were out to teach them otherwise. One of the high priorities in their youth ministry was to show teenagers that Christians could have even more fun than non-Christians. They entered the lives of the young people, bringing them laughter, joy, and a message of Good News. Soon, both Christians and non-Christians hung out with the duo. All the kids wanted to be part of the experience.

Too often we take our faith seriously in the wrong ways. When we present only the somber, quiet side of faith, without expressing the joy, the result is not always so attractive. Christians have gained the reputation of not being too much fun, and nothing should be further from the truth. Being a Christian is the most joy-filled and lively experience we can have. Others need to see that. Live the happiness, laughter, and singing of being a Christian, so the whole world might know.

PRAYER: Never let me forget the intense joy that accompanies being a Christian. Turn my tears to laughter, my sorrow to dancing, and let me spread my delight to everyone. Amen.

They that sow in tears shall reap in joy.
PSALM 126:5

Just when Amy thought her work might go down the drain, a miracle came through. Working with the poor in Atlanta was the best job and the worst job she had ever had. She specifically worked in drug and alcohol rehabilitation, and there was nothing more gratifying than getting someone back on his feet. Yet for every person who got cleaned up, there were a dozen more in need. Money was tight, and things didn't look good. Amy went home at night and cried for all the work left undone and all the people in misery. Then the grant came through: enough money to keep the doors open for a year. Amy felt like God truly did care about what she was doing. All the sweat and tears paid off.

Joy that comes to us in times of despair is twice as sweet. When we care intensely about our world and the people in it, we will be moved to tears; and at times we will even feel like giving up. Thankfully, the tears will turn to joy, for all is in God's hands. He will transform this old world and make all things new. Those who care most deeply will rejoice all the more. Take heart!

PRAYER:

Help me to see a brighter future for my world, O Lord. I get discouraged when it seems like evil triumphs so much of the time. Show me the good, Father.

Amen.

Except the LORD build the house, they labour in vain that build it: except the LORD keep the city, the watchman waketh but in vain.

PSALM 127:1

A great cathedral was constructed to God's glory, while hungry and sick people sat outside its walls. The cathedral was called "The Greatest Achievement in the Name of God." Millions flocked from all over to enter its doors. Thousands went away disturbed that the ministry of the church was contained completely within its walls. As the years passed, the church lost its luster, and it became just another church. The poor were still there, but nothing had yet been done to help them. God looked down on the cathedral and said, "This is the poorest excuse for a church I have seen."

When men and women try to take the church out of God's hands, it ceases to be the church. Only churches built upon the spiritual rock of salvation can claim to be God's churches. Our achievements in the name of God must bear His signature, not our own, otherwise they have been done in vain. God is the author of all that is good; we are merely His helpers. Whatever God builds will last forever, while humankind's creations crumble to the dust.

PRAYER:

Use my talents to do Your will, Lord, not my own. Remind me that I am doing Your work with You, not my own work for You. Bless all my endeavors in Your name. Amen.

*It is vain for you to rise up early, to sit up
late, to eat the bread of sorrows: for so he giveth
his beloved sleep.*

PSALM 127:2

Rodney couldn't sleep. He tossed and turned, thinking of the bills yet to pay, the braces needed for the
children's teeth, the pressures at work, the promises made but not yet fulfilled. Each time he pushed one
demon thought from his mind, another popped in. His
health was beginning to be affected by his lack of sleep.
That added just one more thing to his list of worries.

Worry is the last thing that will help our problems. In
fact, worry can immobilize us from being able to take any
kind of positive steps toward solutions. The only purpose
for worry is to indicate to us that we need to turn our
problems over to God. Once we
enlist the help of our Lord, then
we can rest easy. God will carry us
through any situation, and He
will grant us peace of
mind and peace
of heart.

*PRAYER:
So often I am
haunted by
problems and
concerns, Lord. Lift their
weight from my shoulders, and allow
me to rest. Amen.*

As arrows are in the hand of a mighty man;
so are children of the youth. Happy is the man
that hath his quiver full of them: they shall not be
ashamed, but they shall speak with the enemies in the gate.

PSALM 127:4–5

B everly belonged to a large family. Friends of hers always told her how sorry they were for her being the middle child of nine, but she could never quite understand their sympathy. She liked having lots of sisters and brothers. They were all close, and she never felt lonely or unsupported. Contrary to her friends' belief that there would be less love because it was spread so thin, there was all the more. Beverly couldn't imagine being loved more than she was by her whole family.

God gave families as a blessing. Not only blood families, but church families also qualify as blessings of love. Anyone can belong to a family in God's world, for we are all His family. All it takes is to reach out to others. There is strength, safety, and joy in numbers. The closer we unite, the stronger we will be.

PRAYER:

Draw me close to my sisters and brothers in Christ, O Lord. Expand my family each and every day. Teach me to reach out to those around me. Fill me with a love that never fails. Amen.

Blessed is every one that feareth the LORD;
that walketh in his ways. For thou shalt eat the
labour of thine hands: happy shalt thou be, and
it shall be well with thee.
PSALM 128:1–2

Jack sat down to supper with his family. Even after twenty years, there was something special about a meal that came from their own farm. Jack could imagine thousands of families sitting down to similar meals of produce from his farm. It made him feel like there was purpose to his life. The work was hard, and there were worries about the future, but it was all worth it. The farm was Jack's life. It would never be said that Jack was not fulfilled in his work. He couldn't be happier.

Many people find no satisfaction in the work they do. Their lives lack purpose and meaning. Christians have an alternative source of meaning in their lives. If a Christian does a job—no matter how large or small—to God's glory, that person will find satisfaction. God doesn't much care what we do, but He is always interested in how we do our jobs. If we do our work without grumbling and with a joyful heart, we are witnessing to His power in our lives, and we are pleasing to Him.

PRAYER: Do not let me be so concerned with the prestige of my job, or the salary it pays, or what other people think of it. Instead, assist me to always do the best that I can, to Your glory, Father.

Amen.

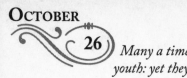
*Many a time have they afflicted me from my
youth: yet they have not prevailed against me.*

PSALM 129:2

Sandra was handicapped. Her hands were twisted beyond usefulness, and she had lived with them since birth. They caused her not only physical pain, but emotional anguish as well. Throughout her childhood, cruel children had mocked her. The damage done to her self-esteem was immense, and for a long period she believed that she could never do anything. In college she had met a friend who led her to Christ. In Christ she found a new desire to succeed and beat her affliction. She received a master's degree in therapy and handicapped services and became a national spokeswoman for a handicap-awareness campaign. Though her detractors always had something to say, Sandra prevailed and rose above her handicap.

The Lord gives us all the ability to rise above the things that limit us. If we will only lean upon Him, He will give us the will and drive to succeed in every situation. His power can be our power when we call upon His holy name.

*PRAYER:
There are
times, dear
Lord, when
I feel I don't
amount to much. My
self-image is bruised, and
my determination is crushed.
Be with me in those times,
and lift me up. Amen.*

The plowers plowed upon my back: they made long their furrows.
PSALM 129:3

The rookie lawyer made his case, then sat down feeling very pleased with himself. Then the fireworks began. The defense picked apart every argument he made and humiliated him before the judge and jury. The judge pulled him aside and told him to put in more time next time, and the opposing lawyer just laughed and thanked him for making his job so easy. With tail tucked between his legs, the young lawyer beat a hasty retreat.

There will be days when things don't just go wrong; they self-destruct totally. When we feel we've gone as low as we possibly can, something else comes along to drive us deeper still. From those depths there is only one place to turn: God. He has seen all, He knows how you feel, and He patiently waits to take you into His arms to comfort and soothe you. When we feel pushed beyond our ability to cope, it is good to know that God is there.

PRAYER:
In times of total
darkness, shine
Your light into my life.
Help me to pick myself up
and start again. Give me strength,
Lord. Amen.

Let them be as the grass upon the housetops,
which withereth afore it growth up.
PSALM 129:6

People who live without God in their lives live without the roots that feed and strengthen all life. They have no protection against the storms of life that can uproot and destroy them. When troubles increase, they wither like plants in a hot sun. God is the true source of all that is needed to grow. Without Him, we can never reach our potential. Like the seed that falls to the rooftop, sprouts, then soon dies for lack of nourishment, so we, too, will die without the saving power of the Almighty in our lives.

PRAYER:

Feed me,
protect me,
nurture me,
and make me
grow, Lord. Send your
life-giving Spirit upon me,
and make me the best person
that I can be. Amen.

Out of the depths have I cried unto thee,
O Lord.
PSALM 130:1

Funny how some people never ask for help until everything comes crashing down upon them. They wait until the last minute, then send out the distress signal. Many people work their relationship with God that way. They call on Him infrequently while things are going well, but when trouble rears its ugly head, they are pounding on His door for help. It is a wise person who learns to include God in everything he does. When God is a full part of your life, you never feel panic when things go wrong. Still, it is good to know that God will hear us when we cry out of the depths, and He will always come to the aid of His children.

PRAYER: Make me to remember You in all times, Lord, not just times of trial. Help me to share my whole life with You and to glory in Your presence. Thank You for staying beside me always. Amen.

I wait for the LORD, my soul doth wait,
and in his word do I hope.
PSALM 130:5

Elizabeth sat by her nightstand, reading from her Bible. Each night before bed, she read from the scriptures. She always claimed that the key to a long and happy life was to keep in contact with God. Each night as she turned out the light, Elizabeth smiled to herself. She wondered how much longer she would live, but not with any fear or dread. She knew that her heavenly home was waiting for her, and that thought held only comfort. As she drifted off to sleep, she prayed for God's will to be done, and she knew in her heart that it would be.

PRAYER:

Lord, do

Your will

in my life.

If I live but one

more day, help me

make it the best day of my

life. If I live for years, help me

to fill them with peace, joy,

contentment, and service.

Amen.

Lord, my heart is not haughty, nor mine eyes lofty: neither do I exercise myself in great matters, or in things too high for me.
PSALM 131:1

When John had started out, all his superiors told him that he was destined to go far in the firm. Now they all shook their heads in wonder that he had never climbed the corporate ladder. John just smiled to himself. Dog-eat-dog was fine for some, but John was content to just do the work he loved. He didn't care what anyone else thought; he was happy, and that was worth more than all the prestige in the world.

Bloom where you're planted, the saying goes. When you find a place of contentment, guard it. Don't be ready to throw it away for what may or may not be better. Too often we get into situations over our heads, and then it is too late to go back. God will not be impressed by your fame or wealth. What pleases the Lord is someone who uses his talents and makes peace for himself in the work that he does.

PRAYER: Make my aspirations for myself realistic and worthwhile. Help me to keep my wits about me, to do the things I like rather than those things that are done merely to impress others. Amen.

Surely I have behaved and quieted myself,
as a child that is weaned of his mother:
my soul is even as a weaned child.

PSALM 131:2

Thomas got so sick of his sister telling him to grow up and act his age. Sure, he blew his temper sometimes, but so what? Everybody does. Who did she think she was, telling him to grow up? He was plenty grown-up. It was other people who needed to grow up, not him. Anybody who thought differently just didn't know what he was talking about.

At some point in our lives, we pass from thinking only of ourselves to thinking of others. We become less defensive and more peaceful. We admit when we are wrong, and we affirm others in their opinions. The apostle Paul says that we must come to a place in our lives where we put aside childish things. Christian maturity comes when we begin to think less of self, more of those around us. There are times in all our lives when the message is clear: We need to grow up.

PRAYER:
Help me to grow and mature in my faith, Lord. Turn my attention to the needs of others. Turn my selfishness into selflessness. Amen.

I will not give sleep to mine eyes, or slumber to mine eyelids, until I find out a place for the LORD, an habitation for the mighty God of Jacob.
PSALM 132:4–5

Rachel closed the door and hung her head. Three o'clock in the morning. She wondered whether the project was ever going to get done. All she wanted to do was collapse in bed, but first there was something she had to do. She dressed for bed, then took the Bible from her dresser and went to the kitchen table to read and to pray. In all her adult life, she had never gone to sleep without first spending time with God. She was determined that nothing would ever come between her and this special time. It made no difference how tired she was; God came before sleep.

When days become hectic and full, it is easy to allow God to be pushed aside. We need to protect our time with the Lord and give it top priority. If we will keep the Lord close to us, He will sustain us and give us strength in tough times. Without Him, we can never hope to be our best.

PRAYER: Convict my heart with the determination to spend time with You. Let nothing come between us, Lord. When other things demand my time, remind me that I gave myself to You first. Amen.

Let thy priests be clothed with righteousness;
and let thy saints shout for joy.

PSALM 132:9

Reverend Fields felt very strongly about the matter. If a person was going to be a representative of the church, he needed to live a clean and upright life. Leaders need to lead by example; therefore, church leaders ministered to others by the way they lived their lives. If a person wasn't ready to steer clear of questionable activities, then maybe he wasn't ready to step into a key role in the church.

All Christians assume the responsibility of being an example to nonbelievers. It is an awesome task, but one we must assume. Christ calls us to a life of perfection. Each day we should strive harder to be more perfect than we were the day before. With God's help, we can clothe ourselves in righteousness, thus sending the message that to be Christian means to be different from the rest of the world. In Christ we are made new. Our newness is a light for all the world to see.

We should strive harder to be more perfect than we were the day before. With God's help, we can clothe ourselves in righteousness, thus sending the message that to be Christian means to be different from the rest of the world. In Christ we are made new. Our newness is a light for all the world to see.

PRAYER:

Clothe me in Your righteousness, Lord, and make me an example of a new life in Christ. Let me serve You through my actions. Move me onward toward perfection. Amen.

*This is my rest for ever: here will I dwell; for
I have desired it.*
PSALM 132:14

The climb was steep and treacherous, and there were no level places to stop. The sun was beating down, and the two climbers were exhausted. Both were beginning to question the wisdom of the climb. Just as they began to despair of ever getting through it alive, a ledge jutted into the cliff, and both climbers pulled themselves up onto it. There, in the cool shade cast by the rock, the climbers were renewed and strengthened, enabled to finish their ascent.

The Lord provides us with a place to rest in this climb of ours through life. He welcomes us, shades us, protects us, and enables us to go forth strengthened and renewed. We are never far from this rest. All we need do is turn to the Lord, and He will grant us respite.

*PRAYER:
Lord, take me into
Your loving arms
to comfort and
energize me. I get so
tired sometimes, and I need
a place to escape. Help me to
turn inward, to dwell with Christ, and
to draw upon His power. Amen.*

Behold, how good and how pleasant it is for brethren to dwell together in unity!
PSALM 133:1

Rob had been through the death of one congregation; he didn't want to see it happen again. There really weren't any problems that couldn't be worked out in Christian love. This church had been through a lot, and there was no reason to believe that it couldn't weather a lot more storms. If everyone would just remember that he or she was there to serve Christ, then everything would work out fine. If Christ could calm the Sea of Galilee, He should have no trouble with the First Church.

Christ built His church as a place for harmony and unity. It is a place for people to come together in celebration and love. Christ rejoices when His family lives together in peace. We, too, can rejoice, for there is nothing better than being able to dwell together in His love.

PRAYER:
Lord,
the best
friends in the
world to have
are those who are
bonded together with me
through my faith. Bring joy to
my relationships, Lord, and
bless me with harmony and
unity. Amen.

Lift up your hands in the sanctuary, and bless the LORD.
PSALM 134:2

It was weird. Jane had never been to a service like it before. All the people murmured the Lord's name during the prayers, raised their hands, and rocked back and forth in the pews. At first, she had been very uncomfortable, but as she got accustomed to the goings-on around her, she began to relax. Suddenly, she realized that everyone didn't have to express their faith the same way. Though she didn't feel comfortable displaying her faith with physical expressions, she found that she readily accepted others who did. The sincerity of the worship and the energy of the congregation excited Jane. A whole new aspect of her faith was opening up to her.

Open-mindedness is the greatest need in our churches today. Somehow we must learn to affirm and respect the other members of the body of Christ who don't choose to function as we do. There is room for any and all honest expressions of love and devotion to our Lord. Whether we approach Him on bended knees deep in the silence of our own hearts, or with hearts, hands, and heads lifted in jubilant praise, we can know beyond doubt that God accepts us and is honored by our expressions of worship.

PRAYER: Receive me as I am, Lord. I worship You in the best way I know how. Help me to be open to new and different expressions of faith, and teach me to grow. Amen.

For I know that the LORD is great,
and that our LORD is above all gods.

PSALM 135:5

Brooke had tried everything. She had started in business, done quite well, then the bottom dropped out. Broke and disillusioned, she moved home with her parents. There she began attending church and studying the Word. Then she was offered a job with a large corporation, and she jumped at the chance. It didn't work out the way she expected, nor did the relationship she got involved in with one of her coworkers. Disillusioned once more, she returned to her hometown. Once more she involved herself with the church, and she was amazed to realize how much she had missed it. The problems she'd been having didn't seem so great anymore. Without even realizing it, Brooke had been developing a faith that helped her through. While everything else in her life changed, mostly for the worse, God stayed the same, and He was waiting to embrace His prodigal daughter the minute she returned.

Our Lord is great, and His love is far beyond our comprehension. No earthly temptation that we try to elevate to the status of a god can ever compare with the one true God. He alone can make our lives worthwhile.

PRAYER: You have changed my life for the better, Father, and I will never again turn from the blessings You alone can supply. Please let nothing ever come between me and Your love. Amen.

Whatsoever the Lord pleased, that did he in heaven, and in earth, in the seas, and all deep places.
PSALM 135:6

Imagine the fun the Lord had creating all the animals of this world. With the power to do whatever He pleased, He concocted a menagerie of some wonderful creatures. Consider the giraffe, or the baboon, or the frog. What a host of funny-looking creatures. Think of the splendor of the eagle, the grace of the gazelle, the power of the tiger. God put so much into making His creation a good one. The same is true of His children. God went to great lengths to make sure His children were good. He even imparted to each and every one of them His own image. He offered them free will and all the blessings they could ever hope for. He did these things because they pleased Him. Our God is a God of love, and nothing pleases Him more than to be able to share that love. Indeed, we may be God's funniest creatures, but that only makes Him love us all the more.

PRAYER: Father, You must have a wonderful sense of humor to put up with children like me. Forgive me for being less than You created me to be. Help me to grow and mature and develop into Your image. Amen.

*O give thanks unto the God of gods: for his
mercy endureth for ever. . . . To him that
made great lights: for his mercy endureth for ever.*

PSALM 136:2, 7

Griffin had gone through college as an atheist. No one could get him to believe that there was a God out there somewhere who made everything work. That was before he began working with the space program. The more he saw the scope and majesty of the cosmos, the more convinced he was that there had to be someone out there who authored all the miracles he saw. To see the power of a billion suns shining through millions of miles of space boggled the mind. They couldn't have just happened. Some great mind had to have a part in bringing it all about. Griffin had come far. His briefcase was always packed with pictures and books, but no book was more important than the Bible that never left his side.

People who don't believe in God reject Him, not because they know so much, but because they just haven't learned enough. Even in the most scientific and complex equation, God can be found. Wisdom comes not when we say we know all we need to, but when we admit there is much left to learn. Open your heart and mind to God, and watch the universe unfold.

PRAYER: A billion stars pierce the infinite darkness of space. Surely Your light can break through the darkness of my ignorance. Shine the light of true wisdom through me, Lord, and let me share in Your glory. Amen.

O give thanks to the Lord of lords: for his mercy endureth for ever. . . . To him which divided the Red sea into parts: for his mercy endureth for ever.

PSALM 136:3, 13

Tracey sat thinking about her troubles. Her mother kept telling her to pray about them, but she didn't know whether that would do any good or not. She wanted to believe, but it seemed a little far-fetched to think praying would really do anything. She wasn't even sure that her prayers got through to God.

Doubt is a killer. It kills faith. Our God is the God who freed the Hebrew people from captivity in Egypt. He parted the waters and let the chosen people through before washing away the Egyptian army. If God could handle the trials of an entire people, then He can handle what we lift up to Him. Give thanks to the Lord, and trust Him with your every thought. His mercy does endure forever.

PRAYER: Hear me, Lord, as I pray for Your guidance and help in my life. I cannot handle all of the problems that come my way, and I need to know You stand with me. Give me that assurance. Amen.

11

*By the rivers of Babylon, there we sat down,
yea, we wept, when we remembered Zion.
We hanged our harps upon the willows in the midst thereof.*

PSALM 137:1–2

W hy fight it? The committee had tried to get more funds to help the aged for three years, and nothing ever got done. Almost everyone on the committee was so discouraged that they wanted to quit. What good did it do to keep hitting your head against a brick wall? No one was willing to listen to their proposals.

We all come up against situations where there just doesn't seem to be any good solution. The Hebrew people grew discouraged in their trek to the Promised Land. They hung up their harps and stopped singing, for the joy and enthusiasm had left them. Their answer was God. He lifted their spirits and filled their hearts with joy. He became their reason for going on, and He can become our reason, too. When we are discouraged, we need to turn to God. He will lift us up and give us the courage we need to continue.

PRAYER:
Lord, there are times when I just want to sit down and cry. Sustain me through these difficult times and fill me with enthusiasm and energy to face new challenges. Amen.

How shall we sing the LORD's song in a strange land?
PSALM 137:4

College was a foreign land for Diane. Even after three years, she felt alienated and alone. Her values just didn't mesh with the values of the people she went to classes with. Sometimes she wondered why she even bothered having morals, with all the immorality rampant on campus. She was thankful that she was a Christian, but there were times when even that was small consolation. God was hard to find in a strange place that obviously didn't know Him very well. Face it, Jesus Christ was not big man on campus. It was hard, but down deep inside Diane knew things would get better. She just hoped it would be soon.

It is hard to be a stranger in a strange land. That is what we become when we ask Christ into our lives. He transforms us into kingdom people while we are yet in our earthly existence. What that does is make us homesick for the one true home above. Thankfully, God is ever with His children, and He will hear our cries. In our times of silence we will hear His song, and we will be able to sing forth ourselves, no matter how strange the land.

PRAYER: Lord, hear my prayers. Let me know that I am not alone, that You are truly close to me. When I feel most lonesome, fill me with Your presence. Amen.

*If I do not remember thee, let my tongue
cleave to the roof of my mouth; if I prefer
not Jerusalem above my chief joy.*

PSALM 137:6

B rett joined the church when he was fourteen. In the
sixty years following his confirmation, he set foot
in a church no more than a half-dozen times. Just
prior to his seventy-fifth birthday, Brett died and stood
before the Lord.

The Lord said, "You joined my church long years ago.
Why?"

Brett stood speechless and ashamed. No answer or
excuse—and Brett had many of them—seemed adequate.
No apology covered his negligence. All Brett could do was
hang his head and cry, for he only now began to realize
why he had needed the church.

If we forget our Lord, we will find
ourselves steeped in shame when we
stand before Him. To call Him Lord,
Master, Guardian, Friend requires
commitment on our part. We cannot
take continually without giving
something back. Remember
the Lord, and speak forth
with joy in His pres-
ence, for you have
known Him, and, in-
deed, He knows you.

*PRAYER:
Lord,
forgive
me when I
neglect You and
turn to other things.
Help me to keep You fully
in my mind and heart. Prepare
me for Your glory. Amen*

O daughter of Babylon, who art to be destroyed; happy shall he be, that rewardeth thee as thou hast served us.

PSALM 137:8

D oesn't God care? Why do evil people get away with all the things they do?"

The question is asked almost every day. Evil seems to be having its way all the time. Don't worry. God sees everything, and He will not forget what evil people have done. Our God, though a God of love, is a God of justice. He will reward those who honor Him, and He will punish those who have rejected Him and His ways. We are responsible for the way God will deal with us. If we choose to ignore Him, we cannot hope for good things, but if we pursue God with all our hearts, we will experience blessings and joy beyond measure.

PRAYER: I know that You care, and I know that You will do right by all who love You. Give me patience to accept what seems unfair now. Make me deserving of Your grace. Amen.

I will praise thee with my whole heart:
before the gods will I sing praise unto thee.
PSALM 138:1

Linda had the chance to sing before a huge audience. Due to an audition at her college, she had chosen to appear on a well-known television show. All her friends made suggestions about what she should sing, but Linda had ideas of her own. Her grandmother had always loved the song "Amazing Grace" and told Linda that she should always look for ways to let people know what she believed. This was a chance to do just that. Linda would sing her heart out—for her grandmother and for her Lord.

Perhaps singing is not your talent, but each of us can find ways to proclaim the power of Christ in our lives. If God is really important in our lives, we should be excited to let the whole world know how we feel. Praise God with your whole heart, and sing forth His glory always.

PRAYER:
I cannot express how grateful I am to have You in my life, Father. Help me to share Your love with the people I meet this day. Amen.

I will worship toward thy holy temple,
and praise thy name for thy lovingkindness
and for thy truth: for thou hast magnified thy
word above all thy name.
PSALM 138:2

I believe in God, but I have no use for the Bible. People take it and twist it, and it's no good to anyone. The Bible just gives some people an excuse to feel superior to other people."

The young man who expressed these sentiments is right. . .to some extent. God's Word has been misused many times throughout history. It is a destructive component when used by the wrong people for the wrong reasons, but that is no reason to reject it. What God intends for His Word and what people do with it are two completely different things. God does reveal Himself through His Word, and it is nearly impossible to come to a deep understanding of Him apart from the holy scriptures. God has magnified Himself through His Word, and He enables us to know Him when we read it in a spirit of openness, with a desire for the truth.

PRAYER:
Illuminate the
pages of Your
Word, Lord. Bless me
with understanding of Your
holy scripture, and help me to keep
an open mind as I learn and grow.
Amen.

*All the kings of the earth shall praise thee,
O LORD, when they hear the
words of thy mouth.*

PSALM 138:4

Wouldn't it be wonderful if all the leaders on earth suddenly found their hearts filled with love and compassion and justice? What would happen if they all decided that top priority would be to take care of others first? Perhaps then we would have a taste of what God originally intended. We want to believe that our leaders are listening for the voice of God as they make their difficult decisions, but often we can only wonder. Perhaps one day all the kings of earth will stop their quarreling long enough to hear the gentle urgings of God. Until then, it is the responsibility of every Christian to pray for the leaders and ask God that He might work for good in spite of them, when it is impossible to work with or through them.

PRAYER:
Amidst
the chaos
of our world,
Lord, You are the
center of sanity and
reason. Inspire our leaders
to work together for the
greatest good. Help them to
do what is pleasing in Your
sight. Amen.

Though I walk in the midst of trouble, thou wilt revive me: thou shalt stretch forth thine hand against the wrath of mine enemies, and thy right hand shall save me.

PSALM 138:7

Chet and Alex had been great friends since elementary school. Now they were starting together on the high school football team—Alex the star running back and Chet his number-one blocker. Chet opened the holes to let Alex get running room, and Alex took off. Throughout their lives together, things had worked pretty much the same way. Chet was always looking out for Alex, making sure he was okay. Together they were an unbeatable pair.

Life sometimes feels like a football game. We've got the ball, and everybody else is out to flatten us. In that case, we want to have the best blocker in front of us that we can. God will assume that role for us, if we ask Him to. God sticks with us in the midst of trouble. He picks us up when we fall, He reaches out to help us along when we get bogged down, and He clears our way to deal with problems rather than let us be beaten by them. Nothing can harm us so long as God is on our side.

PRAYER:
There are days, Lord, when I feel like I'm losing ground all the time. I get tired of trying so hard to make things work out and feeling like they just get worse. When I face those times, O God, be with me to lift me up and make me a conqueror.
Amen.

O Lord, thou hast searched me,
and known me.
PSALM 139:1

Kent really wanted the new security job. The aeronautics company was one of the largest and was considered to be the up-and-coming industry leader. His job could possibly become one of the most important around. He sat down at the desk of his interviewer. The man pulled out Kent's file, which appeared to be about three hundred pages thick. The company had sent a team of investigators to find out everything they could about Kent. Though he knew it was necessary, he couldn't help feeling a little angry and alarmed that they were able to find out so much about him. It was frightening to see someone hold your life's stories and secrets in his hands.

Our Lord holds the complete file on each and every one of us. He knows us much better than we even know ourselves. Yet that is nothing to be alarmed about. In His infinite love, He has forgiven us for all that we have done wrong, and He is able to help us in our deepest need.

PRAYER:

It is strange to think that You know me so well, Lord, but I am thankful that You do. Only someone who knows me as You do could possibly understand what I go through and what I need. Thank You. Amen.

*Thou knowest my downsitting and mine
uprising, thou understandest my thought
afar off.*
PSALM 139:2

Peter and Jeanne had been through a lot together.
Peter's wife had died a few years before, and Jeanne's
husband had left her. They had spent many long
hours talking to each other, pulling each other through
dismal times. They had grown so close that they knew
each other's thoughts and moods without a word passing
between them. In time they decided to marry, and theirs
was a match to truly honor God. Their love was a fine
example of how wonderful love can be.

We need someone to turn to who knows us and whom
we can trust. God is that Someone. Perhaps we will find
an earthly partner who understands us so well, but even if
we don't, God will hear us. He knows us, and
He will comfort us. He is never
too busy for us, and He knows
our hearts before we even call
upon Him. Talk to the Lord.
Take your deepest desires
to Him, and rejoice
in the blessings
He has to
give.

*PRAYER: I need
Your counsel,
Father. Thank
You for knowing
me so well and for being
there when I need You. Watch
over me, Lord, and fill me with the
assurance of Your nearness. Amen.*

For there is not a word in my tongue,
but, lo, O LORD, thou knowest it altogether.

PSALM 139:4

Kirk loved working with the young actors and actresses. They had such enthusiasm, and they wanted so hard to please. Kirk had many offers to move on to more "serious" theater opportunities, but he always chose to stay with the high school crowd. Little did it matter that each opening night gave him gray hairs. He nearly died every time one of his kids muffed a line, but the feeling of triumph after every show made it worthwhile. He would live and die for his kids. He loved them.

Like the director of a play who knows all his actors' lines by heart, so God knows the thoughts and words we possess. He stands anxiously, waiting to see if we will use our mouths to glorify and uplift, or if we will muff our lines and turn to other things. He always knows what He would like us to say, but He still allows us the freedom to choose what will actually come out. Let us use our tongues to the glory and honor of God. Proclaim the love of God, and you'll never muff a line.

PRAYER:

O Lord, may the words of my mouth and the meditations of my heart be truly acceptable in Your sight, for You are the source of my strength and my salvation. Amen.

Whither shall I go from thy spirit? or
whither shall I flee from thy presence?
PSALM 139:7

B enjy ran away from home about three times a week.
His mother always left the door unlocked, counted
to a hundred, then listened for the door to creak
open and Benjy's soft footsteps on the hallway carpet.
Benjy always got to the end of the block, assessed his options, realized he didn't have any, and headed for home.

We're all Benjys now and then. We wonder why God
isn't doing all He ought to be doing, we get discouraged,
and then we turn away a little bit. But, just like Benjy, when
we look at the options, we find that nothing comes close
to our Lord Jesus Christ. Wherever
we go, whatever we do, whatever
our need might be, God is right
there with us. Nothing can do
for us what God can. We might
as well stay home, because
we can't ever have it any
better than we have it
right now.

PRAYER:
I may think that
other solutions
will work in
dealing with my life's
problems, Lord, but bring
me back to the realization that
nothing will do more for me than You
can. There is nowhere that I would rather
be than with You. Amen.

*If I take the wings of the morning, and
dwell in the uttermost parts of the sea;
even there shall thy hand lead me,
and thy right hand shall hold me.*

PSALM 139:9–10

The man sat alone in the prison cell. Seldom did he get to see the light of day. His cell was a cubicle of about five square feet. He could not even stretch out to lie down. He had a straw mat and a can, and that completed the inventory of his possessions. A window three inches wide and one foot high opened to the outside world, but it was at least five feet above his head. The man sat and wept, believing that even God would not find him in such a place as this.

Then, as he sat on the floor, he saw a spider in the corner, weaving a delicate web. It peacefully spun and created an object of beautiful symmetry. The man watched closely as the hours passed. In his heart, he knew that God would be with him; that He did know where he was. With nothing more to hold on to, the man was able to wait out his sentence in peace and quiet joy.

PRAYER:
No matter where I may go, Father, be there with me. Help me to know that You are always near and I have not been abandoned. With You by my side, I can make it through anything. Amen.

Yea, the darkness hideth not from thee; but the night shineth as the day: the darkness and the light are both alike to thee.
PSALM 139:12

Sam stuck close to his dad. The old building was dark, and Sam wasn't sure what might be out in that darkness. All he knew for sure was that his dad was big and brave, and he wasn't afraid of the dark. Sam hoped that one day he would be like his dad: able to walk in darkness just like he would in broad daylight.

Our Lord goes with us into the dark times of our lives. He holds us by the hand and lets us know that we have nothing to fear. Darkness and light are the same to the Lord. He will lead us through our times of fear and bring us back into the light every time.

PRAYER:
When I am fearful, Lord, I will reach out to You. Walk with me through the dark times. Fill me with Your courage. Teach me to walk in Your light always. Amen.

I will praise thee; for I am fearfully and
wonderfully made: marvellous are thy works;
and that my soul knoweth right well.

PSALM 139:14

The potter sat at his wheel, turning the clay into beautiful pots. It was hypnotizing to watch. After a time, the pot looked as though it were emerging directly from the potter's hand. With love and care, the potter put his style and mark on every piece he created. Each piece was different, but each bore the striking mark of its maker.

We, too, are fearfully and wonderfully made. We are individual, yet we bear the stamp of our maker. God's image dwells within us all. With love and care we are fashioned, emerging from the Father's hand, and one day we will return to Him, where we will be afforded a place of honor and love. God's works are marvelous, and His Spirit fills them all.

PRAYER:
By Your hand I came into being. Make me useful, Lord, to do that which I was created for. Then, when the time comes, I may stand before You, fulfilled and confident that I have served You well. Amen.

Thine eyes did see my substance, yet being unperfect; and in thy book all my members were written, which in continuance were fashioned, when as yet there was none of them.
PSALM 139:16

Sonia played the violin beautifully, but few ever got to hear her. She practiced day and night. She worked on her talent and technique constantly. She decided that when she could play her pieces perfectly, then she would allow others to listen to her. The problem was that Sonia set her own standards for perfection, and she was never satisfied. Many people were deprived of much beauty because Sonia was afraid to perform before she thought she was perfect.

If we wait until we're perfect before we move out into the world to share our talents, we won't ever get too far. Even more important, we should be very thankful that our acceptance by God is not conditional on how close to being perfect we are. God knows that we have a long way to go, but He is willing to accept us anyway. Our names are written in the book of life the minute we turn our lives over to Christ, not when we become perfect. Rejoice! The Lord loves you just as you are.

*PRAYER:
I am far from perfect, Lord, but I am striving to always grow and be better each day. Help me and bless me in that pursuit. Amen.*

How precious also are thy thoughts unto me,
O God! how great is the sum of them!

PSALM 139:17

Luke was considered by many to be one of the most influential men in American business. He controlled millions of dollars, was responsible for employing millions of workers, and made decisions that affected millions of people's lives. He spent time with most of the truly important people in the world, but no one more important, in Luke's mind, than the Lord. Schedules were always packed full, but never so full that Luke couldn't spend time in prayer and scripture each day. No day went by when Luke didn't take some time with God. No decision was made without consulting the Lord. When so much depended on the integrity of Luke's decisions, he wanted to make sure he took into consideration the Word of the Lord. To do less would be absurd.

The counsel of the Lord should be precious to us all. God holds the sum of all wisdom and knowledge. He is the ground of all common sense. Why wouldn't we want to consult the Lord when we make the important decisions in our lives? Doing less is absurd.

PRAYER:
Fill my mind with Your own thoughts, O God. Help me to see problems through Your eyes and meet them with Your solutions. Teach me to use the gifts of reason, logic, and wisdom that You have given me. Amen

Search me, O God, and know my heart: try me, and know my thoughts: and see if there be any wicked way in me, and lead me in the way everlasting.

PSALM 139:23–24

C arrie hated criticism. She wanted to be a good journalist, but she hated to feel she wasn't good enough. Her editor kept turning her pieces away, forcing her to write and rewrite a half-dozen times. Now, she had done the piece of her life. Never had she been so proud of her work before, and she was afraid to show it to her editor for fear of what he might say. The only thing was, if she didn't show him and get his comments, how could she ever hope to get better? With all her courage and resolution, Carrie marched into the editor's office to see what he thought.

To grow means to be willing to change. God has great things in mind for us, but we must be able to accept criticism and guidance. The Lord can only do with us what we allow Him to. Examine yourself daily in the light of Christ, willing to see the flaws and weaknesses, and ask God to help you change. The results may surprise you.

PRAYER:
Lord, make me over and over again, until I begin to resemble the dream You have for me. Break down my defensiveness and my walls of resistance. Help me to grow, Lord. Amen.

O God the Lord, the strength of my salvation, thou hast covered my head in the day of battle.

PSALM 140:7

Larry had to face the fact: His surgery was less than three days away, and he was scared. He'd hardly been sick a day in his life, and now he was preparing to go under the knife for heart surgery. Nothing had ever prepared him for something like this. He lay back and closed his eyes and began to pray. As he did, an image came into his mind. He was dressed as a soldier, and the surgery ahead was a foe to defeat. But Larry didn't stand alone. God was with him, and beside the awesome image of God, the foe didn't look large at all. When Larry ended his prayer, he opened his eyes with a renewed sense of hope and a heart that was strangely calm. The Lord had prepared him for battle, and Larry felt that it was already won.

PRAYER:

Lord, I put my trust in You. As I face the challenges of everyday life, help me to remember that You stand with me, supplying my strength and my courage. Amen.

Let not an evil speaker be established in the earth: evil shall hunt the violent man to overthrow him.

PSALM 140:11

The committee was worried. They had elected a new chairman who was becoming vocal about some very unpopular ideas. People were getting the idea that the committee endorsed these ideas, just because the new chair so freely shared them. Some of his ideas were quite biased and offensive. Quick action was being taken to replace him, but the damage done was almost too great to measure.

The words of our mouth are powerful weapons. We can do great good by a few well-placed words, or we can wreak total destruction. The words of an evil person spread like a cancer. However, the words spoken by righteous men and women can be our greatest source of healing. Be careful how you speak, for you hold great power and responsibility within your words.

PRAYER:

Guide the words I speak, Lord. Spice them with Your love and concern. Make my speech a joy to others, not a burden. Steer me away from evil, I pray.

Amen.

I know that the LORD will maintain the cause of the afflicted, and the right of the poor.

PSALM 140:12

John sat back in his chair, folded his arms, and said, "Look, if poor and starving people were doing what they were supposed to, they wouldn't be having the problems they do! God would take care of them if they were worth taking care of."

As cruel and narrow as they may sound, comments like these are made all the time. Somehow, some people believe that the poor and needy in our world are that way because they've done something to deserve it. They figure God would solve the problem if it was supposed to be solved. They don't realize that God is trying to solve the problem, but that the solution involves us. We are God's eyes, hands, and feet. He has blessed us with the resources needed to solve the problem.

PRAYER: All that remains is for us to find the *As Your* love and compassion within ourselves *Son came* to make God's plan a reality. As we *into this world* prepare to share the blessings of Christmas, it is good to think *to save others, so* of ways we might repay the *send me, that I might* Lord for the greatest gift *help give life to those in* ever given. How better *need. Use me to solve the* can we return thanks *problem of poverty. Amen.* for the life of Christ than to share in saving the life of another?

*Incline not my heart to any evil thing,
to practise wicked works with men that
work iniquity: and let me not eat of their dainties.*
PSALM 141:4

The company had been after some low-income housing property for over a year. They hoped to put the new headquarters in what was fast becoming the disgrace of the city. Minority families lived in an apartment complex that had gone to ruin. Now, three weeks before Christmas, the company took ownership. The task ahead was to get the tenants moved out; the sooner, the better. As David sat looking at the notices, he felt sick to his stomach. He knew what the property meant to the company, but he also thought about what the housing meant to the people. He poised his pen over the notices a number of times, but something would not allow him to sign them. After hours of struggle, David turned in the blank notices, along with a resignation letter that stated he could not in good conscience continue to work for a firm with such shady values. Walking into the wintry air, David found that he was not sorry to leave, but that Christmas had come a little early.

*PRAYER:
Help me to stand firm against that which is evil. Let me not kid myself into believing that I can remain unaffected by the wickedness that surrounds me. Guide me to new avenues by which I might do good. Amen.*

*Let the righteous smite me; it shall be a
kindness: and let him reprove me; it shall
be an excellent oil, which shall not break my head:
for yet my prayer also shall be in their calamities.*

PSALM 141:5

"You were really out of line back there."

Alan looked over at Barbara and nodded. He had been angry about a mix-up at the bank and had taken out his wrath on a poor, innocent teller. His temper often got him into hot water. Without a word, the two turned around and headed back to the bank. Though the line was long, Alan waited until he could return to the same teller, where he then apologized.

We need to have loving friends around us who will let us know when we are doing something wrong. If we are to grow, we need to have our shortcomings pointed out to us, so we can turn our weaknesses into strengths. Loving, constructive criticism will not hurt us; in fact, it will make us feel better. Love each other enough to criticize, for in caring criticism is the seed of maturity.

PRAYER: I do so many foolish things. I allow my own emotions to get the best of me at times. Channel my passions into constructive streams, and show me the better ways to go. Amen.

I poured out my complaint before him; I shewed before him my trouble.
PSALM 142:2

Benson was sure he knew what his boss wanted him for. He had been late quite frequently because his wife was very sick. Now he was sure he was going to get fired. His boss ushered him into his office, sat him down, and said, "Thomas told me this morning how sick your wife is. Why didn't you tell me? I was ready to fire you because I didn't think there was a good reason for you to be late all the time. I am a reasonable man. Let's work something out. And by the way, the next time there's something wrong, let me know."

At times we may feel that there is nothing to gain by sharing our burdens. Often, however, just talking about them may make us feel better, and it may lead us to new solutions. God wants us to pour out our complaints to Him, and He hopes that we will share with each other. Much good can come from opening up and letting our troubles out.

PRAYER: Hear me when I pray, O Lord. Help me to shoulder my burdens and walk on paths that lead to solutions. Let me be open to others who need to share, as You are open to me. Amen.

I looked on my right hand, and beheld, but there was no man that would know me: refuge failed me; no man cared for my soul.

PSALM 142:4

Terry knew he was in big trouble. He had stolen the test answers along with three of his friends, but they all took off, and he was the only one caught. He tried to tell the principal, but all he got was a lecture on not getting his friends in trouble and facing his punishment like a man. His friends had no intention of coming forth with the truth. He was alone in this mess, and there was no one to bail him out.

Often friends desert us, allies are hard to find, and we stand alone in what we do, right or wrong. Sometimes we face the music for sins we have committed. Other times we stand alone for something we believe in. Comfort comes to us when we realize that, no matter how many earthly friends desert us, God is always standing right beside us. We need face no trial alone. Whether we have sinned or stood up for what is right, God will be near to us, to protect and defend us.

PRAYER: Lord, I need to have You near me. I feel alone and abandoned sometimes. Stand with me, hold me in Your arms, and fill me with Your love. Amen.

Bring my soul out of prison, that I may
praise thy name: the righteous shall compass
me about; for thou shalt deal bountifully with me.
PSALM 142:7

Mikhail was released after seven years in prison. Because of his political views, he had been detained in a small cell, isolated from the other prisoners. His only human contact had been with his jailor, who brought him food once a day. Walking into the sunlight, Mikhail lifted his head skyward, tears flowed down his cheeks, and he began praising God. Many thought he had gone mad in captivity, but others knew that he was merely giving thanks to the One who had sustained him through his imprisonment.

When we find ourselves trapped by situations that have no end in sight, we need to draw on the courage and power of the Lord Jesus Christ. He will enable us to survive any trial, whether it be long or short. We have the assurance that God is greater than any problem that might arise. Call upon the Lord, and He will lift you up.

PRAYER: Lord, I need to feel Your presence near me. Alone, I get so tired and afraid. This life has many trials that I'm not ready to deal with. Free me from the captivity of my fears and doubts, and empower me to praise Your name always. Amen.

And enter not into judgment with thy servant: for in thy sight shall no man living be justified.

PSALM 143:2

Claire found fault with everyone. The mailman was always late, the grocery clerk was always slow, the paperboy was always rude, the minister was always boring, her friends were always too loud, too quiet, too fat, too skinny, too immoral, too prudish. In Claire's eyes, no one was really worth much at all.

Forgiveness was one word that was not found in Claire's vocabulary. She could not forgive people for being human. Thankfully, God does acknowledge our humanness, and He loves us just the same. God has yet to see the perfect human being, apart from Jesus Christ, but that doesn't change His feelings for us. When we see others through the eyes of God's love, we find that we can accept their failings and love them as they are.

PRAYER: Help me to find the lovable in all people, Lord. Destroy in me the tendency to be judgmental. Instead, teach me new ways to affirm others and spread Your grace. Amen.

Hear me speedily, O LORD: my spirit faileth:
hide not thy face from me, lest I be like unto
them that go down into the pit.
PSALM 143:7

The road was slick with ice and snow. Cars were traveling along too fast for the conditions. Molly gripped the wheel and gritted her teeth. Suddenly, a car veered in front of her and went into a skid. Wide-eyed, Molly gasped, "Oh, Lord, help!"

The car passed by her with mere inches to spare, righted itself, and Molly was able to come to a stop, frightened but unharmed. Once more Molly breathed out a short prayer, saying merely, "Thanks."

In our times of greatest need, lengthy prayers just won't come. Our sentiments and needs are already in God's heart, so all we need to do is express them as our situation demands. The prayers of "help" and "thanks" are both acceptable in the sight of the Lord. Those two words say more than many wordy and pious prayers offered up in quieter times. How we pray is not so important as remembering to pray. The Lord hears them all.

PRAYER:
There are times
when I need Your
answer right away,
Lord. In times of distress,
please be near at hand. Hear my
short prayers, and heed them quickly.
Amen.

LORD, what is man, that thou takest knowledge of him! or the son of man, that thou makest account of him!

PSALM 144:3

Ricky walked home from school past the front of the church. He noticed that the nativity scene had been set up, so he stopped long enough to check it out. All of the figures towered above him, but one in particular caught his eye. An angel looked down from the roof of the crèche, and Ricky thought it was looking right at him. He thought to himself, *I wonder if real angels are watching me right now. I wonder if God is.* Ricky left the nativity scene in awe, thinking maybe he was being watched over, and the thought filled him with joy.

Though we cannot fathom why God would love us so much, He does indeed watch over us. He knows all our movements and thoughts, and He cares deeply about the things we face in life. Know that the Lord is mindful of you, and be glad. In God's sight you are precious.

PRAYER:

Watch over me, Lord. Thank You for making me important by loving me so much. I am a new person in Your love. Use me to spread Your joy. Amen.

Every day will I bless thee; and I will praise thy name for ever and ever.
PSALM 145:2

Janet, Ann, and Jenny all agreed. This year they were going to get together daily to pray together and share their experiences. Over the past few months they had spent more time in fellowship with one another, and it was the best part of their weeks. They all worked in the same office, ate lunch together, went to church together, and they lived close enough that they could meet at one another's homes when necessary. In covenant with God and one another, they promised to get together for praise and prayer.

Perhaps such a setup is not feasible for everyone, but it is easier and more enjoyable when we can share our faith with others. Other people hold us accountable to the commitment we make in a way that God does not. He will not force anyone to make time for Him. It is from a willing heart that God wants our time with Him to come. Friends and prayer partners can help us remember God every day, and thereby help us praise Him always.

PRAYER: Every day will I praise You, Lord. I will try to take time each day to reflect on the great gifts I have been given and the wonderful love that is in my heart. Thank You for that love. Amen.

Great is the LORD, and greatly to be praised;
and his greatness is unsearchable.

PSALM 145:3

Four children were engaged in the timeless "My Dad" argument.

Tim said, "My dad works for the largest computer company in the world, and he travels everywhere."

Kip replied, "Well, my father owns a shipping business with hundreds of boats, and even airplanes. I get to ride on boats and planes whenever I want."

Darryl chipped in, "My father works for the government, and he even gets to talk to the president sometimes. We have security men at our house all the time."

Stanley stood quietly for a moment, because his father had died not long before. Finally he said, "My dad is in heaven and gets to see God every day."

The other boys tried to think of something to say that could top that, but nothing came to mind.

Nothing can top the Lord our God. He is above all else. Nothing compares with Him. Therefore, nothing else in this world is more worthy of our worship and devotion. Great is the Lord, and greatly to be praised. His glory endures forever.

PRAYER:

Hear my words of praise, O Lord. Search my heart to see the love I have for You. Bless me with Your grace, O God. Amen.

The LORD is nigh unto all them that call upon him, to all that call upon him in truth.
PSALM 145:18

Florence had fallen twice, and she was deathly afraid of falling again. The last time, she had lain in her apartment for hours before anyone discovered her. The problem was solved when her daughter brought her a beeper that was directly patched into the local hospital. Should Florence fall again, all she had to do was push the button on the beeper, and the ambulance would come immediately. The fear of being left without help was resolved, and Florence could get on with a normal life again.

We need a lifeline like Florence's. For our spiritual needs, we have one in the person of Jesus Christ. Christ is always as close as a prayer. In our times of need, we can call out to Him, and He will be there with us immediately. Christ gives us the assurance we need to live full lives, for we need have no fear of life when He is present with us.

PRAYER:

In times of joy, in times of sorrow, in times of need, I thank You, Lord, for being there when I call upon You. Amen.

Put not your trust in princes, nor in the son of man, in whom there is no help.
PSALM 146:3

Jack called a meeting in the chairman's absence. During the meeting, he outlined a new proposal for restructuring a part of the firm. It was voted on and approved, ignoring the rules that stated that no action could be taken in the chair's absence. When the chairman returned, he reconvened the meeting, overturned the decision, and reminded the entire council of their bylaws. Jack was reprimanded for usurping authority that was not his, and things got back to normal.

It is always wise to seek answers from the true authority. Decisions made by people unqualified to make them often end in disaster. When we put our trust in the wrong places, we may end up being hurt. The only safe place to put our trust is in God. He will guide us in our decisions. He will give us sound direction, and He will always be honest and truthful with us.

PRAYER:

I look to many sources for guidance, Lord, but no one can offer me the help You can. Help me place my total trust in You. Amen.

The LORD preserveth the strangers; he reliveth the fatherless and widow: but the way of the wicked he turneth upside down.
PSALM 146:9

Teri had never been on her own before. She had married fresh out of high school, and her husband had taken care of her for twenty years. When he died, she was suddenly faced with making it on her own for the first time in her life. The whole idea frightened her. More than anything else, she was afraid of being alone. She thought she could make it, if only she had someone to turn to for help and consolation.

God is our consolation and help. When we are alone against the world, we most need His strength. He offers us all the help we need, if we will but ask. He loves to help His children, and He will not turn us away.

PRAYER:
Lord, grant me
rest in Your loving
arms. I can handle
anything, as long as I
know that You are with me.
Preserve me in times of weakness
and frustration. Amen.

He healeth the broken in heart,
and bindeth up their wounds.

PSALM 147:3

Mae sat by the window of her apartment, watching the children playing in the snow below. She wished she could have fun like that once more. Even the companionship and feeling of belonging would be nice. At present, all she had was her cat, Morgan, and he wasn't much for conversation.

Mae was shaken from her reverie by a knock at the door. As she opened it, she was met by the greetings of her neighbors from one floor below. Bearing gifts of food and drink, they asked if they might come in to share the evening with her. Glowing with warmth long forgotten, Mae invited them in to celebrate a new, blossoming friendship.

We have been given the power to bring joy to the lives of others. In this season of God's gift of joy to us, we ought to think of ways that we might spread happiness to those who have little to be happy about. God heals the broken hearts of His children, often through His servants: you and me. Reach out in love to heal the wounds of loneliness and despair.

PRAYER:
Make me
an agent
of Your love
and care, Father.
Send me forth with a
message of mercy and joy.
Use me to heal the emotional
wounds of my neighbors.
Amen.

Great is our Lord, and of great power: his understanding is infinite.
PSALM 147:5

The snow was falling in clumps now. The blizzard had begun six hours ago, and the world had ground to a halt, at least, the world in northeast New York State. It was astonishing to watch the snow accumulate: not into mounds, but into mountains. Somewhere, Stuart had learned in his childhood that no two snowflakes were ever the same. Incredible! The Lord never ceased to create. Billions of snowflakes fell to earth, and not one matched any other. How could people doubt that some creative force was behind the universe?

When we stop to admire the many miracles in nature, we are met with the indisputable evidence of a mastermind who brought everything into being. The power of the Lord is beyond our comprehension, and His wisdom and understanding are beyond our knowing. We should be thankful that the Lord has given us so much beauty. We are blessed by the Lord's continuing creativity.

PRAYER: Dear Father, You have shared so many good things with me. Let me fully appreciate them all. Show me the wonders of this world, and let me receive them with the wonder and amazement of a child. Amen.

The LORD lifteth up the meek: he casteth the wicked down to the ground.

PSALM 147:6

The message came to the small town: "I will arrive to select one of you to dine with Me. Put on your best behavior. You will be judged accordingly." The townspeople knew that Jesus was a special man, and so they dressed in their finest clothes. The merchant stood at the front of the line, followed by the carpenter, the tent-maker, and the miller. A poor girl came along and tried to get in line. The merchant shoved her aside and called her a name. The carpenter threatened to hit her, and the tent-maker pushed her into the dirt. The miller raised a boot to kick her, but stopped. The four men realized that they were being watched. They looked up to see Jesus watching their behavior. Christ stepped forward and took the girl by the hand. He said, "Come. Dine with Me."

To the others, He said, "Depart from Me. You know me not, and so I neither know you."

PRAYER:

In my desire to impress You, Lord, let me not neglect my duty to my neighbor. Stretch forth my hands as You would Your own. Help me to help others. Amen.

This story was written almost 1,700 years ago. Though it is not from the Bible, it reflects well the sentiment of God toward the poor and abused. He will raise up the afflicted, but the abuser will He cast aside. Look kindly upon the poor, viewing them with Christ's own eyes. Then He will be real in you.

He giveth snow like wool: he scattereth the hoarfrost like ashes. He casteth forth his ice like morsels: who can stand before his cold?

PSALM 147:16–17

Toby wasn't afraid of anything, but that made him foolish rather than brave. He had heard the weather forecast and had laughed it off. After all, he was a good driver, and nothing would happen to him as long as he was careful. But the roads were treacherous, and the snow was blinding. He wasn't sure exactly where he was, and the gas gauge was near empty. Toby cursed himself for always thinking he could handle every situation. It was beginning to dawn on him that maybe there were things bigger than he was.

God is too powerful to take lightly. He has created in nature awesome forces, which are much too big for any one person to handle. Winter is a keen reminder of the power of nature. The cold temperatures, the ice and snow, and the darkness: they all add to the tremendous power. The wise woman or man will acknowledge his limitations, conceding to nature its supremacy and admitting to God that He, indeed, reigns above all else.

PRAYER: Wisdom is the one thing I lack most often, Lord. Teach me to be honest with myself. Let me do the things I can, but help me to understand what things I cannot do. Amen.

Praise ye him, all his angels:
praise ye him, all his hosts.
PSALM 148:2

B ecky was an angel in the school play. She and a group of her friends got to tell the whole world about the birth of the baby Jesus. Becky realized what an important part she had. If it weren't for her, the shepherds wouldn't know about Jesus, and the kings wouldn't find their way. No one would watch over Jesus if it weren't for the angels. Yes, Becky knew that Mary and Joseph were important, but she thought that just maybe the angels were the most important characters in the entire story.

The angels in heaven above are still rejoicing over the birth of the Lord Jesus Christ. Two thousand years have not diminished their enthusiasm. Likewise, all the angels in heaven above rejoice when a soul is saved. Let all the earth and all of heaven praise the Lord, for He alone is worthy to be praised.

PRAYER:
Let my voice join the heavenly host in worshipping and praising You, O Lord. Thank You for Your unending love.
Amen.

Praise ye him, sun and moon: praise him,
all ye stars of light.
PSALM 148:3

All the children were so disappointed. The snows had been so heavy that the power lines had been knocked out. No Christmas lights twinkled. No stereos played carols. With the trees unlit, something seemed to be missing.

Then, a wonderful thing happened. The clouds parted, and a huge, glowing moon peeked through. The ice and snow below sparkled with brilliant light. The landscape came alive, and in the breeze, the icicles twinkled in the branches. Children came forth from every house to see the most spectacular display of lights ever imagined. God had supplied what the power company could not. In all their lives, the children could not hope to find trees and lights more beautiful than the ones God gave them this Christmas.

PRAYER:
Everything we create, Lord, is a poor imitation of the beauty You have created in nature. Let our lives be lit up with Your glorious stars, suns, and moons. Let each of these lights be reminders of Your light.
Amen.

Let them praise the name of the LORD:
for he commanded, and they were created.

PSALM 148:5

The shepherds sat in their fields, watching over their flocks. The evening was mild, and the night sky was clear. The stars shone brilliantly, especially the one toward Bethlehem. The sheep were calm and silent.

Little did the band of shepherds know that a visit was being planned for them. So great was their devotion, belief, and faithfulness that they were to be among the first to know of the Messiah's birth. The shepherds had a special tie with their God. They lived each day of their lives close to His creation. They depended upon Him to provide for their needs. They continually praised the name of the Lord, for He took good care of them.

Those who live in close communion with God have a better understanding of His will and His ways. If we will devote ourselves to God, He will reveal Himself to us in so many ways. Rejoice in God's creation. Embrace it, and know God.

PRAYER:

I wait in anxious anticipation of the coming of Your Son once more. Reveal Him to me in new ways, Lord. Let Him be born in my heart anew. Amen.

*Kings of the earth, and all people; princes,
and all judges of the earth. . .let them praise
the name of the LORD: for his name alone is excellent;
his glory is above the earth and heaven.*

PSALM 148:11, 13

The wise men never took their eyes from the star. They had spent the better part of their adult lives watching for this very star to usher in the new Messiah. A new age was come upon the earth, and they devoted everything they had to meet it when it started. They had traveled for months, hoping for little more than a glimpse of the new babe who would set the world straight. Three of the most powerful men of the world committed themselves to worshipping the baby Jesus. Nothing was more important in all the world.

Is that true for us? Is Jesus the most important thing in all the world? Christ comes to us anew each Christmas, and we must ask ourselves what He means to us. For some, He will make us willing to give up everything to follow Him. For others, He will make us willing to begin the journey of faith. Regardless of where we are in our faith, He will come to meet us there, and He will come with love and understanding.

*PRAYER:
Come to me, O Lord. Search my heart to find where I am in my walk of faith. Walk with me, Lord. Help me to make Christ the most important person in my life. Amen.*

*Praise ye the LORD. Sing unto the LORD
a new song, and his praise in the
congregation of saints.*

PSALM 149:1

Pete took his dinner from the oven and sat down at the table to eat. He hadn't decided whether or not to go to church. For some reason the spirit just didn't seem to be moving him. Maybe he was getting too old for Christmas. As he bowed his head to pray over his meal, he heard the voices of distant carolers singing familiar old Christmas songs. His head flooded with the joyous memories of the days of Christmases past. The spirit so absent moments before surged through him. With a lightness of heart, Pete dug into his meal, eating quickly to ensure that he wouldn't be late for the Christmas Eve service.

PRAYER: Fill my heart with songs of praise and joy. Send the light of the world into my life, and shine forth through me so that others might see how wonderful You are. Amen.

For the LORD taketh pleasure in his people:
he will beautify the meek with salvation.
PSALM 149:4

Jesus looked around at the people of Nazareth. There were people of all kinds there. He knew that He had been sent to them all, but He also knew that there were some who would reject Him. He knew there would also be those who would accept Him readily: His people. His people were the poor and oppressed. They were the slaves and the widows and the orphans. They were the outcasts: prostitutes and tax collectors and lepers. In a world where so much value was placed on beauty, His people were the dregs. But He had something to offer them that would make them beautiful. Through His grace, His people would be elevated to the level of angels, and even higher. In God's wisdom, the last—His people—would be first, and the first would be last. Jesus set out, looking to find His people.

Are we His people? Do we accept Him and fashion our lives to His will, or do we reject Him, continuing to live by our own rules? Christ will beautify the meek with salvation. It is in our meekness that we realize our need for God. Let God beautify you, and you will find His pleasure.

PRAYER: Make me meek, Lord. Break my spirit of willfulness and re-create me with Your beauty. Amen.

Let them praise his name in the dance:
let them sing praises unto him with the
timbrel and harp.
PSALM 149:3

A man once said, "I couldn't enjoy myself in heaven. There's too much singing and dancing there for my taste. They started up a long time ago, and it doesn't look like they're anywhere near ready to stop. Ever since Jesus was born, they've had one big, long celebration."

Indeed, since the birth of Jesus Christ, there has been great reason to dance. Death lost all its power, and eternity was opened to all who would choose it. There is reason to dance and sing. Christ came among us, and He is with us to this day. He has given us eternal life and has offered us everything we need to live happy and full lives on earth. Rejoice! Christ has come this day. And He will never leave us alone.

PRAYER:

Come into my heart, dear Lord. I have waited for Your coming, and I am ready to share my life with You. Be close by me, Lord, and fill me with song and dance and joy. Amen.

Let the saints be joyful in glory: let them sing aloud upon their beds.
PSALM 149:5

Carol dreaded going into the nursing home. She had been in others in the past, and she had never felt very good about them. There was something very sad and depressing about them. As she entered the front door, she was surprised that she wasn't met with moans and groans, but with the sound of singing. She followed the sound to a large community room. There, dozens of men and women sat together around a piano, singing songs from their younger days. None of the people looked unhappy. Quite the contrary, they looked joyful and content. Carol moved quietly into the group and began to sing along. Perhaps at last she had found a place where she could be comfortable.

The older segment of our population is a wonderful resource that we have. Too often they are shoved out of the way and not allowed to enjoy their golden years. God loves His oldest children. When they join together, they have a blessed opportunity to continue to grow and enjoy life.

PRAYER:
Number me among the saints of the body of Christ, O Lord. When I feel like groaning about the way things are, fill my heart with song instead. Amen.

Praise ye the LORD. Praise God in his sanctuary: praise him in the firmament of his power.

PSALM 150:1

Before there were churches, before there were preachers, before Christ came to this earth, God had created His sanctuaries. On the mountaintops, God was worshipped. In the valleys, God was worshipped. In the forests, by lakesides, in caves wherever God's handiwork was found, there He was worshipped.

We can praise God anywhere. Church isn't a place; it is an entity made up of living parts. Wherever we gather in the name of God, there is His sanctuary. Life your voices to the Lord. Praise Him wherever you may be. He is with you where you are.

PRAYER:
I will
praise and
worship You
with all my heart
and mind and soul.
Hear my words, Lord, and
be pleased by the love I have
for You. Amen.

Praise him for his mighty acts: praise him according to his excellent greatness.

PSALM 150:2

Jeff was beside himself. His wife had gone into labor hours ago, and a nurse had just come out to tell him that there were complications. There was a good chance that they might lose either the mother or the child. Jeff could only wait and pray. Time passed slowly, but when everything was finally done, both mother and child were fine, and Jeff offered a silent prayer of thanks.

God does mighty acts in our lives. There are times when things don't always work out the way we want them, but God is there to pick us up and help us deal with our trials. Praise the Lord that He is good and kind. His goodness is unending, and we are always in His care.

PRAYER: I cannot begin to understand all that You have done, Lord, but I praise You for what I have seen and felt. You have given so much. Thank You. Amen.

Praise him with the sound of the trumpet: praise him with the psaltery and harp.

PSALM 150:3

The choir prepared to sing. They had come from all over the state to be a part of this event. Hundreds of people were joining their voices together in praise of God. They hoped that other people would take notice. God was worthy of their time, talents, and devotion. Many in the choir felt they had little else to give other than their voices. They sang beautifully. They poured out their hearts. Hundreds of people heard them, and the Spirit of God was shared by them all.

PRAYER: Music is a language that speaks to us all. Let me make a joyful noise unto You, Lord. My heart sings Your praises forever and ever. Amen.

Praise him with the timbrel and dance:
praise him with stringed instruments
and organs. Praise him upon the loud
cymbals: praise him upon the high sounding cymbals.
PSALM 150:4–5

The short-term mission trip to Haiti had pushed Lucy way out of her comfort zone. On her second day, she attended a church service that felt more like an ethnic festival with dancing and singing to fast drum beats and unidentifiable musical instruments. The whole experience was a far cry from the piano, organ, and occasional acoustic guitar at her church back in the States.

But as Lucy got to know the Haitian culture, the people, and their heart for the Lord, she began to understand that their outward expression of worship was filled with powerful praise to the same Creator that she loved. Lucy's appreciation of her Christian brothers and sisters in Haiti widened as she prayed, worked, and lived with them. As she stood among the Haitian congregation the day before returning home, Lucy felt her arms raising in thankful clapping and her toes tapping to the beat of the melodious praise.

PRAYER: You are a God who loves creativity, and you give us a multitude of ways to express our praise to you. Forgive me when I limit my own practice of worship to my comfort zone. Let every moment of my day be a time for praise. Amen.

Let every thing that hath breath praise the
LORD. Praise ye the LORD.
PSALM 150:6

God looked down upon His creation and saw that it was good. In time, God's creation looked back and saw that God was good. Together they formed a unity of love and devotion. Through their covenant, all creation was brought into harmony. The Lord loves His children, and many of His children love Him back. Praise the Lord with all of your being. With each breath you take, remember that the Lord is God. Nothing you do is done apart from Him. Wherever you go, God is there. He will never leave those who love Him. He gives us new years and new challenges, and He helps us to grow and learn. As we approach the new year, we can enter it confident that God goes forth with us. Praise the Lord, one and all. The Lord has been very good to His children.

PRAYER:
I thank You for the year just past—the challenges and the joys—and I look forward to the future, asking Your blessing upon it. Be with me, Lord, and with all my loved ones. Keep me in Your care. Shine Your light upon my path, and make me acceptable in Your sight. Amen.

Bible Readings for January

January 1 - Luke 5:27–39, Genesis 1–2, Psalm 1
January 2 - Luke 6:1–26, Genesis 3–5, Psalm 2
January 3 - Luke 6:27–49, Genesis 6–7, Psalm 3
January 4 - Luke 7:1–17, Genesis 8–10, Psalm 4
January 5 - Luke 7:18–50, Genesis 11, Psalm 5
January 6 - Luke 8:1–25, Genesis 12, Psalm 6
January 7 - Luke 8:26–56, Genesis 13–14, Psalm 7
January 8 - Luke 9:1–27, Genesis 15, Psalm 8
January 9 - Luke 9:28–62, Genesis 16, Psalm 9
January 10 - Luke 10:1–20, Genesis 17, Psalm 10
January 11 - Luke 10:21–42, Genesis 18, Psalm 11
January 12 - Luke 11:1–28, Genesis 19, Psalm 12
January 13 - Luke 11:29–54, Genesis 20, Psalm 13
January 14 - Luke 12:1–31, Genesis 21, Psalm 14
January 15 - Luke 12:32–59, Genesis 22, Psalm 15
January 16 - Luke 13:1–17, Genesis 23, Psalm 16
January 17 - Luke 13:18–35, Genesis 24, Psalm 17
January 18 - Luke 14:1–24, Genesis 25, Psalm 18
January 19 - Luke 14:25–35, Genesis 26, Psalm 19
January 20 - Luke 15, Genesis 27:1–45, Psalm 20
January 21 - Luke 16, Genesis 27:46–28:22, Psalm 21
January 22 - Luke 17, Genesis 29:1–30, Psalm 22
January 23 - Luke 18:1–17, Genesis 29:31–30:43, Psalm 23
January 24 - Luke 18:18–43, Genesis 31, Psalm 24
January 25 - Luke 19:1–27, Genesis 32–33, Psalm 25
January 26 - Luke 19:28–48, Genesis 34, Psalm 26
January 27 - Luke 20:1–26, Genesis 35–36, Psalm 27
January 28 - Luke 20:27–47, Genesis 37, Psalm 28
January 29 - Luke 21, Genesis 38, Psalm 29
January 30 - Luke 22:1–38, Genesis 39, Psalm 30
January 31 - Luke 22:39–71, Genesis 40, Psalm 31

Bible Readings for February

February 1 - Luke 23:1–25, Genesis 41, Psalm 32
February 2 - Luke 23:26–56, Genesis 42, Psalm 33
February 3 - Luke 24:1–12, Genesis 43, Psalm 34
February 4 - Luke 24:13–53, Genesis 44, Psalm 35
February 5 - Hebrews 1, Genesis 45:1–46:27, Psalm 36
February 6 - Hebrews 2, Genesis 46:28–47:31, Psalm 37
February 7 - Hebrews 3:1–4:13, Genesis 48, Psalm 38
February 8 - Hebrews 4:14–6:12, Genesis 49–50, Psalm 39
February 9 - Hebrews 6:13–20, Exodus 1–2, Psalm 40
February 10 - Hebrews 7, Exodus 3–4, Psalm 41
February 11 - Hebrews 8, Exodus 5:1–6:27, Proverbs 1
February 12 - Hebrews 9:1–22, Exodus 6:28–8:32, Proverbs 2
February 13 - Hebrews 9:23–10:18, Exodus 9–10, Proverbs 3
February 14 - Hebrews 10:19–39, Exodus 11–12, Proverbs 4
February 15 - Hebrews 11:1–22, Exodus 13–14, Proverbs 5
February 16 - Hebrews 11:23–40, Exodus 15, Proverbs 6:1–7:5
February 17 - Hebrews 12, Exodus 16–17, Proverbs 7:6–27
February 18 - Hebrews 13, Exodus 18–19, Proverbs 8
February 19 - Matthew 1, Exodus 20–21, Proverbs 9
February 20 - Matthew 2, Exodus 22–23, Proverbs 10
February 21 - Matthew 3, Exodus 24, Proverbs 11
February 22 - Matthew 4, Exodus 25–27, Proverbs 12
February 23 - Matthew 5:1–20, Exodus 28–29, Proverbs 13
February 24 - Matthew 5:21–48, Exodus 30–32, Proverbs 14
February 25 - Matthew 6:1–18, Exodus 33–34, Proverbs 15
February 26 - Matthew 6:19–34, Exodus 35–36, Proverbs 16
February 27 - Matthew 7, Exodus 37–38, Proverbs 17
February 28 - Matthew 8:1–13, Exodus 39–40, Proverbs 18

Bible Readings for March

March 1 - Matthew 8:14–34, Leviticus 1–2, Proverbs 19
March 2 - Matthew 9:1–17, Leviticus 3–4, Proverbs 20
March 3 - Matthew 9:18–38, Leviticus 5–6; Proverbs 21
March 4 - Matthew 10:1–25, Leviticus 7–8, Proverbs 22
March 5 - Matthew 10:26–42, Leviticus 9–10, Proverbs 23
March 6 - Matthew 11:1–19, Leviticus 11–12, Proverbs 24
March 7 - Matthew 11:20–30, Leviticus 13, Proverbs 25
March 8 - Matthew 12:1–21, Leviticus 14, Proverbs 26
March 9 - Matthew 12:22–50, Leviticus 15–16, Proverbs 27
March 10 - Matthew 13:1–23, Leviticus 17–18, Proverbs 28
March 11 - Matthew 13:24–58, Leviticus 19, Proverbs 29
March 12 - Matthew 14:1–21, Leviticus 20–21, Proverbs 30
March 13 - Matthew 14:22–36, Leviticus 22–23, Proverbs 31
March 14 - Matthew 15:1–20, Leviticus 24–25, Ecclesiastes 1:1–11
March 15 - Matthew 15:21–39, Leviticus 26–27, Ecclesiastes 1:12–2:26
March 16 - Matthew 16, Numbers 1–2, Ecclesiastes 3:1–15
March 17 - Matthew 17, Numbers 3–4, Ecclesiastes 3:16–4:16
March 18 - Matthew 18:1–20, Numbers 5–6, Ecclesiastes 5
March 19 - Matthew 18:21–35, Numbers 7–8, Ecclesiastes 6
March 20 - Matthew 19:1–15, Numbers 9–10, Ecclesiastes 7
March 21 - Matthew 19:16–30, Numbers 11–12, Ecclesiastes 8
March 22 - Matthew 20:1–16, Numbers 13–14, Ecclesiastes 9:1–12
March 23 - Matthew 20:17–34, Numbers 15–16, Ecclesiastes 9:13–10:20
March 24 - Matthew 21:1–27, Numbers 17–18, Ecclesiastes 11:1–8
March 25 - Matthew 21:28–46, Numbers 19–20, Ecclesiastes 11:9–12:14
March 26 - Matthew 22:1–22, Numbers 21, Song of Solomon 1:1–2:7
March 27 - Matthew 22:23–46, Numbers 22:1–40,
        Song of Solomon 2:8-3:5
March 28 - Matthew 23:1–12, Numbers 22:41–23:26,
        Song of Solomon 3:6–5:1
March 29 - Matthew 23:13–39, Numbers 23:27–24:25,
        Song of Solomon 5:2–6:3
March 30 - Matthew 24:1–31, Numbers 25–27, Song of Solomon 6:4–8:4
March 31 - Matthew 24:32–51, Numbers 28–29, Song of Solomon 8:5–14

Bible Readings for April

April 1 - Matthew 25:1–30, Numbers 30–31, Job 1
April 2 - Matthew 25:31–46, Numbers 32–34, Job 2
April 3 - Matthew 26:1–25, Numbers 35–36, Job 3
April 4 - Matthew 26:26–46, Deuteronomy 1–2, Job 4
April 5 - Matthew 26:47–75, Deuteronomy 3–4, Job 5
April 6 - Matthew 27:1–31, Deuteronomy 5–6, Job 6
April 7 - Matthew 27:32–66, Deuteronomy 7–8, Job 7
April 8 - Matthew 28, Deuteronomy 9–10, Job 8
April 9 - Acts 1, Deuteronomy 11–12, Job 9
April 10 - Acts 2:1–13, Deuteronomy 13–14, Job 10
April 11 - Acts 2:14–47, Deuteronomy 15–16, Job 11
April 12 - Acts 3, Deuteronomy 17–18, Job 12
April 13 - Acts 4:1–22, Deuteronomy 19–20, Job 13
April 14 - Acts 4:23–37, Deuteronomy 21–22, Job 14
April 15 - Acts 5:1–16, Deuteronomy 23–24, Job 15
April 16 - Acts 5:17–42, Deuteronomy 25–27, Job 16
April 17 - Acts 6, Deuteronomy 28, Job 17
April 18 - Acts 7:1–22, Deuteronomy 29–30, Job 18
April 19 - Acts 7:23–60, Deuteronomy 31–32, Job 19
April 20 - Acts 8:1–25, Deuteronomy 33–34, Job 20
April 21 - Acts 8:26–40, Joshua 1–2, Job 21
April 22 - Acts 9:1–25, Joshua 3:1–5:1, Job 22
April 23 - Acts 9:26–43, Joshua 5:2–6:27, Job 23
April 24 - Acts 10:1–33, Joshua 7–8, Job 24
April 25 - Acts 10:34–48, Joshua 9–10, Job 25
April 26 - Acts 11:1–18, Joshua 11–12, Job 26
April 27 - Acts 11:19–30, Joshua 13–14, Job 27
April 28 - Acts 12, Joshua 15–17, Job 28
April 29 - Acts 13:1–25, Joshua 18–19, Job 29
April 30 - Acts 13:26–52, Joshua 20–21, Job 30

Bible Readings for May

May 1 - Acts 14, Joshua 22, Job 31
May 2 - Acts 15:1–21, Joshua 23–24, Job 32
May 3 - Acts 15:22–41, Judges 1, Job 33
May 4 - Acts 16:1–15, Judges 2–3, Job 34
May 5 - Acts 16:16–40, Judges 4–5, Job 35
May 6 - Acts 17:1–15, Judges 6, Job 36
May 7 - Acts 17:16–34, Judges 7–8, Job 37
May 8 - Acts 18, Judges 9, Job 38
May 9 - Acts 19:1–20, Judges 10:1–11:33, Job 39
May 10 - Acts 19:21–41, Judges 11:34–12:15, Job 40
May 11 - Acts 20:1–16, Judges 13, Job 41
May 12 - Acts 20:17–38, Judges 14–15, Job 42
May 13 - Acts 21:1–36, Judges 16, Psalm 42
May 14 - Acts 21:37–22:29, Judges 17–18, Psalm 43
May 15 - Acts 22:30–23:22, Judges 19, Psalm 44
May 16 - Acts 23:23–24:9, Judges 20, Psalm 45
May 17 - Acts 24:10–27, Judges 21, Psalm 46
May 18 - Acts 25, Ruth 1–2, Psalm 47
May 19 - Acts 26:1–18, Ruth 3–4, Psalm 48
May 20 - Acts 26:19–32, 1 Samuel 1:1–2:10, Psalm 49
May 21 - Acts 27:1–12, 1 Samuel 2:11–36, Psalm 50
May 22 - Acts 27:13–44, 1 Samuel 3, Psalm 51
May 23 - Acts 28:1–16, 1 Samuel 4–5, Psalm 52
May 24 - Acts 28:17–31, 1 Samuel 6–7, Psalm 53
May 25 - Romans 1:1–15, 1 Samuel 8, Psalm 54
May 26 - Romans 1:16–32, 1 Samuel 9:1–10:16, Psalm 55
May 27 - Romans 2:1–3:8, 1 Samuel 10:17–11:15, Psalm 56
May 28 - Romans 3:9–31, 1 Samuel 12, Psalm 57
May 29 - Romans 4, 1 Samuel 13, Psalm 58
May 30 - Romans 5, 1 Samuel 14, Psalm 59
May 31 - Romans 6, 1 Samuel 15, Psalm 60

Bible Readings for June

June 1 - Romans 7, 1 Samuel 16, Psalm 61
June 2 - Romans 8 1 Samuel 17:1–54, Psalm 62
June 3 - Romans 9:1–29, 1 Samuel 17:55–18:30, Psalm 63
June 4 - Romans 9:30–10:21, 1 Samuel 19, Psalm 64
June 5 - Romans 11:1–24, 1 Samuel 20, Psalm 65
June 6 - Romans 11:25–36, 1 Samuel 21–22, Psalm 66
June 7 - Romans 12, 1 Samuel 23–24, Psalm 67
June 8 - Romans 13, 1 Samuel 25, Psalm 68
June 9 - Romans 14, 1 Samuel 26, Psalm 69
June 10 - Romans 15:1–13, 1 Samuel 27–28, Psalm 70
June 11 - Romans 15:14–33, 1 Samuel 29–31, Psalm 71
June 12 - Romans 16, 2 Samuel 1, Psalm 72
June 13 - Mark 1:1–20, 2 Samuel 2:1–3:1, Daniel 1
June 14 - Mark 1:21–45, 2 Samuel 3:2–39, Daniel 2:1–23
June 15 - Mark 2, 2 Samuel 4–5, Daniel 2:24–49
June 16 - Mark 3:1–19, 2 Samuel 6, Daniel 3
June 17 - Mark 3:20–35, 2 Samuel 7–8, Daniel 4
June 18 - Mark 4:1–20, 2 Samuel 9–10, Daniel 5
June 19 - Mark 4:21–41, 2 Samuel 11–12, Daniel 6
June 20 - Mark 5:1–20, 2 Samuel 13, Daniel 7
June 21 - Mark 5:21–43, 2 Samuel 14, Daniel 8
June 22 - Mark 6:1–29, 2 Samuel 15, Daniel 9
June 23 - Mark 6:30–56, 2 Samuel 16, Daniel 10
June 24 - Mark 7:1–13, 2 Samuel 17, Daniel 11:1–19
June 25 - Mark 7:14–37, 2 Samuel 18, Daniel 11:20–45
June 26 - Mark 8:1–21, 2 Samuel 19, Daniel 12
June 27 - Mark 8:22–9:1, 2 Samuel 20–21, Hosea 1:1–2:1
June 28 - Mark 9:2–50, 2 Samuel 22, Hosea 2:2–23
June 29 - Mark 10:1–31, 2 Samuel 23, Hosea 3
June 30 - Mark 10:32–52, 2 Samuel 24, Hosea 4:1–11

Bible Readings for July

July 1 - Mark 11:1–14, 1 Kings 1, Hosea 4:12–5:4
July 2 - Mark 11:15–33, 1 Kings 2, Hosea 5:5–15
July 3 - Mark 12:1–27, 1 Kings 3, Hosea 6:1–7:2
July 4 - Mark 12:28–44, 1 Kings 4-5, Hosea 7:3–16
July 5 - Mark 13:1–13, 1 Kings 6, Hosea 8
July 6 - Mark 13:14–37, 1 Kings 7, Hosea 9:1–16
July 7 - Mark 14:1–31, 1 Kings 8, Hosea 9:17–10:15
July 8 - Mark 14:32–72, 1 Kings 9, Hosea 11:1–11
July 9 - Mark 15:1–20, 1 Kings 10, Hosea 11:12–12:14
July 10 - Mark 15:21–47, 1 Kings 11, Hosea 13
July 11 - Mark 16, 1 Kings 12:1–31, Hosea 14
July 12 - 1 Corinthians 1:1–17, 1 Kings 12:32–13:34, Joel 1
July 13 - 1 Corinthians 1:18–31, 1 Kings 14, Joel 2:1–11
July 14 - 1 Corinthians 2, 1 Kings 15:1–32, Joel 2:12–32
July 15 - 1 Corinthians 3, 1 Kings 15:33–16:34, Joel 3
July 16 - 1 Corinthians 4, 1 Kings 17, Amos 1
July 17 - 1 Corinthians 5, 1 Kings 18, Amos 2:1–3:2
July 18 - 1 Corinthians 6, 1 Kings 19, Amos 3:3–4:3
July 19 - 1 Corinthians 7:1–24, 1 Kings 20, Amos 4:4–13
July 20 - 1 Corinthians 7:25–40, 1 Kings 21, Amos 5
July 21 - 1 Corinthians 8, 1 Kings 22, Amos 6
July 22 - 1 Corinthians 9, 2 Kings 1–2, Amos 7
July 23 - 1 Corinthians 10, 2 Kings 3, Amos 8
July 24 - 1 Corinthians 11:1–16, 2 Kings 4, Amos 9
July 25 - 1 Corinthians 11:17–34, 2 Kings 5, Obadiah
July 26 - 1 Corinthians 12, 2 Kings 6:1–7:2, Jonah 1
July 27 - 1 Corinthians 13, 2 Kings 7:3–20, Jonah 2
July 28 - 1 Corinthians 14:1–25, 2 Kings 8, Jonah 3
July 29 - 1 Corinthians 14:26–40, 2 Kings 9, Jonah 4
July 30 - 1 Corinthians 15:1–34, 2 Kings 10, Micah 1
July 31 - 1 Corinthians 15:35–58, 2 Kings 11, Micah 2

Bible Readings for August

August 1 - 1 Corinthians 16, 2 Kings 12–13, Micah 3
August 2 - 2 Corinthians 1:1–2:4, 2 Kings 14, Micah 4:1–5:1
August 3 - 2 Corinthians 2:5–3:18, 2 Kings 15–16, Micah 5:2–15
August 4 - 2 Corinthians 4:1–5:10, 2 Kings 17, Micah 6
August 5 - 2 Corinthians 5:11–6:13, 2 Kings 18, Micah 7
August 6 - 2 Corinthians 6:14–7:16, 2 Kings 19, Nahum 1
August 7 - 2 Corinthians 8, 2 Kings 20–21, Nahum 2
August 8 - 2 Corinthians 9, 2 Kings 22:1–23:35, Nahum 3
August 9 - 2 Corinthians 10, 2 Kings 23:36–24:20, Habakkuk 1
August 10 - 2 Corinthians 11, 2 Kings 25, Habakkuk 2
August 11 - 2 Corinthians 12, 1 Chronicles 1–2, Habakkuk 3
August 12 - 2 Corinthians 13, 1 Chronicles 3–4, Zephaniah 1
August 13 - John 1:1–18, 1 Chronicles 5–6, Zephaniah 2
August 14 - John 1:19–34, 1 Chronicles 7–8, Zephaniah 3
August 15 - John 1:35–51, 1 Chronicles 9, Haggai 1–2
August 16 - John 2, 1 Chronicles 10–11, Zechariah 1
August 17 - John 3:1–21, 1 Chronicles 12, Zechariah 2
August 18 - John 3:22–36, 1 Chronicles 13–14, Zechariah 3
August 19 - John 4:1–26, 1 Chronicles 15:1–16:6, Zechariah 4
August 20 - John 4:27–42, 1 Chronicles 16:7–43, Zechariah 5
August 21 - John 4:43–54, 1 Chronicles 17, Zechariah 6
August 22 - John 5:1–18, 1 Chronicles 18–19, Zechariah 7
August 23 - John 5:19–47, 1 Chronicles 20:1–22:1, Zechariah 8
August 24 - John 6:1–21, 1 Chronicles 22:2–23:32, Zechariah 9
August 25 - John 6:22–59, 1 Chronicles 24, Zechariah 10
August 26 - John 6:60–71, 1 Chronicles 25–26, Zechariah 11
August 27 - John 7:1–24, 1 Chronicles 27–28, Zechariah 12
August 28 - John 7:25–52, 1 Chronicles 29, Zechariah 13
August 29 - John 8:1–20, 2 Chronicles 1:1–2:16, Zechariah 14
August 30 - John 8:21–47, 2 Chronicles 2:17–5:1, Malachi 1:1–2:9
August 31 - John 8:48–59, 2 Chronicles 5:2–14, Malachi 2:10–16

Bible Readings for September

September 1 - John 9:1–23, 2 Chronicles 6, Malachi 2:17–3:18
September 2 - John 9:24–41, 2 Chronicles 7, Malachi 4
September 3 - John 10:1–21, 2 Chronicles 8, Psalm 73
September 4 - John 10:22–42, 2 Chronicles 9, Psalm 74
September 5 - John 11:1–27, 2 Chronicles 10–11, Psalm 75
September 6 - John 11:28–57, 2 Chronicles 12–13, Psalm 76
September 7 - John 12:1–26, 2 Chronicles 14–15, Psalm 77
September 8 - John 12:27–50, 2 Chronicles 16–17, Psalm 78:1-20
September 9 - John 13:1–20, 2 Chronicles 18, Psalm 78:21–37
September 10 - John 13:21–38, 2 Chronicles 19, Psalm 78:38–55
September 11 - John 14:1–14, 2 Chronicles 20:1–21:1,
          Psalm 78:56–72
September 12 - John 14:15–31, 2 Chronicles 21:2–22:12,
          Psalm 79
September 13 - John 15:1–16:4, 2 Chronicles 23, Psalm 80
September 14 - John 16:4–33, 2 Chronicles 24, Psalm 81
September 15 - John 17, 2 Chronicles 25, Psalm 82
September 16 - John 18:1–18, 2 Chronicles 26, Psalm 83
September 17 - John 18:19–38, 2 Chronicles 27–28, Psalm 84
September 18 - John 18:38–19:16, 2 Chronicles 29, Psalm 85
September 19 - John 19:16–42, 2 Chronicles 30, Psalm 86
September 20 - John 20:1–18, 2 Chronicles 31, Psalm 87
September 21 - John 20:19–31, 2 Chronicles 32, Psalm 88
September 22 - John 21, 2 Chronicles 33, Psalm 89:1–18
September 23 - 1 John 1, 2 Chronicles 34, Psalm 89:19–37
September 24 - 1 John 2, 2 Chronicles 35, Psalm 89:38–52
September 25 - 1 John 3, 2 Chronicles 36, Psalm 90
September 26 - 1 John 4, Ezra 1–2, Psalm 91
September 27 - 1 John 5, Ezra 3–4, Psalm 92
September 28 - 2 John, Ezra 5–6, Psalm 93
September 29 - 3 John, Ezra 7–8, Psalm 94
September 30 - Jude, Ezra 9–10, Psalm 95

Bible Readings for October

October 1 - Revelation 1, Nehemiah 1–2, Psalm 96
October 2 - Revelation 2, Nehemiah 3, Psalm 97
October 3 - Revelation 3, Nehemiah 4, Psalm 98
October 4 - Revelation 4, Nehemiah 5:1–7:4, Psalm 99
October 5 - Revelation 5, Nehemiah 7:5–8:12, Psalm 100
October 6 - Revelation 6, Nehemiah 8:13–9:37, Psalm 101
October 7 - Revelation 7, Nehemiah 9:38–10:39, Psalm 102
October 8 - Revelation 8, Nehemiah 11, Psalm 103
October 9 - Revelation 9, Nehemiah 12, Psalm 104:1–23
October 10 - Revelation 10, Nehemiah 13, Psalm 104:24–35
October 11 - Revelation 11, Esther 1, Psalm 105:1–25
October 12 - Revelation 12, Esther 2, Psalm 105:26–45
October 13 - Revelation 13, Esther 3–4, Psalm 106:1–23
October 14 - Revelation 14, Esther 5:1–6:13, Psalm 106:24–48
October 15 - Revelation 15, Esther 6:14–8:17, Psalm 107:1–22
October 16 - Revelation 16, Esther 9–10, Psalm 107:23–43
October 17 - Revelation 17, Isaiah 1–2, Psalm 108
October 18 - Revelation 18, Isaiah 3–4, Psalm 109:1–19
October 19 - Revelation 19, Isaiah 5–6, Psalm 109:20–31
October 20 - Revelation 20, Isaiah 7–8, Psalm 110
October 21 - Revelation 21–22, Isaiah 9–10, Psalm 111
October 22 - 1 Thessalonians 1, Isaiah 11–13, Psalm 112
October 23 - 1 Thessalonians 2:1–16, Isaiah 14–16,
        Psalm 113
October 24 - 1 Thessalonians 2:17–3:13, Isaiah 17–19, Psalm 114
October 25 - 1 Thessalonians 4, Isaiah 20–22, Psalm 115
October 26 - 1 Thessalonians 5, Isaiah 23–24, Psalm 116
October 27 - 2 Thessalonians 1, Isaiah 25–26, Psalm 117
October 28 - 2 Thessalonians 2, Isaiah 27–28, Psalm 118
October 29 - 2 Thessalonians 3, Isaiah 29–30, Psalm 119:1–32
October 30 - 1 Timothy 1, Isaiah 31–33, Psalm 119:33–64
October 31 - 1 Timothy 2, Isaiah 34–35, Psalm 119:65–96

Bible Readings for November

November 1 - 1 Timothy 3, Isaiah 36–37, Psalm 119:97–120
November 2 - 1 Timothy 4, Isaiah 38–39, Psalm 119:121–144
November 3 - 1 Timothy 5:1–22, Jeremiah 1–2,
          Psalm 119:145–176
November 4 - 1 Timothy 5:23–6:21, Jeremiah 3–4, Psalm 120
November 5 - 2 Timothy 1, Jeremiah 5–6, Psalm 121
November 6 - 2 Timothy 2, Jeremiah 7–8, Psalm 122
November 7 - 2 Timothy 3, Jeremiah 9–10, Psalm 123
November 8 - 2 Timothy 4, Jeremiah 11–12, Psalm 124
November 9 - Titus 1, Jeremiah 13–14, Psalm 125
November 10 - Titus 2, Jeremiah 15–16, Psalm 126
November 11 - Titus 3, Jeremiah 17–18, Psalm 127
November 12 - Philemon, Jeremiah 19–20, Psalm 128
November 13 - James 1, Jeremiah 21–22, Psalm 129
November 14 - James 2, Jeremiah 23–24, Psalm 130
November 15 - James 3, Jeremiah 25–26, Psalm 131
November 16 - James 4, Jeremiah 27–28, Psalm 132
November 17 - James 5, Jeremiah 29–30, Psalm 133
November 18 - 1 Peter 1, Jeremiah 31–32, Psalm 134
November 19 - 1 Peter 2, Jeremiah 33–34, Psalm 135
November 20 - 1 Peter 3, Jeremiah 35–36, Psalm 136
November 21 - 1 Peter 4, Jeremiah 37–38, Psalm 137
November 22 - 1 Peter 5, Jeremiah 39–40, Psalm 138
November 23 - 2 Peter 1, Jeremiah 41–42, Psalm 139
November 24 - 2 Peter 2, Jeremiah 43–44, Psalm 140
November 25 - 2 Peter 3, Jeremiah 45–46, Psalm 141
November 26 - Galatians 1, Jeremiah 47–48, Psalm 142
November 27 - Galatians 2, Jeremiah 49–50, Psalm 143
November 28 - Galatians 3:1–18, Jeremiah 51–52, Psalm 144
November 29 - Galatians 3:19–4:20, Lamentations 1–2, Psalm 145
November 30 - Galatians 4:21–31, Lamentations 3–4, Psalm 146

Bible Readings for December

December 1 - Galatians 5:1–15, Lamentations 5, Psalm 147
December 2 - Galatians 5:16–26, Ezekiel 1, Psalm 148
December 3 - Galatians 6, Ezekiel 2–3, Psalm 149
December 4 - Ephesians 1, Ezekiel 4–5, Psalm 150
December 5 - Ephesians 2, Ezekiel 6–7, Isaiah 40
December 6 - Ephesians 3, Ezekiel 8–9, Isaiah 41
December 7 - Ephesians 4:1–16, Ezekiel 10–11, Isaiah 42
December 8 - Ephesians 4:17–32, Ezekiel 12–13, Isaiah 43
December 9 - Ephesians 5:1–20, Ezekiel 14–15, Isaiah 44
December 10 - Ephesians 5:21–33, Ezekiel 16, Isaiah 45
December 11 - Ephesians 6, Ezekiel 17, Isaiah 46
December 12 - Philippians 1:1–11, Ezekiel 18, Isaiah 47
December 13 - Philippians 1:12–30, Ezekiel 19, Isaiah 48
December 14 - Philippians 2:1–11, Ezekiel 20, Isaiah 49
December 15 - Philippians 2:12–30, Ezekiel 21–22, Isaiah 50
December 16 - Philippians 3, Ezekiel 23, Isaiah 51
December 17 - Philippians 4, Ezekiel 24, Isaiah 52
December 18 - Colossians 1:1–23, Ezekiel 25–26, Isaiah 53
December 19 - Colossians 1:24–2:19, Ezekiel 27–28, Isaiah 54
December 20 - Colossians 2:20–3:17, Ezekiel 29–30, Isaiah 55
December 21 - Colossians 3:18–4:18, Ezekiel 31–32, Isaiah 56
December 22 - Luke 1:1–25, Ezekiel 33, Isaiah 57
December 23 - Luke 1:26–56, Ezekiel 34, Isaiah 58
December 24 - Luke 1:57–80, Ezekiel 35–36, Isaiah 59
December 25 - Luke 2:1–20, Ezekiel 37, Isaiah 60
December 26 - Luke 2:21–52, Ezekiel 38–39, Isaiah 61
December 27 - Luke 3:1–20, Ezekiel 40–41, Isaiah 62
December 28 - Luke 3:21–38, Ezekiel 42–43, Isaiah 63
December 29 - Luke 4:1–30, Ezekiel 44–45, Isaiah 64
December 30 - Luke 4:31–44, Ezekiel 46–47, Isaiah 65
December 31 - Luke 5:1–26, Ezekiel 48, Isaiah 66